Artificial

Neural Networks

for Image

Understanding

Arun D. Kulkarni

VNR VAN NOSTRAND REINHOLD
New York

Copyright © 1994 by Van Nostrand Reinhold

Library of Congress Catalog Card Number 93-4892
ISBN 0-442-00921-6

I(T)P Van Nostrand Reinhold is an International Thomson Publishing company. ITP logo is a trademark under license.

Printed in the United States of America.

10736522

Van Nostrand Reinhold
115 Fifth Avenue
New York, NY 10003

ITP Germany
Königswinterer Str. 418
53227 Bonn
Germany

International Thomson Publishing
Berkshire House, 168–173
High Holborn, London, WC1V 7AA
England

International Thomson Publishing Asia
38 Kim Tian Rd., #0105
Kim Tian Plaza
Singapore 0316

Thomas Nelson Australia
102 Dodds Street
South Melbourne 3205
Victoria, Australia

International Thomson Publishing Japan
Kyowa Building, 3F
2-2-1 Hirakawacho
Chiyada-Ku, Tokyo 102
Japan

Nelson Canada
1120 Birchmount Road
Scarborough, Ontario
M1K 5G4, Canada

16 15 14 13 12 11 10 9 8 7 6 5 4 3 2 1

Library of Congress Cataloging in Publication Data
Kulkarni, Arun D., 1947–
    Artificial neural networks for image understanding / by Arun D. Kulkarni.
        p.   cm.
    Includes bibliographical references and index.
    ISBN 0-442-00921-6
    1. Neural networks (Computer science)   2. Image processing.
    I. Title.
    QA76.87.K84   1993
    006.3′7—dc20
                                                    93-4892
                                                    CIP

Dedicated to the memory of my father.

CONTENTS

PREFACE

During the past few years there have been phenomenal developments in artificial neural networks. Artificial neural networks have been used successfully for many image-processing and pattern recognition tasks. Researchers in such application areas as remote sensing, medical image processing, robot vision, military reconnaissance, cartography, and geology are now exploring the possibilities of employing neural network algorithms and models for their processing tasks. This book is written mainly for such professionals. It explains various neural network architectures and algorithms as applied to tasks such as image enhancement, feature extraction, classification, clustering, associative storage, and recall. It demonstrates the utility of neural networks with a number of illustrative examples.

There have been many research papers on neural networks as applied to image understanding, which involves image processing and pattern recognition. This book thus spans three disciplines—neural networks, image processing, and pattern recognition—and discusses fundamental concepts from all three areas. Neural network algorithms are compared with conventional methods, important concepts are explained in simple English, and informal mathematical treatments are included to clarify explanations. For complicated derivations the reader is guided to appropriate references, which together constitute an extensive bibliography of important writings.

Every effort has been made to produce a book that is easy to understand without oversimplification of the material. The book assumes its readers have the mathematical background of senior college students in a technical discipline such as engineering or computer science, including at least some preparation in mathematical analysis, matrix theory, probability, and computer programming. The book need not be read from cover to cover. Every chapter is intended to be self-contained, assuming familiarity only with the first chapter. Practicality has been a primary objective. By studying the chapters carefully, it should be possible to implement most of the networks on a general-purpose computer. The book can be used as a reference book by professionals or as a textbook for a one-semester graduate course in a discipline such as electrical engineering or computer science.

ACKNOWLEDGMENTS

I wish to thank all those who enabled me to see this book grow from dream to reality. I am especially indebted to all those who granted permission for use of their copyrighted figures. I would also like to thank my colleagues for their useful discussions, and my students for their help in software development work. Last but not least, I want to thank my wife Vasanti and our children Himani, Prathit, and Shradha for their encouragement and tolerance during the months I spent preparing this manuscript.

ARUN D. KULKARNI

1

Introduction

1.1. ARTIFICIAL NEURAL NETWORK MODELS

Vision has long fascinated researchers from such disciplines as psychology, neural science, computer science, and engineering. Vision has been defined as a process of recognition of objects of interest, and it deals with image understanding. Artificial neural networks (ANNs) have been used to model the human vision system. They are biologically inspired, and contain a large number of simple processing elements that perform in a manner that is analogous to the most elementary functions of neurons. ANN models learn by experience, generalize from previous experiences to new ones, and can make decisions.

Neural elements of a human brain have a computing speed of a few milliseconds, whereas the computing speed of electronic circuits is of the order of microseconds. In spite of its very low processing speed, the human brain resolves vision and language problems much faster than the fastest computers. ANN models mimic the human brain. They provide a computing architecture that is radically different from the computers that are widely used today: they are massively parallel systems.

ANN models have been used for pattern recognition since the 1950s (Rosenblatt, 1958, 1962). In 1949 Hebb provided the learning law that became the starting point for artificial neural network training algorithms. Early successes of ANN models produced a burst of activity and optimism. The earliest single-layer ANN models were analyzed by Minsky and Papert (1969), who pointed out

1

that they were theoretically incapable of solving many simple problems. This discouraged many researchers. Nevertheless, a few dedicated scientists such as Teuvo Kohonen, Stephen Grossberg, Bernard Widrow, John Hopfield, and James Anderson continued their efforts. Gradually, a theoretical foundation emerged, and the past few years have seen phenomenal developments in ANN architecture and learning algorithms. Theories have been translated into applications, and new corporations dedicated to commercialization of the technology have appeared.

ANN models are preferred for image-understanding tasks because of their parallel processing capabilities as well as learning and decision-making abilities. Image understanding deals with recognition of various objects in a scene. It includes image processing and pattern recognition. Often, the ultimate aim in developing an image-understanding system is to perform tasks that are normally performed by a human vision system.

Interest in digital image-processing methods stems from two principal application areas: improvement of pictorial information for human interpretation and processing of scene data for machine perception. Image processing is concerned with manipulation and analysis of pictures. Its major subareas include (1) digitization and compression, (2) enhancement, restoration, and reconstruction, and (3) matching, description, and recognition. Digitization and compression techniques deal with converting pictures to discrete form and efficient coding or approximation of pictures so as to save storage space or channel capacity. Enhancement and restoration techniques are concerned with improving the quality of low-contrast, blurred, noisy images. Matching and description techniques deal with comparing and superimposing pictures with one another, segmenting pictures into parts, and measuring relationships among the parts. Textbooks such as those by Andrews (1970), Rosenfeld and Kak (1982), Gonzalez and Wintz (1987), and Jain (1989) deal with digital image-processing techniques.

Pattern recognition deals with identification of objects from observed patterns or images. In conventional pattern recognition, an observation vector is first mapped onto a feature space. The decision process deals with partitioning of the feature space. Typical pattern recognition techniques include discriminant functions and parametric and nonparametric statistical methods (Duda and Hart, 1973). During the past 30 years many digital, optical techniques have been developed for image-processing and pattern recognition tasks and are now used in such practical applications as robot vision, character recognition, speech recognition, remote sensing, military reconnaissance, signature identification, medical image diagnosis, mineral resources, and geological surveys. Textbooks such as those by Duda and Hart (1973), Ullman (1973), Tou and Gonzalez (1974), Fu (1977), and James (1988) deal with pattern recognition techniques.

ANN models are also known as connectionist models of parallel distributed processing (PDP) models. PDP models are well described in the definitive book by Rumelhart et al. (1986). Many other books describing neural network models are now available (Grossberg, 1988; Pao, 1989; Wasserman, 1989; Dayhoff, 1990; Hecht-Nielsen, 1990; Khanna, 1990). Review articles such as those by Casasent (1985) and Lippmann (1987) deal with neural network classifiers and feature extraction techniques. The functional synthesis of these models consists of establishing a relationship among several inputs and one or more outputs.

The human nervous system consists of cells called neurons. There are hundreds of billions of neurons, each connected to hundreds or thousands of other neurons. Each neuron is capable of receiving, processing, and transmitting electrochemical signals over the neural pathways that comprise the brain's communication system. The neurons consist of four basic parts: the cell body, synapse, axon, and dendrite (Figure 1.1). Dendrites are the branch-like structures that provide the input to a cell body. Dendrites receive signals from other neurons at connection points called synapses. On the receiving side of a synapse these inputs are connected to the cell body. The cell body essentially sums the membrane potentials provided by the dendrites. When the cumulative excitation in the cell body exceeds the threshold, the cell fires, sending a signal down the axon to another neuron.

ANNs consist of a large number of neurons or simple processing units, also referred to as neurodes. An artificial neuron (Figure 1.2) mimics the characteristics of the biological neuron. Here, a set of inputs are applied, each representing an output of another neuron. Each input is multiplied by a corresponding

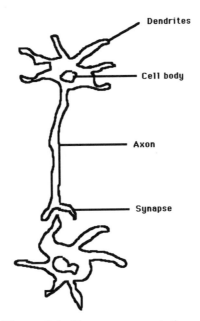

Figure 1.1. *Neuron representation.*

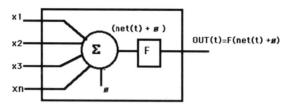

Figure 1.2. *Artificial neuron representation.*

weight, analogous to synaptic strengths. The weighted inputs are summed to determine the activation level of the neuron. The connection strengths or the weights represents the knowledge in the system. Information processing takes place through the interaction among these units.

Let $x = (x_1, x_2, \ldots, x_n)$ represents the n inputs applied to the artificial neuron. The net input to the neuron at time t is given by:

$$net(t) = \sum_{i=1}^{n} x_i w_i \qquad (1.1)$$

The net input, $net(t)$, is further processed by an activation function F to produce neuron's output signal, $O(t)$. Often activation values are restricted in a range $[0, 1]$. A number of activation functions can be used to define neuron characteristics. Commonly used activation functions are shown in Figure (1.3). Often a sigmoid function of the following form is preferred

$$F(x) = 1/\{1 + \exp[-(x + \phi)]\} \qquad (1.2)$$

where ϕ is a constant. The output of the neuron with the above activation function is then given by

$$O(t) = 1/(1 + \exp\{-[net(t) + \phi]\}) \qquad (1.3)$$

These outputs pass through unidirectional synaptic connections. This simple model of the artificial neuron ignores many characteristics of the biological neuron. It does not take into account the delays that affect the dynamics of the system. It does not include the effects of the frequency modulation function of the biological neuron. Nevertheless, the simple model of an artificial neuron is very useful in developing complex ANN models.

A number of considerations must be taken into account in designing an ANN model. One must first decide on the structure of the model. Usually the models consist of a number of layers. The number of layers and the number of units in each layer must be chosen. They depend on the application for which the network is being designed. The most general model assumes complete intercon-

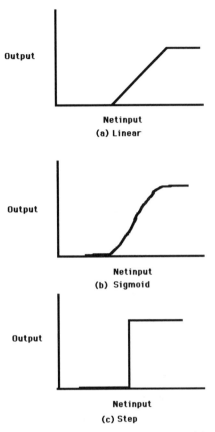

Figure 1.3. *Commonly used activation functions. (a) Linear. (b) Sigmoid. (c) Step.*

nections between all units and handles nonconnected units by setting the corresponding connection strengths equal to zero.

Some of the commonly used neural network architectures and the corresponding weight matrix configurations are shown in Figures 1.4 through 1.7. Elements of these matrices indicate the presence or absence of a connection between any two units. Here units are sequentially numbered. The presence and absence of a connection between any two units are indicated by the symbol × or a blank, respectively, as the corresponding matrix element. ANNs can be synchronous or asynchronous. Synchronous networks are controlled by clock pulses, whereas in asynchronous networks, units respond instantaneously to incoming inputs. One may also describe the types of interconnections between the units: the connections can be bidirectional or unidirectional. The activation function and the activation values to be used also need to be specified. The connection strengths or weights in a network represent the knowledge in the

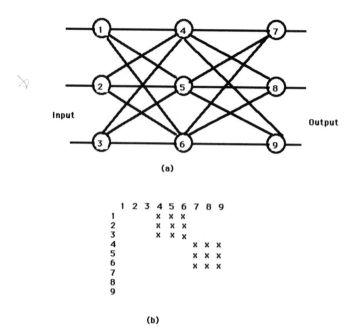

(a)

```
    1 2 3 4 5 6 7 8 9
1         x x x
2         x x x
3         x x x
4               x x x
5               x x x
6               x x x
7
8
9
```

(b)

Figure 1.4. *A three-layer feed-forward network (a) and a weight matrix for the network (b).*

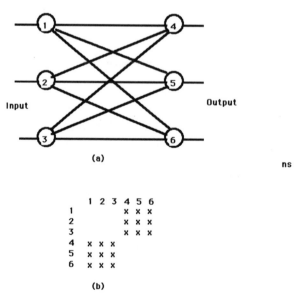

(a)

ns

```
    1 2 3 4 5 6
1         x x x
2         x x x
3         x x x
4   x x x
5   x x x
6   x x x
```

(b)

Figure 1.5. *A two-layer network with bidirectional connections (a) and its weight matrix (b).*

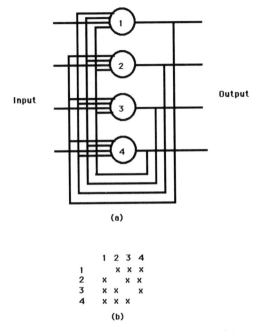

(a)

```
        1 2 3 4
    1     x x x
    2   x   x x
    3   x x   x
    4   x x x
```

(b)

Figure 1.6. *A single-layer network with feedback (a) and its weight matrix (b).*

system, and they are often updated iteratively during the learning phase. The advantages of ANN models are that (1) they can be implemented electrically, optically, or electrooptically, or can be modeled on a general-purpose computer; (2) they are fault tolerant and robust; (3) they work in parallel; and (4) many learning paradigms or algorithms are available in practice. ANN models have been used successfully for many image-processing and recognition applications.

1.2. IMAGE UNDERSTANDING

The recognition of an object in an image is a complex task that involves a broad range of techniques. Various steps involved in an image-understanding system are shown in Figure 1.8. The system consists of six stages: image acquisition, preprocessing, feature extraction, associative storage, knowledge base, and recognition. These stages essentially correspond to the low-level, intermediate-level, and high-level processing.

The first step in the process is image acquisition: acquiring a digital image. The term *image* refers to a two-dimensional light intensity function $f(x, y)$, where x and y are spatial coordinates and the value of f at any point (x, y) is proportional to the brightness or gray level of the image at that point. A

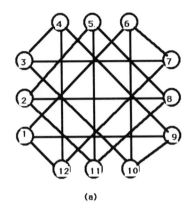

(a)

	1	2	3	4	5	6	7	8	9	10	11	12
1				x	x	x	x	x	x	x	x	x
2				x	x	x	x	x	x	x	x	x
3				x	x	x	x	x	x	x	x	x
4	x	x	x				x	x	x	x	x	x
5	x	x	x				x	x	x	x	x	x
6	x	x	x				x	x	x	x	x	x
7	x	x	x	x	x	x				x	x	x
8	x	x	x	x	x	x				x	x	x
9	x	x	x	x	x	x				x	x	x
10	x	x	x	x	x	x	x	x	x			
11	x	x	x	x	x	x	x	x	x			
12	x	x	x	x	x	x	x	x	x			

(b)

Figure 1.7. *A multilayer network with bidirectional connections (a) and its weight matrix (b).*

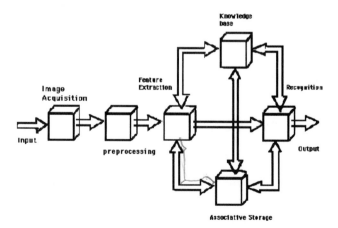

Figure 1.8. *Model for image recognition system.*

digitized image is an image $f(x, y)$ in which both spatial coordinates and brightness have been digitized. A digitized image can be considered as a matrix in which each row and column identify a point in the image and the corresponding matrix element value represents the gray level at that point. The elements of such a digitized array are called picture elements or pixels. The image acquisition stage is concerned with sensors that capture images. The sensor can be a camera or a scanner. The nature of the sensor and the image it produces are determined by the application.

After a digitized image has been obtained, the next step is preprocessing, which corresponds to early vision processing or low-level processing. A number of preprocessing techniques are available in practice. These include gray scale manipulation, noise filtering, isolation of regions, geometric correction, restoration, reconstruction, and segmentation. Image enhancement techniques can be classified into two broad categories: spatial domain and frequency domain methods. Spatial domain methods are based on the direct manipulation of gray values of pixels in the image. Frequency domain processing techniques are based on modifying the Fourier transform of an image. In the gray scale manipulation technique the enhancement at any point in the image may depend on the gray value at that point, or it may depend on the gray values at that point and its neighbors. The former category is referred to as point processing. Approaches wherein the enhancement at any pixel depends on the gray value of the pixel and those of its neighbors make use of masks or windows that define the neighborhood of the pixel. Many hardware and software implementations are available in practice to implement the above enhancement techniques.

ANN models provide an alternative approach to implement enhancement techniques. Researchers such as Grossberg (1988) have considered properties of the human vision system and have proposed neural network architectures for brightness perception under constant and variable illumination conditions. The human visual system takes variability in illumination into account. The preprocessing stage in a machine recognition system may deal with brightness perception, as well as problems such as image restoration and reconstruction. Image acquisition systems in practice are not perfect. They are of finite resolution. Image restoration methods deal with estimating an original image from a degraded one. Restoration techniques compensate for system degradation that the image might have undergone, and recently, ANN models have been developed for image restoration.

The next level of processing is the intermediate level. The processing on this level attempts to build a coalition of tokens that are obtained in the low-level processing and to extract meaningful entities. One well-known intermediate-level processing technique is feature extraction, which consists of mapping an observation vector onto a feature space. The main purpose of feature extraction is to reduce data by measuring certain features that distinguish the input patterns. To extract features, one may select a subset of the observed input vector, or one may transform the input observation vector to a feature vector using some orthogonal basis functions. In many applications, the observation vector is obtained by sampling an input image that represents highly correlated data. In order to reduce the dimensionality while retaining most information, the observation vector is mapped onto a feature space domain. The data in the transformed domain can then be ranked according to the degree of significance of the information content and the quality of the retrieved pattern.

During the past 30 years many techniques have been developed for feature extraction. These include the Fourier transform, moment invariants, the Wigner distribution, the Hough transform, orthogonal polynomials, Gabor functions, etc. Many ANN models have been suggested for feature extraction. The problem of invariant object recognition is often tackled at a feature-extraction stage. This is because in order to consider translation, rotation, and scale differences in the image, the recognition system needs to be trained over a large number of training samples. To obtain invariant features, the properties of the Fourier transform are often used. The human visual system is also sensitive to textural variations in the object's surfaces. Texture features are often used to recognize objects. Texture is generally recognized as being fundamental to perception. Many statistical and structural methods as well as ANN models for texture analysis are available in practice. Statistical methods of texture analysis are based on the relationship between gray values of pixels in the image. Recently, ANN models based on Gabor functions (Daugman, 1988) have been used for texture segmentation. The usage of Gabor functions has evolved because the receptive fields of neurons in a visual cortex are known to have shapes that approximate two-dimensional Gabor functions. The feature-extraction stage also deals with the extraction of texture features.

The last three stages—associative storage, knowledge base, and the recognition stage—correspond to high-level processing. The human memory can often recall complete information from partial information or subtle clues. Associative memories are content-addressable memories. The ability to get from one internal representation to another or to infer a complex representation from a portion forms the basis of an associative memory. The basic functions of an associative memory are to store associative pairs of patterns through a self-organizing process and to produce an appropriate response pattern on the presentation of the corresponding stimulus pattern. Associative memories are also useful for invariant object recognition. In the past few years there has been renewed interest in associative memory models. Textbooks such as those by Kohonen (1988), and Hinton and Anderson (1989) describe associative memories.

The recognition stage deals with classification. It assigns a label to an object based on the information provided by its descriptors. Conventional classification techniques are grouped into two categories: supervised and unsupervised techniques. In a supervised mode, classifiers learn with the help of training sets; in the case of an unsupervised mode, classifiers learn without training sets. Neural networks represent a powerful and reasonable alternative to conventional classifiers. ANN models with learning algorithms such as back-propagation are being used as supervised classifiers, and self-organizing neural networks with learning algorithms such as competitive learning, or adapative resonance theory (ART) are being used as unsupervised classifiers. Statistical methods and neural network classifiers are being used successfully in many recognition problems. However, there are many problems in practice where statistical methods are inappropriate and descriptive methods are more suitable. Descriptive methods are often based on the classification rules that map the input feature vectors to the output categories. The classification rules in this case can be stored in a knowledge base. The interaction between the knowledge base and other modules in a recognition system is shown in Figure 1.8. The knowledge base interacts not only with the feature-extraction and recognition stages but also with the associative storage. Often any prior knowledge about an object can also be encoded in the knowledge base. The knowledge may be as simple as detailing regions of an image where the information of interest is known to be located, thus limiting the search that has to be conducted in seeking that information. The knowledge base may be complex. The design of a machine recognition system needs to encompass all of the above processing stages.

In Chapter 2, we discuss algorithms and neural network models used in the preprocessing stage, including techniques for gray scale manipulation, segmentation, and edge detection, noise removal, restoration, and interpolation. Chapter 3 deals with feature extraction. Conventional methods of feature extraction such as moment invariants, and Fourier coefficients are discussed. We also introduce neural network architecture for transformed domain feature extraction. Chapter 4 deals with texture features and texture analysis. Chapter 5 and Chapter 6 deal with supervised and unsupervised classification techniques, respectively. Associative memories are discussed in Chapter 7. The human visual system is very sensitive to motion of objects in a scene. It also extracts depth information from stereo images. Temporal images are often used to extract motion parameters. Temporal analysis deals with sequences of images. The problem of temporal pattern recognition has been studied via both pattern recognition and the neural network approach. The techniques used in temporal image analysis and stereo vision are discussed in Chapter 8. Chapter 9 deals with neurocomputing. Neurocomputing is a technological discipline concerned with parallel, distributed, and adaptive information-processing systems based on the implementation and execution of neural algorithms (Hecht-Nielsen, 1990). Chapter 10 illustrates practical applications of ANN models.

REFERENCES

Andrews, H. C. (1970). *Computer Techniques in Image Processing*. Academic Press, New York.

Casasent, D. (1985). Hybrid optical/digital image pattern recognition: A review. *Proceedings of SPIE* 528:64–82.

Daugman, J. G. (1988). Complete discrete 2-D Gabor transforms by neural networks for image analysis and compression. *IEEE Transactions on Acoustics, Speech and Signal Processing 36*:1169–1179.

Dayhoff, J. (1990). *Neural Network Architectures*. Van Nostrand Reinhold, New York.

Duda, R. O., and Hart, P. E. (1973). *Pattern Classification and Scene Analysis*. John Wiley & Sons, New York.

Fu, K. S. (1977). *Syntactic Methods in Pattern Recognition: Applications*. Springer Verlag, New York.

Gonzalez, R. C., and Wintz, P. (1987). *Digital Image Processing*. Addison-Wesley, Reading, MA.

Gonzelez, R. C., and Woods, R. E. (1992). *Digital Image Processing*. Addison-Wesley, Reading, MA.

Grossberg, S. (1988). *Neural Networks and Natural Intelligence*. Bradford Books, MIT Press, Cambridge, MA.

Hebb, D. O. (1949). *The Organizational Behaviors*. John Wiley & Sons, New York.

Hecht-Nielsen, R. (1990). *Neurocomputing*. Addison-Wesley, Reading, MA.

Hinton, G., and Anderson, J. (1989). *Parallel Models of Associative Memory*. Lawrence Erlbaum Associates, Hillsdale, NJ.

Jain, A. K. (1989). *Fundamentals of Digital Image Processing*. Prentice Hall, Englewood Cliffs, NJ.

James, M. (1988). *Pattern Recognition*. John Wiley & Sons, New York.

Khanna, T. (1990). *Foundations of Neural Networks*. Addison-Wesley, Reading, MA.

Kohonen, T. (1988). *Self Organization and Associative Memory* (ed. 2). Springer-Verlag, Berlin.

Kulkarni, A. D. (1990). Neural networks for pattern recognition. In: *Progress In Neural Networks*, Vol. I, O. Omidvar (ed.), pp. 197–219, Ablex, New York.

Lippman, R. P. (1987). An introduction to computing with neural nets. *IEEE Transactions on Acoustics, Speech, and Signal Processing 32*:4–22.

Minsky, M., and Papert, S. (1969). *Perceptrons*. MIT Press, Cambridge, MA.

Pao, Y. H. (1989). *Adaptive Pattern Recognition and Neural Networks*. Addison-Wesley, Reading, MA.

Rosenblatt, F. (1958). The perceptron: A probablistic model for information storage and organization in brain. *Psychology Review*, 65:386–408.

Rosenblatt, F. (1962). *Principles of Neurodynamics: Perceptron and the Theory of Brain Mechanism*. Spartan Books, Washington, DC.

Rosenfeld, A., and Kak, A. (1982). *Digital Image Processing*, Vols. I and II. Academic Press, Orlando, FL.

Rumelhart, D. E., McClelland, J. L., and the PDP Group, (1986). *Parallel Distributed Processing*, Vol. I. MIT Press, Cambridge, MA.

Tou, J. T., and Gonzalez, R. C. (1974). *Pattern Recognition Principles: Trainable Pattern Classifiers—the Deterministic Approach*. Addison-Wesley, Reading, MA.

Ullman, J. R. (1973). *Pattern Recognition Techniques*. Butterworth, London.

Wasserman, P. D. (1989). *Neural Computing Theory and Practice*. Van Nostrand Reinhold, New York.

2

Preprocessing

2.1. INTRODUCTION

The first stage in an image-understanding system is the preprocessing stage, which deals with early vision processing. Its main function is to develop useful canonical descriptions of shapes and surfaces in a given image. Images are acquired by recording reflected light energy from the object surfaces. Four main factors contribute to the intensity value of a pixel in an image: (1) the geometry, (2) reflectances of visible surfaces, (3) illumination of the scene, and (4) the viewpoint. In a given image all these factors are muddled up. The purpose of early vision processing is to sort out which changes are caused by what factors and to create representations in which the four factors are separated (Marr, 1984).

In an image-understanding system, the preprocessing stage often performs functions such as the gray scale manipulation, edge detection, developing descriptions of objects or shapes in the image, image restoration, and geometric correction. Intensity changes yield important clues about the structure of a visible surface. In the preprocessing stage we try to capture this information. There are a number of image-processing operations that can be performed with virtually no knowledge about the contents of the image. These operations include gray scale manipulation, filtering, noise removal, edge detection, segmentation, and restoration. Image enhancement techniques deal with improvement in the image quality. Conventional techniques, as well as artificial neural network (ANN) models used in preprocessing, are discussed in this chapter.

2.2. GRAY SCALE MANIPULATION TECHNIQUES

In order to make maximum use of the available information or to extract features in the image, some sort of enhancement is usually needed. Many textbooks and review articles such as those by Andrews (1970), Huang et al. (1971), Rosenfeld and Kak (1982), and Gonzalez and Wintz (1987) deal with enhancement techniques. Gray scale manipulation techniques deal with point-to-point mapping. Filtering techniques consider neighboring pixels to calculate gray values of pixels in the output image. Operations such as the gray scale manipulation and filtering are also performed by the early vision system. Researchers have tried to develop artificial neural network architectures to perform early vision tasks (Grossberg and Mingolla, 1987; Carpenter and Grossberg, 1987; Grossberg, 1988).

Gray scale manipulation is an intensity-mapping technique in which each pixel is assigned a new gray value to improve the contrast in the image. In gray scale manipulation, often the gray level difference between the object and background is increased. Gray scale manipulation techniques can be defined as:

$$g'(i,j) = T[g(i,j)] \qquad (2.1)$$

where g' is the enhanced imagery, g is the original imagery, $T(g)$ is the transform function, and (i,j) represents the column and row number of the pixel. Most commonly used transfer functions are shown in Figure 2.1. In order to implement these transfer functions, look-up tables are often constructed. Pixels are mapped from the input image to the output image using the look-up

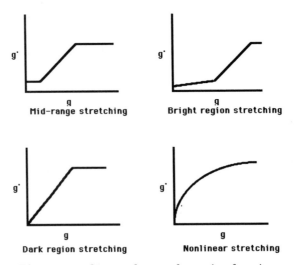

Figure 2.1. *Gray scale transformation functions.*

table. The original and enhanced imageries using a linear transfer function are shown in Figures 2.2 and 2.3, respectively.

Histogram equalization is one of the commonly used gray scale manipulation techniques. The typical histograms of a set of input and output images are shown in Figure 2.4. It can be seen from Figure 2.4 that gray values in the output image are uniformly distributed. The cumulative distribution function

Figure 2.2. *Original image (satellite data). (From Kulkarni, 1986, with permission. © 1986 Academic Press.)*

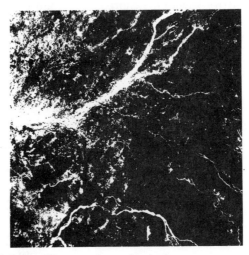

Figure 2.3. *Enhanced by stretching. (From Kulkarni, 1986, with permission. © 1986 Academic Press.)*

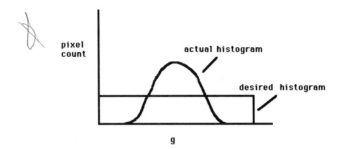

Figure 2.4. *Histogram equalization.*

(CDF) of a typical image is shown in Figure 2.5. The desired linear CDF corresponds to the equalized histogram and is also shown in Figure 2.5. The CDF linearization procedure can be formulated as:

$$g'(i,j) = (g_{\max} - g_{\min})p[g(i,j)] + g_{\min} \tag{2.2}$$

where g' represents the enhanced imagery, g represents the input imagery, $p[g(i,j)]$ is the value of the CDF at a gray level $g(i,j)$, and $g_{\min}$ and $g_{\max}$ are the minimum and maximum gray levels, respectively.

Filtering techniques are used to remove noise or to enhance edges and small details in an image. The filtering can be carried out in the spatial frequency domain or in the space domain. Any given image can be decomposed into its Fourier series. The low-frequency components correspond to homogeneous objects and background, whereas the high-frequency components correspond to edges and small details in the image. Low-pass and high-pass filters are used to smoothe the image or to enhance edges and small details. Duda and Hart (1973)

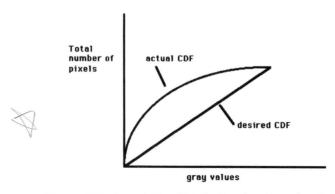

Figure 2.5. *Cumulative distribution function of an image.*

considered the low-pass filter with the transfer function

$$H(u,v) = [(\cos \pi u)(\cos \pi v)]^{\alpha} \tag{2.3}$$

where $\alpha \geq 1$; and the high-pass filter with the transfer function

$$H(u,v) = 1 - [(\cos \pi u)(\cos \pi v)]^{\alpha} \tag{2.4}$$

where $\alpha \geq 1$. In Eq. 2.3 and 2.4, u and v represent spatial frequencies in the x and y directions, respectively.

Filtering can also be carried out in the the spatial domain. Filtering in a spatial domain can be represented as

$$g'(i,j) = C_1[g_L(i,j)] + C_2[g(i,j) - g_L(i,j)] \tag{2.5}$$

where g' is the enhanced imagery, g is the input or original imagery, C_1 and C_2 are constants such that $C_1 \leq 1$ and $C_2 \geq 1$, (i,j) corresponds to the row and column numbers of the pixel, and g_L is the local gray level mean. It can be seen that with $C_1 = 1$ and $C_2 = 0$, the operation is simple smoothing. With $C_1 \leq 1$ and $C_2 \geq 1$, edges and fine details in the image are enhanced. The original image and the high-pass version obtained by spatial filtering are shown in Figure 2.6a, and b, respectively. Spatial filtering methods are often used in practice.

2.3. EDGE ENHANCEMENT TECHNIQUES

In edge enhancement, we attempt to make edges more visually prominent within the image. Edge enhancement techniques essentially increase the gray level difference between the boundaries of two regions. Most of the edge operators used in practice are local. A step edge and its derivatives are shown in Figure 2.7. The line edge and its derivatives are shown in Figure 2.8. It is obvious that for a step edge, the first derivative shows a maximum at the edge point, whereas for the line edge the first derivative is zero at the edge point. The second derivative, in the case of a step edge is zero. However, for the line edge the second derivative is maximum at the edge point. Hence, the edges in the image can be detected by fixing a threshold on the values of the first and second derivatives. Because the images are two dimensional, the derivatives in both directions need to be considered. Since the gray value variations are different for different types of edges, the threshold for detecting edges is a subjective matter. The presence of noise in the image also causes difficulty in detecting edges.

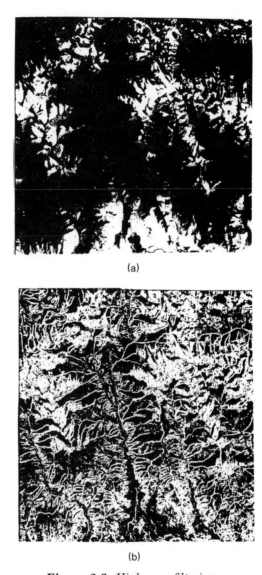

(a)

(b)

Figure 2.6. *High-pass filtering.*

To detect edges in the image, operators such as the Laplacian, gradient, and Robert's may be applied. These can be described as:

$$g'(i,j) = abs[4g(i,j) - g(i+1,j) - g(i,j+1) - g(i-1,j) - g(i,j-1)]$$

$$\text{(2.6)}$$

$$g'(i,j) = \left\{[g(i,j) - g(i,j-1)]^2 + [g(i,j) - g(i-1,j)]^2\right\}^{1/2} \quad \text{(2.7)}$$

$$g'(i,j) = abs[g(i,j) - g(i+1,j+1)] \quad \text{(2.8)}$$

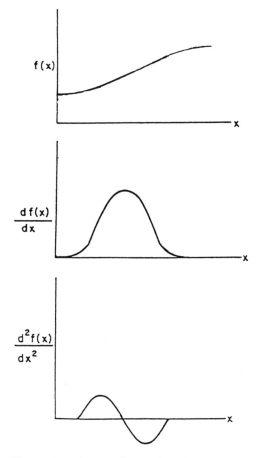

Figure 2.7. *A step edge and its derivatives.*

In Eq. 2.6, 2.7, and 2.8, $g(i, j)$ corresponds to the input image gray value at (i, j); $g'(i, j)$ corresponds to the output image gray value at (i, j). In order to determine whether a pixel at (i, j) is an edge pixel or not an edge pixel, some threshold T is employed; i.e.,

if $g'(i, j) \geq T$, the pixel is an edge pixel, whereas
if $g'(i, j) < T$, the pixel is not an edge pixel.

Edge operators can also be defined in terms of masks. Considering a region of the size 3×3 as shown in Figure 2.9, with g_5 as the central pixel, the gray values in the region can be represented by a vector $\boldsymbol{g} = [g_1, g_2, \ldots, g_9]$. The weighting coefficient vector can be represented by $\boldsymbol{w} = [w_1, w_2, \ldots, w_9]$. The edges can be detected by fixing a threshold on the value of S, which is given by

$$S = \boldsymbol{g} \cdot \boldsymbol{w} = \sum_{i=1}^{9} g_i w_i \qquad (2.9)$$

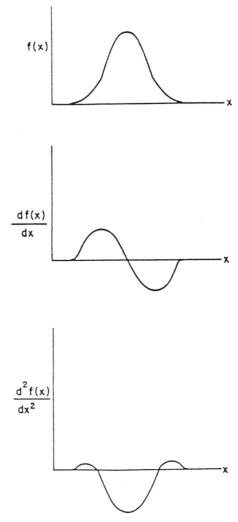

Figure 2.8. *A line and its derivatives.*

Different masks can be used in detecting edges in different directions. The masks for Sobel and Khrish operators are shown in Figures 2.10 and 2.11, respectively. Several masks have been proposed in the literature for detection of edges and lines by fitting a hypersurface to an image in the neighborhood of each pixel. Hueckel (1973) treated the surface fitting using a polar version of the orthogonal Fourier basis. Haralick (1980, 1981), Morgenthaler and Rosenfeld (1981), and Chittineni (1982, 1983) used multidimensional orthogonal polynomials as the basis functions.

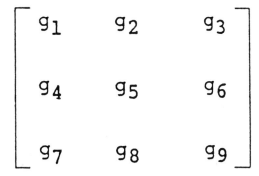

Figure 2.9. *A 3 × 3 image window.*

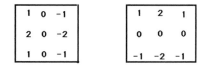

Figure 2.10. *Masks for Sobel operator.*

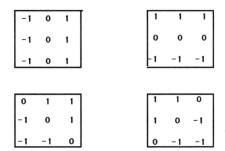

Figure 2.11. *Krisch templates.*

2.4. ANN MODELS FOR BRIGHTNESS PERCEPTION AND BOUNDARY DETECTION

Grossberg and Todorovic (1988) have considered properties of a human visual system and have proposed a neural network architecture for brightness perception under constant and variable illumination conditions. The architecture consists of a feature counter system (FCS) and a boundary counter system (BCS). A fundamental issue in visual perception and the design of a real machine vision system is how the visual system transforms the incoming distribution of illuminance to generate the perceived brightness distribution.

The transformation of illuminance into brightness is a complex process. To mimic a human visual system, we need to consider two phenomena: brightness constancy and brightness contrast. The phenomenon of brightness constancy can be explained by the fact that two identical pieces of paper will look about equally bright even when one is well illuminated and other is in shadow. The visual system takes into account the variability of the illumination. The phenomenon of brightness contrast can be explained by the fact that the same gray piece of paper looks brighter against a black background than against a white background. Thus, the appearance of a portion of a visual field not only depends on the conditions within that region but also is dependent on context (Grossberg and Todorovic, 1988). The boundary counter system is a segmentation and boundary completion process based on luminance differences across the image. As proposed by Grossberg and Mingolla (1987), the BCS contains two successive subsystems: an orientation contrast (OC) filter and a cooperative competitive (CC) loop. The OC filter obtains the amplitude, direction, and location of luminance gradients within an image. The CC loop subsystem is a four-layer neural network that allows interaction between the oriented receptive field data. Van Allen and Kolodzy (1988) have developed software to simulate the BCS on a general-purpose computer. They have considered two images: the Kanizsa square and the Ehrenstein figure. The images before and after processing are shown in Figures 2.12 and 2.13. The BCS produced visible contrast at locations where no illuminance contrast existed in the original image.

Recently, Carpenter et al. (1989) developed a neural network architecture called the CORT-X filter for boundary segmentation in the presence of noise. The model detects, regularizes, and completes sharp image boundaries. The basic element of their model is a contrast-sensitive cell that detects the direction and amount of contrast between gray levels. The output of a simple cell is given by:

$$output = \max[\, L_s(x, k) - \alpha_s R_s(x, k) - \beta_s, 0\,] \tag{2.10}$$

where

$$L_S(x, k) = \int_{\substack{\text{left} \\ \text{half}}} I(y)\, dy \Big/ \int_{\substack{\text{left} \\ \text{half}}} dy$$

and

$$R_S(x, k) = \int_{\substack{\text{right} \\ \text{half}}} I(y)\, dy \Big/ \int_{\substack{\text{right} \\ \text{half}}} dy$$

where x represents the position of the receptive field center, k is the orientation of the receptive field, α_s is a contrast parameter $(1 < \alpha_s)$, β_s is a threshold parameter such that $0 < \beta_s < 1$, $L_s(x, k)$ is the total activation of the left half of the receptive field, $R_s(x, k)$ is the total activation of the right half of the

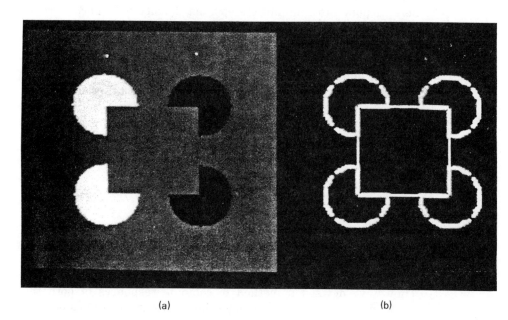

(a)   (b)

Figure 2.12. The Kanizsa square (a) before processing and (b) after processing. (From Van Allen and Kolodzy, 1988, with permission. © 1988 IEEE.)

(a)   (b)

Figure 2.13. The Ehrenstein figure (a) before processing and (b) after processing. (From Van Allen and Kolodzy, 1988, with permission. © 1988 IEEE.)

receptive field, and $I(y)$ represents illuminance at y. The simple cell described here responds to luminance steps, dot density differences, gradual changes in luminance, and other contrast changes.

The next processing step is the detector that is sensitive to orientation, amount, and spatial scale of contrast at a given image location but not to the direction of contrast. This type of detector may be compared to the complex cell in the visual cortex. The response $C_s(x, k)$ of a complex cell centered at position x and orientation k can be obtained by using a pair of simple cells with the same direction but of opposite contrast.

$$C_s(x, k) = \max[\, L_s(x, k) - \alpha_s R_s(x, k) - \beta_s, 0\,]$$
$$+ \max[\, R_s(x, k) - \alpha_s L_s(x, k) - \beta_s, 0\,] \tag{2.11}$$

In order to detect edges in the presence of noise, one may use filters of different sizes. Simple and complex cells are shown in Figure 2.14. Carpenter et al. (1989) have shown that smaller filters do a better job of boundary localization than a larger filter, whereas the larger filter does a better job of noise suppression. They have devised a method to combine responses of both the smaller and larger filters, in order to achieve the desirable properties of both. The interaction is defined by

$$B_{12}(x) = D_1(x) \sum_y D_2(y) U(y, x) \tag{2.12}$$

In Eq. 2.12 the unoriented excitatory kernel $U(y, x)$ is the nearest-neighbor kernel such that $\sum U(y, x) = 1$. The factors $D_1(x)$ and $D_2(y)$ represent the hypercomplex activation patterns corresponding to the smaller and higher filters, respectively. The factor $D_1(x)$ is generally positive on the boundary and zero close to the boundary; it thus accurately localizes boundary segments and suppresses noise near the boundary. The factor $D_2(x)$ suppresses noise far from the boundary (Carpenter et al., 1989). Software to simulate the CORT-X filters

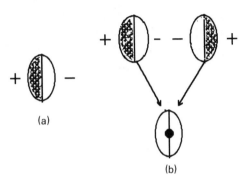

Figure 2.14. *Simple and complex cells.*

has been developed and tested with test images (Seedle, 1989). The results are shown in Figures 2.15a through d. Figure 2.15a represents the original image; Figures 2.15b and 2.15c show the outputs obtained by 3×3 and 5×5 filters, respectively. The combined response of both filters is shown in Figure 2.15d.

Dhawan and Dufresne (1990) have suggested a self-organizing neural network to enhance and restore gray level images for application in low-level image processing. The model consists of a multilayered neural network called the "neuron pyramid" for image representation and recognition. Each layer in the network presents a description of the image with a specific primitive such as a pixel, an edge, a region. The results from the first layer in their model are presented here. Each pixel is represented by a neuron with a state $o(j, k) = 1, 2, \ldots, N$; which is equal to the gray level value of the pixel for $j = 1, 2, \ldots, J$; $k = 1, 2, \ldots, K$, where $J \times K$ is the image size. Each unit is linked with other neighboring units with mth-order links. The strengths of these links are proportional to the contrast between the pixels.

The network layer analyzes the state of each unit with respect to the strengths of connected links under a local homogeneity-based constrained environment. Any change in the value of the unit state establishes a focus of attention of analysis and tries to propagate the change to neighboring units. The states of units are thus updated, and the process is iterated until it converges to the stopping criterion set by the image evaluation function. The links between the two units are defined as contrast values, which are computed as

$$w_m(i, j, k, l) = [f(i, j) - f(k, l)]/N \tag{2.13}$$

where $m = 1$ corresponds to the first-order links and $m = 2$ corresponds to the second-order links, N is the number of gray levels in the image, and $f(i, j)$ represents the gray value of pixel (i, j).

Dhawan and Dufresne (1990) have considered the first- and second-order contrast links. The first-order contrast links are defined as nearest neighbors, whereas the second-order contrast links are defined as the two pixels jumping over the central pixel, as shown in Figure 2.16. The initial states of units are set equal to the gray level values of the respective pixels. To start, a random unit is picked. The state of the unit is analyzed on the basis of the weighted link strengths. The weighted linked strength is defined as

$$w_\tau(i, j) = \alpha \sum_{k, l \in R_1} w_1(i, j, k, l) + \beta \sum_{k, l \in R_2} w_2(i, j, k, l) \tag{2.14}$$

where R_1 and R_2 represent the first-order and second-order regions, respectively, and α and β are the constants. The weighted sum of link strength $w_\tau(i, j)$ is compared with a threshold T to update the unit state. If $w_\tau(i, j)$ is

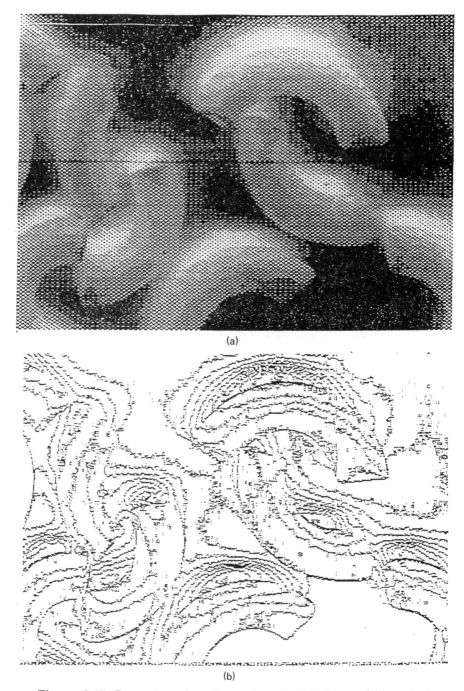

(a)

(b)

Figure 2.15. Processing of an image by CORT-X filters. (a) Original image. (b) Output from a 3 × 3 CORT-X filter. (c) Output from a 5 × 5 CORT-X filter. (d) Combined response.

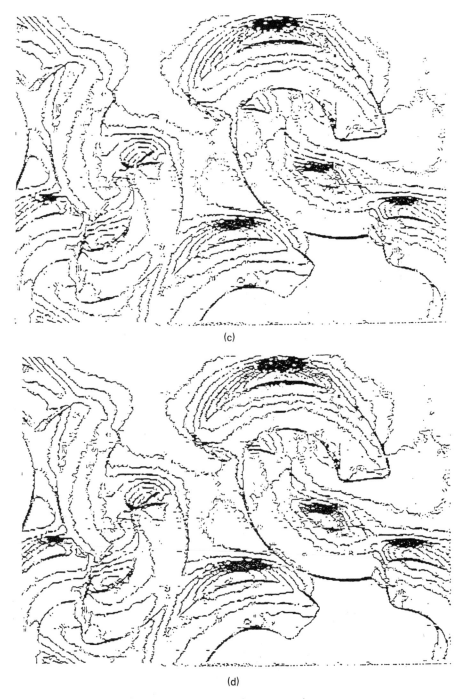

(c)

(d)

Figure 2.15. *(Continued.)*

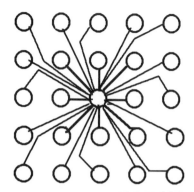

Figure 2.16. *First- and second-order links.*

greater than the threshold T, then only the state of the unit (i, j) is changed by adding or subtracting 1 to the current gray value. It can be noted that high values of $w_T(i, j)$ correspond to nonhomogeneous regions or edges in the image. Adding or subtracting 1 increases the contrast at such nonhomogeneous regions. This processing is essentially similar to high-pass filtering in the space domain. The choice of the threshold T is critical.

Dhawan and Dufresne (1990) also assign an inhibitory status, a probability indicating the likelihood of updating the unit state. In the beginning all units are active, as the inhibitory status of all the units is set to 0. After a few iterations the inhibitory status of many units becomes 1. The inhibitory status of each unit is changed such that the focus of attention is extended from the active area to an inactive area. To stop the iterative process, they have used a selective criterion influenced by the local homogeneity. They selected three spatially distributed regions with minimum variance in contrast links that are well separated. After each iteration, the change in variances of these selected regions is computed and normalized. If the combined weighted variance exceeds three times the initial variance measure, the iterations are stopped. The result of the last iteration is used as the final solution. As an illustration, they tested the algorithm with a test image. The original and enhanced images are shown in Figures 2.17a and b, respectively.

2.5. NOISE REMOVAL TECHNIQUES

If an image contains noise, smoothing techniques are used to clean the noise. However, some smoothing techniques blur the image. Thus, edge enhancement may be needed afterwards. The simplest smoothing technique is equal to a weighted averaging over the neighborhood of a pixel. It can be expressed as

$$g'(i, j) = \sum_{p=-m}^{m} \sum_{q=-n}^{n} w(p, q)g(i - p, j - q) \qquad (2.15)$$

(a) (b)

Figure 2.17. *Enhancement by ANN model. (a) Original image. (b) En-*
hanced by neural network. (From Dhawan and Dufresne, 1990, with
permission. © 1990 IEEE.)

where the weighting coefficients $w(p, q)$ are given by

$$w(p, q) = 1/(2m + 1)(2n + 1) \qquad (2.16)$$

Eq. 2.15 replaces the gray value at (i, j) by a gray value averaged over a $(2m + 1) \times (2n + 1)$ rectangular neighborhood surrounding (i, j), and $g'(i, j)$ represents the output image. This simple averaging technique removes noise; however, it blurs the image. To reduce the blurring effect, several unequal weighted smoothing techniques have been suggested. These are

$$W = \begin{vmatrix} 0.25 & 0.5 & 0.25 \\ 0.5 & 1.0 & 0.5 \\ 0.25 & 0.5 & 0.25 \end{vmatrix} \qquad (2.17)$$

$$W = \begin{vmatrix} 1 & 1 & 1 \\ 1 & 2 & 1 \\ 1 & 1 & 1 \end{vmatrix} \qquad (2.18)$$

The unequal weighted masks improve the signal-to-noise ratio in the output image and cause less blurring than the simple averaging technique.

There are many methods that make use of statistical properties of pixels. Yasuoka and Haralick (1983) have proposed a scheme using a slope facet model, with a t test for cleaning the pepper-and-salt noise. In their linear stochastic model, the gray value of any pixel can be expressed as

$$g(i, j) = \alpha i + \beta j + \gamma + \rho \varepsilon(i, j) \qquad (2.19)$$

where i represents the row number, j is the column number, ε represents the independent identically distributed random noise with standard deviation ρ, and α, β, γ, and ρ are the parameters of the model.

Each pixel is checked for noise by considering a 3×3 neighborhood. The model is fitted for a 3×3 block. The estimated $\hat{\alpha}$, $\hat{\beta}$, $\hat{\gamma}$, and $\hat{\rho}$ are found by the criterion function J, which in this case is a total mean-squared error for the block Ω.

$$J = \sum_{i,j \in \Omega} [g(i,j) - \alpha i - \beta j - \gamma]^2 \tag{2.20}$$

By minimizing J with reference to α, β, and γ, we get

$$\hat{\alpha} = \sum_{i,j} ig(i,j) \Big/ \sum_{i,j} i^2 \tag{2.21}$$

$$\hat{\beta} = \sum_{i,j} jg(i,j) \Big/ \sum_{i,j} j^2 \tag{2.22}$$

$$\hat{\gamma} = \sum_{i,j} g(i,j) \Big/ \sum_{i,j} 1 \tag{2.23}$$

In all of the above summations, i and j vary from -1 to $+1$. From these estimates ρ is found as below

$$\hat{\rho}2 = \left[\sum_{i,j} g(i,j) - \hat{\alpha} i - \hat{\beta} j - \hat{\gamma} \right]^2 \Big/ N \tag{2.24}$$

where N is the number of elements in the block (in this case $N = 9$). The estimated gray value of the pixel can now be expressed as

$$g(i,j) = \hat{\alpha} i + \hat{\beta} j + \hat{\gamma} + \hat{\rho} \epsilon(i,j) \tag{2.25}$$

The t test is used to test the hypothesis H_0: $g(i,j) = \hat{g}(i,j)$; i.e., the estimated value and the actual values are equal, and hence $g(i,j)$ is not a noise pixel. Here t' is defined as

$$t' = [g(i,j) - \hat{g}(i,j)]/\rho\sqrt{N}$$

For $N = 9$ and $\rho = \hat{\rho}$, the threshold value of t' is taken as $t(N - 1, 0.05)$ using 95% confidence level, and the value of t can read from tables. If $t' < t(N - 1, 0.05)$, we accept the hypothesis H_0; i.e., $g(i,j)$ is not a noise element and is not replaced. If $t' \geq t(N - 1, 0.05)$, we reject the hypothesis H_0; i.e., $g(i,j)$ is a noise element, and we replace it by $\hat{g}(i,j)$. The scheme is amenable to iterations. A software simulation of the above algorithm has been developed and

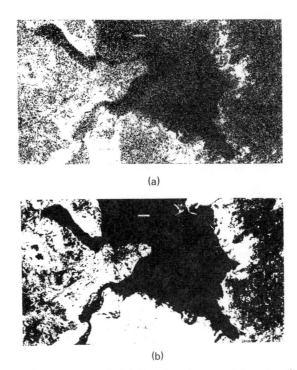

(a)

(b)

Figure 2.18. *Noise removal. (a) Landsat image with noise. (b) Landsat image without noise. (From Kulkarni, 1986, with permission. © Academic Press.)*

implemented. The algorithm has been applied to a test image. The original image with noise is shown in Figure 2.18a, and the image after filtering is shown in Figure 2.18b (Kulkarni, 1986).

2.6. IMAGE RESTORATION

No imaging system in practice is perfect, and images obtained in practice are always degraded. Restoration techniques are applied to compensate for system degradations such as motion blur, atmospheric turbulence, and optical diffractions (Huang et al., 1971, Sahasrabudhe and Kulkarni, 1979). Many methods for image restoration have been suggested in practice. They include the mean squared error filters, singular value decomposition technique, and others. In all of these methods imaging systems are modeled by a linear system, and the systems are characterized by their point spread functions. Restoration techniques basically deal with inversion of the degrading process. Software implementations of conventional restoration methods are often time-consuming and not useful for real-time applications. Recently, a few ANN models for image restoration have been suggested (Zhou et al., 1988; Kulkarni, 1991; Farehat and

Bai, 1989). The model suggested by Zhou et al. (1988) uses the Hopfield network, whereas the model suggested by Kulkarni (1990a, 1991) is a six-layer feed-forward network, and it is based on the singular value decomposition technique. ANN models for image restoration are discussed in subsequent sections.

Many imaging systems can be modeled in practice by an integral equation (Huang et al., 1971):

$$g(x, y) + \varepsilon(x, y) = \int_a^b \int_a^b f(x', y')h(x, x'; y, y') \, dx' \, dy' \qquad (2.26)$$

for $a \le x, y \le b$ where $f(x', y')$ is an object (ideal image), and $h(x, x'; y, y')$ is the impulse response function of the recording system. The degraded image is given by $g(x, y)$, and $\varepsilon(x, y)$ represents the random additive noise in the measurement of $g(x, y)$. $\varepsilon(x, y)$ may represent detector noise and/or round-off errors. It is often possible to reduce Eq. 2.26 by using the scanning or stacking operation to a Fredholm integral equation of the first kind:

$$g(y) + \varepsilon(y) = \int_a^b f(x)h(x, y) \, dx \qquad (2.27)$$

for $a \le y \le b$.

The problem of restoration reduces to solving Eq. 2.27 for $f(x)$, when $g(y)$ and $h(x, y)$ are known. The family of allowed functions $\varepsilon(y)$ defines a family of functions $f(x)$; however, most of these solutions are physically meaningless. To solve Eq. 2.27 numerically or by ANN models, it is necessary to make the variables discrete and replace the integral equation by a set of finite linear equations. Continuous variables x and y can be replaced by sets of finite mesh points.

$$a \le y_1 \le y_2 \cdots \le y_{n_1 - 1} \le y_{n_1} \le b$$

$$a \le x_1 \le x_2 \cdots \le x_{n_2 - 1} \le x_{n_2} \le b$$

where $n_1 \ge n_2$. The integral equations then can be replaced by a set of equations.

$$g(y_i) + \varepsilon(y_i) = \int_a^b h(y_i, x)f(x) \, dx$$

$$= \sum_{j=1}^{n_2} d_j h(y_i, x_j)f(x_j) \qquad (2.28)$$

where $i = 1, 2, \ldots n_1$ and $j = 1, 2, \ldots n_2$, and $d_1, d_2, \ldots d_{n2}$ are the weighting coefficients for the quadrature formula used. In order to write Eq. 2.28 in a matrix form, we define vectors f, g, ε and matrix H as $f = f(x_j)$, $\varepsilon = \varepsilon(y_i)$, $g = g(y_i)$, and $H = d_j h(y_i, x_j)$. With the above notation, Eq. 2.28 can be rewritten as

$$Hf = g + \varepsilon \qquad (2.29)$$

The solution of the system of equations in Eq. 2.29 by direct inversion is given by

$$f = H^{\dagger}(g + \varepsilon) \qquad (2.30)$$

where $H^{\dagger}$ represents the g-inverse of H.

Many researchers have suggested numerical methods to solve Eq. 2.30. Phillips (1962) assumed the desired solution to be reasonably smooth. He chose the second derivative to be minimum as a smoothness criterion. Twomey (1963) simplified Phillips' method by generalizing it to use prior constraints. Sahasrabudhe and Kulkarni (1977, 1979) assumed an image to be a sample function of a homogeneous random field in a two-dimensional parameter space and have used the autocorrelation function as a priori knowledge (Habibi and Wintz, 1971; Kretzmer, 1952). They suggested a singular value decomposition (SVD) approach. Kulkarni (1991) has developed an ANN model based on the SVD approach in which weights in the network are initialized using the SVD components. The "critical weights" in the network are updated iteratively to obtain a smooth solution. The main advantages of neural network implementation are that the neural network model is massively parallel and can be implemented electronically or electrooptically. The ANN model can be used along with a recording system to obtain the restored image.

The model suggested by Kulkarni (1991) is a linear feedforward network as shown in Figure 2.19. Recently, there has been renewed interest in the study of linear neural networks. This is because the linear networks serve as a basis for understanding qualitatively the behavior of more efficient nonlinear networks, whose analysis is otherwise difficult. The model makes use of sigma units as well as pi units. If the net input for a unit is the sum of all weighted inputs, then the unit is called a sigma unit. Other kinds of units are pi units. The pi units and their neurobiological interpretation have been discussed recently by Durbin and Rumelhart (1989). In pi units the net input of any unit is a product of all weighted inputs. In some situations, such as calculating autocorrelation coefficients, pi units are very useful.

Consider Eq. 2.30; by using the singular value decomposition (SVD) of matrix H we have

$$f = U[D, 0]V^T(g + \varepsilon) \qquad (2.31)$$

where columns of U are eigenvectors of $H^T H$, the rows of V are eigenvectors of HH^T, $D = \mathrm{diag}[1/\mu_1, 1/\mu_2, \ldots, 1/\mu_n]$, and the μ_i are the singular values of H.

In Figure 2.19, the weights connecting layers $L_1 L_2$, $L_2 L_3$ and $L_3 L_4$ are initialized using the elements of matrices $\boldsymbol{V}^T$, $[\boldsymbol{D}, \boldsymbol{0}]$, and $\boldsymbol{U}$, respectively. Input to the network is the observation vector $\boldsymbol{g}$. The output vector $\boldsymbol{f}$ obtained at layer L_4 is given by

$$f_i = \sum_{j=1}^{n_2} U_{ij} \beta_j \omega_j \tag{2.32}$$

where β_j are elements of vector β, which is given by $\beta = \boldsymbol{V}^T(\boldsymbol{g} + \varepsilon)$, and $\omega_j = 1/\mu_j$.

The β_j components in Eq. 2.32 differ from their true values because of the presence of noise ε in the measurement of $\boldsymbol{g}$. It can be seen from Eq. 2.32 that the solution $\boldsymbol{f}$ is sensitive to errors in β values that correspond to small singular values; whereas the solution is insensitive to errors in β components that correspond to large singular values. The distinction between large and small singular values can be made as follows. In solving Eq. 2.30, ϕ_1, the signal-to-noise ratio in solution $\boldsymbol{f}$, and ϕ_2, the signal-to-noise ratio in the

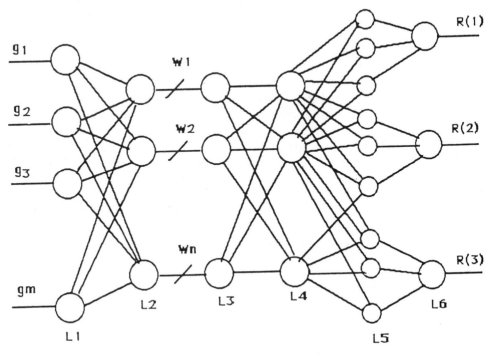

Figure 2.19. ANN model for image restoration. (From Kulkarni, 1991, with permission.)

measurement of g, are related by

$$\phi_1 \leq (1/C)\phi_2 \qquad (2.33)$$

where the condition number C is the ratio of the largest to the smallest singular value of H. In a physical situation, depending on the accepted lower bound on ϕ_1 ($\phi_{1\,min}$) and precision in measurement of g (i.e., $\phi_2 = \|g\|/e_2$, as determined by detector noise, truncation and roundoff errors, etc.), the singular values μ_i for which the inequality $\phi_{1\,min} \leq (\mu_{max}/\mu_i)\phi_2$ is satisfied are considered small singular values, and the corresponding weights $\omega_i = 1/\mu_i$ are considered critical weights.

The estimated autocorrelation or the output at layer L_6 is given by

$$\hat{R}(k) = \sum_{i=1}^{n_2-k} f_i f_{i+k} \qquad (2.34)$$

where $k = 1, 2, \ldots, K$. If we compare the estimated autocorrelation function $\hat{R}(i)$ with the known autocorrelation function $R(i)$, we get a system of equations given by

$$R(i) - \hat{R}(i) = 0 \qquad (2.35)$$

for $i = 1, 2, \ldots, K$. Using Eq. 2.32 and 2.34, we can rewrite Eq. 2.35 as

$$F_i(\omega_{n_2-m+1}, \ldots, \omega_{n_2-1}, \omega_{n_2}) = 0 \qquad \text{for } i = 1, 2, \ldots, K \qquad (2.36)$$

where F_i represents a quadratic equation with m critical weights. The critical weights have been considered to be unknown.

To solve the system in Eq. 2.36, consider the function

$$S(\omega_{n_2-m+1}, \ldots, \omega_{n_2-1}, \omega_{n_2}) = \sum_{i-1}^{K} \left[F_i(\omega_{n_2-m+1}, \ldots, \omega_{n_2-1}, \omega_{n_2}) \right]^2 \qquad (2.37)$$

The solution of the system of equations in Eq. 2.37 reduces the function S to zero; contrariwise, the values of the weights for which the error is minimized are the roots of the system of equations in Eq. 2.36. The function S represents the mean square error in the autocorrelation function. The critical weights in the model are adjusted such that the mean squared error in the autocorrelation function is minimized. The algorithm for updating the weights is described in the steps below (Kulkarni, 1991):

1. Initialize the weights using eigenvalues and eigenvectors of matrix H.
2. Propagate the input vector g to obtain the solution f and autocorrelation coefficients $R(i)$.

3. Obtain the mean squared error as

$$\Delta E = \sum_{i=1}^{K} [R(i) - \hat{R}(i)]^2 \tag{2.38}$$

4. The change in critical weights is given by

$$\Delta \omega_i = \begin{cases} \alpha \, \Delta E \, \omega_i & \text{if } |\Delta \omega_i| \le |\omega_i| \\ 0 & \text{otherwise} \end{cases} \tag{2.39}$$

where α is a constant.

5. Update the weights as

$$\omega(t + 1) = \omega(t) - |\Delta \omega| \qquad \text{for all } i \tag{2.40}$$

6. Repeat steps 2 through 5 until the error ΔE becomes smaller than some constant $E_{\min}$ or the change in weights $\Delta \omega$ becomes zero.

The constant α in Eq. 2.39 is determined so that the weights representing the small singular values to which the solution is sensitive are reduced; i.e., the critical weights that contribute most to the error are reduced with each iteration. This causes the solution to be smoother with each iteration. The algorithm terminates when the mean squared error in the autocorrelation coefficients reduces to $E_{\min}$. In the extreme case the critical weights become zero, and the network yields the smoothest solution. Thus, the algorithm is guaranteed to converge for smooth solutions.

Kulkarni (1991) has developed a software simulation of the model and has considered two images: the image representing circles and the one obtained from satellite data. The sensor used to obtain the satellite image is called the thematic mapper, which provides data in seven spectral bands. The images were blurred using the kernel given by

$$K(z) = \begin{cases} 1 + \cos(2\pi z/3) & \text{for } z \le 3 \\ 0 & \text{otherwise} \end{cases} \tag{2.41}$$

The plot for Eq. 2.41 is shown in Figure 2.20. It was assumed that the blur is in the x direction only. This can be achieved by suitably orienting the coordinate system. The original images are shown in Figures 2.21a and 2.22a. The degraded images are shown in Figures 2.21b and 2.22b. The images obtained by direct inversion are shown in Figures 2.21c and 2.22c. The images restored by the ANN model are shown in Figures 2.21d and 2.22d. The images were restored line by line. Measurements of the kernel or the point spread function for degradations such as motion degradation, atmospheric turbulence, or lens aberrations are often available in practice. Also, measurements of autocorrelation functions for various classes of images are available in practice. The

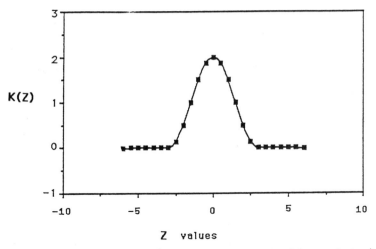

Figure 2.20. *Kernel function. (From Kulkarni, 1991, with permission.)*

accuracy of the solution depends on the signal-to-noise ratio of the observation vector g, the accuracy of the true correlation coefficients, and the condition number of the degrading kernel. The noise in g includes recording media noise, roundoff errors, and truncation errors. Also, since the solution f is of finite size, the correlation coefficients are known with a finite accuracy. The suggested architecture can be implemented electronically or electrooptically, and it is of significance, as it can be used for real-time applications.

An alternative approach for image restoration is to use the mean square error criterion. The most straightforward method to solve Eq. 2.30 is to find the mean squared solution that minimizes the error function E given by

$$E = \tfrac{1}{2}\|g - Hf\|^2 \tag{2.42}$$

Zhou et al. (1988) have used a Hopfield network to obtain the solution by minimizing the function E. In order to do this, it is necessary to map the function E to the energy function of the Hopfield network. A Hopfield network consists of a single layer, as shown in Figure 2.23. Each unit has a single activation function that sums the inputs from other units. A Hopfield network can be described by a system of nonlinear differential equations (Hopfield and Tank, 1985).

$$C_i(du_i/dt) = \sum_{j=1}^{N} T_{ij}v_i - u_i/R_i + I_i \qquad \text{for } i = 1, 2, \dots, N \tag{2.43}$$

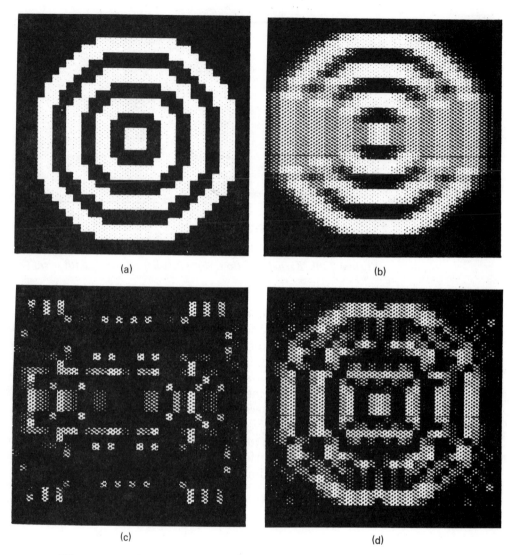

Figure 2.21. *Image restoration. (a) Original image. (b) Degraded image. (c) Image restored by direct inversion. (d) Image restored by ANN model. (From Kulkarni, 1991, with permission.)*

where
$$C_i = \text{capacitance of unit } i$$
$$u_i = \text{input potential}$$
$$T_{ij} = \text{synaptic strength between } i \text{ and } j$$
$$v_i = g(u_i)$$
$$g(\cdot) = \text{Sigmoid function describing how output voltage changes}$$
$$R_i = \text{internal resistance}$$
$$I_i = \text{external current}$$

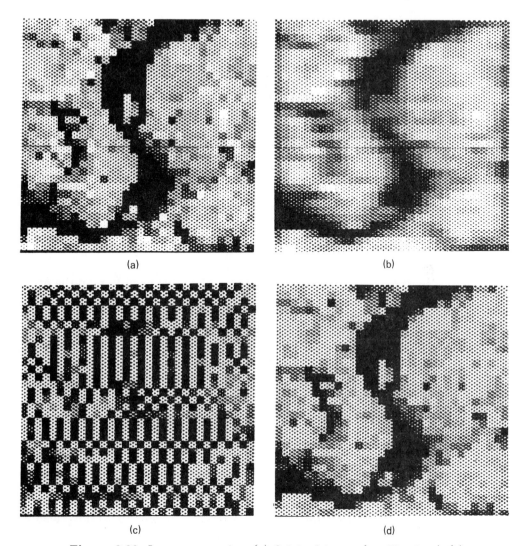

Figure 2.22. *Image restoration. (a) Original image (satellite data). (b) Degraded image. (c) Image restored by direct inversion. (d) Image restored by ANN model. (From Kulkarni, 1991, with permission.)*

An important property of the Hopfield network is that given a symmetrical connectivity matrix (i.e., $T_{ij} = T_{ji}$, $T_{ii} = 0$), the output vector $\boldsymbol{v} = v_1, v_2, \ldots, v_n$ will converge to a stable state. The energy function for the Hopfield network is given by

$$E = -\frac{1}{2} \sum_{i=1}^{N} \sum_{j=1}^{N} T_{ij} v_i v_j - \sum_{i=1}^{N} I_i v_i \qquad (2.44)$$

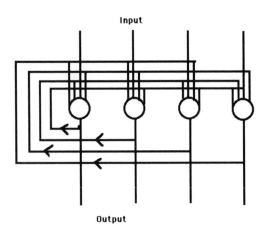

Figure 2.23. *Hopfield network.*

In order to solve the restoration problem, we need to map the error function in Eq. 2.42 to the energy function in Eq. 2.44 of the Hopfield network. The network parameters such as the interconnection strengths and bias inputs are determined in terms of the energy function of the network. Zhou et al. (1988) have considered this mapping. Their model consists of $L^2 \times M$ mutually interconnected units, where L is the size of the image and M is the maximum value of the gray level function. Their model can be explained as follows.

Let $V = \{v_{i,k}, \ 1 \le i \le L^2, \ 1 \le k \le M\}$ be a binary state set of the neural network with $v_{i,k}$ denoting the state of (i, k)th unit. Let $T_{i,k;j,l}$ denote the strength of the interconnection between unit (i, k) and unit (j, l).

$$T_{i,k;j,l} = T_{j,l;i,k} \tag{2.45}$$

for $1 \le i, \ j \le L^2$ and $1 \le i, \ k \le M$. Zhou et al. (1988) have also assumed that the units have self-feedback. The input image is represented by a finite set of gray level functions $\{x(i, j); \ 1 \le i, j \le L\}$, and the gray level function is given by a simple sum of neuron state variables as

$$x(i, j) = \sum_{k=1}^{M} v_{m,k} \tag{2.46}$$

where $m = i \times L + j$.

If we scan a 2-D image by rows and stack them as a long vector, then the degraded vector can be represented as Eq. 2.47.

$$\boldsymbol{y} = \boldsymbol{H}\boldsymbol{x} + \varepsilon \tag{2.47}$$

where H is the $L^2 \times L^2$ matrix representing the point spread function, and x, y and ε are the original, degraded and noise vectors, respectively. The energy function of the neural network can be written as

$$E = \frac{1}{2} \sum_{i=1}^{L^2} \sum_{j=1}^{L^2} \sum_{k=1}^{M} \sum_{l=1}^{M} T_{i,k;j,l} v_{i,k} v_{j,l} + \sum_{i=1}^{L^2} \sum_{k=1}^{M} I_{i,k} v_{i,k} \qquad (2.48)$$

Comparing terms in the expansion of Eq. 2.42 with the corresponding terms in Eq. 2.48, we can determine the interconnection strengths and the bias inputs:

$$T_{i,k;j,l} = - \sum_{p=1}^{L^2} h_{p,i} h_{p,j}$$

and

$$I_{i,k} = \sum_{p=1}^{L^2} y_p h_{p,i} \qquad (2.49)$$

From Eq. 2.49, one can see that the interconnection strengths are determined by the degrading function. Hence, $T_{i,k;j,l}$ can be computed without any error provided the degrading kernel is known. If the image is degraded by a shift-invariant blur function only, then $I_{i,k}$ can be estimated perfectly. Once the parameters $T_{i,k;j,l}$ and $I_{i,k}$ are obtained using Eq. 2.49, each neuron can randomly and asynchronously evaluate its state and readjust using Eq. 2.43. When one of the quasiminimum energy points is reached, the image can be reconstructed using Eq. 2.43. The algorithm described above is difficult to simulate on a conventional computer because of the high computational complexity. Zhou et al. (1988) have simplified the algorithm and have suggested a practical method. The results of their experiment are shown in Figures 2.24a through 2.24d.

2.7. INTERPOLATION

Interpolation is a process of estimating intermediate values of a continuous function from discrete samples. Interpolation is used extensively in image processing for magnification and reduction of images. The limitations of classical polynomial interpolation approaches are discussed by Hou and Andrews (1978). They developed an algorithm for interpolation using cubic spline functions. Keys (1981) developed an algorithm for interpolation by cubic convolution. Other algorithms such as the nearest-neighbor, bilinear interpolation, and hypersurface fitting are also used in practice. The cubic convolution interpolation method is more accurate than the nearest-neighbor or bilinear interpolation methods. However, it is not as accurate as the cubic spline interpolation method. The conventional methods of interpolation are discussed below.

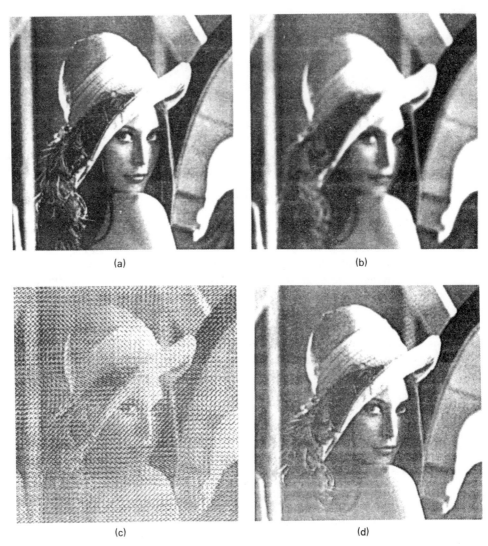

Figure 2.24. *Image restoration using a Hopfield network. (a) Original image. (b) Degraded image. (c) Image restored by direct inversion. (d) Image restored by ANN model. (From Zhou et al., 1988, with permission. © 1988 IEEE.)*

For equispaced one-dimensional data, the continuous interpolation function can be written as

$$g(x) = \sum_{k} C_k U[(x - x_k)/h] \tag{2.50}$$

where $g(x)$ is the interpolated, continuous function corresponding to a sampled function $f(x_k)$, and x_k are the interpolation nodes. C_k are the coefficients that depend on $f(x_k)$, and h is the sampling interval. The kernels for the nearest-neighbor, bilinear, and cubic convolution interpolation are given by Eq. 2.51, 2.52, and 2.53, respectively (Stucki, 1979).

$$U(s) = \begin{cases} 1 & \text{for } 0 \le |s| \le 0.5 \\ 0 & \text{otherwise} \end{cases} \tag{2.51}$$

$$U(s) = \begin{cases} 1 - |s| & \text{for } |s| \le 1 \\ 0 & \text{otherwise} \end{cases} \tag{2.52}$$

$$U(s) = \begin{cases} |s|^3 - 2|s|^2 + 1 & \text{for } |s| < 1 \\ -|s|^3 + 5|s|^2 - 8|s| + 4 & \text{for } 1 \le |s| \le 2 \\ 0 & \text{otherwise} \end{cases} \tag{2.53}$$

In the nearest-neighbor, bilinear, and cubic convolution interpolation methods, the coefficients C_k are the sampled data functions $f(x_k)$. Images are two-dimensional in nature. The continuous interpolated function in two dimensions is given by

$$g(x, y) = \sum_{k=-n}^{n} \sum_{l=-m}^{m} C_{i+k, j+l} U\left[(x - x_i)/h_x, (y - y_j)/h_y\right] \tag{2.54}$$

where $C_{i+k, j+1}$ are the coefficients that depend on the sampled data, and h_x and h_y are the sampling intervals. The parameters i and j are given by

$$i = \text{int}(x/h_x + 0.5)$$

$$j = \text{int}(y/h_y + 0.5) \tag{2.55}$$

In the case of the nearest-neighbor, bilinear, and cubic convolution methods, the kernels are separable. Hence, the two-dimensional interpolation can be carried out by interpolating the image, first in the x direction and then in the y direction. The original image and the enlarged images obtained by using the nearest-neighbor, bilinear, and cubic convolution techniques are shown in Figures 2.25a through 2.25c.

The interpolation also can be carried out using the hypersurface representation with orthogonal polynomials as the basis functions (Beaudt, 1978). The

Figure 2.25. *Image interpolation. (a) Original image. (b) Image interpolated by nearest-neighbor technique. (c) Image interpolated by cubic convolution. (d) Image interpolated by hypersurface fitting. (From Kulkarni and Sivaraman, 1984, with permission.)*

$$\frac{1}{9} \begin{bmatrix} -1 & 2 & -1 \\ 2 & 5 & 2 \\ -1 & 2 & -1 \end{bmatrix} \qquad \frac{1}{6} \begin{bmatrix} -1 & -1 & -1 \\ 0 & 0 & 0 \\ 1 & 1 & 1 \end{bmatrix} \qquad \frac{1}{6} \begin{bmatrix} -1 & 0 & 1 \\ -1 & 0 & 1 \\ -1 & 0 & 1 \end{bmatrix}$$
$$B_0 \qquad\qquad\qquad B_1 \qquad\qquad\qquad B_2$$

$$\frac{1}{6} \begin{bmatrix} 1 & 1 & 1 \\ -2 & -2 & -2 \\ 1 & 1 & 1 \end{bmatrix} \qquad \frac{1}{4} \begin{bmatrix} 1 & 0 & -1 \\ 0 & 0 & 0 \\ -1 & 0 & 1 \end{bmatrix} \qquad \frac{1}{6} \begin{bmatrix} 1 & -2 & 1 \\ 1 & -2 & 1 \\ 1 & -2 & 1 \end{bmatrix}$$
$$B_{11} \qquad\qquad\qquad B_{12} \qquad\qquad\qquad B_2$$

Figure 2.26. *Matrices for hyper-surface fitting.*

continuous function $g(x, y)$ at point (x, y), can be written as:

$$g(x, y) = b_0 + b_1 s_1 + b_2 s_2 + b_{11} s_1^2 + b_{22} s_2^2 + b_{12} s_1 s_2 \qquad (2.56)$$

where $s_1 = |x - x_i|/h_x$ and $s_2 = |y - y_j|/h_y$, and x_i, y_j are sampling nodes that correspond to i and j given by Eq. 2.55. Eq. 2.56 defines a continuous function $g(x, y)$ at (x, y) and the coefficients b are evaluated from discrete data points in region of size 3×3 centered around the interpolation node $f(x_i, y_j)$. Eq. 2.56 can be rewritten (Kulkarni and Sivaraman, 1984):

$$g(x, y) = \sum_{k=i-1}^{i+1} \sum_{l=j-1}^{j+1} \Big[(B_0(k - i + 2, l - j + 2) + B_1(k - i + 2, l - j + 2)s_1$$

$$+ B_2(k - i + 2, l - j + 2)s_2 + B_{11}(k - i + 2, l - j + 2)s_1^2$$

$$+ B_{22}(k - i + 2, l - j + 2)s_2^2$$

$$+ B_{12}(k - i + 2, i - j + 2)s_1 s_2) f(x_i, y_j) \Big] \qquad (2.57)$$

In Eq. 2.57, $g(x, y)$ represents the continuous function at (x, y) in the 3×3 neighborhood centered at (i, j), and $f(x_i, y_j)$ represents the discrete image function. B_0, B_1, B_2, B_{11}, B_{22}, and B_{12} are the matrices shown in Figure 2.26. The image obtained by interpolation using the above method is shown in Figure 2.25d.

ANN models work in parallel. This ability of ANN models is useful in implementing interpolation algorithms. Consider a simple two-layer feed-forward network as shown in Figure 2.27. Here, layer L_1 represents the input image, and layer L_2 represents the output image. Units in layer L_1 represent input image pixels, and units in layer L_2 represent pixels in the output image.

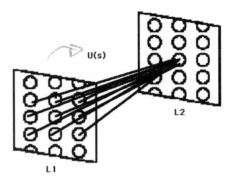

Figure 2.27. *ANN model for interpolation.*

Each unit has N states that correspond to N discrete gray levels in the image. Connection strengths or weights connecting units in layers L_1 and L_2 are given by the kernel function $U(s)$. The kernel function $U(s)$ depends on the interpolation technique used. Kernel functions for nearest-neighbor, bilinear, and cubic convolution interpolation are given by Eq. 2.51 through 2.53. The weights between layers L_1 and L_2 can also be evaluated using interpolation techniques; for example, interpolation by hypersurface fitting can also be used. By choosing appropriate weights a simple two-layer feed-forward network can be developed to implement any of the above interpolation methods.

2.8. SUMMARY

Early vision processing corresponds to preprocessing. It is also known as low-level processing. In a machine vision system a typical preprocessing stage performs functions such as gray scale manipulation, edge enhancement, filtering, and segmentation. In this chapter we discussed techniques that perform these tasks. We also discussed ANN models to perform these tasks, including the boundary counter system (BCS), which takes into account properties of the human vision system. ANN models for image restoration were introduced and discussed; these are of significance as they can be used along with the recording system for real-time applications.

REFERENCES

Andrews, H. C. (1970). *Computer Techniques in Image Processing.* Academic Press, New York.

Beaudt, P. R. (1978). Rotationally invariant image operators. *Proceedings of the Fourth International Conference on Pattern Recognition, Kyoto,* pp. 579–583.

Carpenter, G. A., and Grossberg, S. (1987). A massively parallel architecture for a self organizing neural pattern recognition machine. *International Journal of Computer Vision, Graphics and Image Processing* 37:54–115.

Carpenter, G. A., et al. (1989). Invariant recognition of cluttered scenes by a self organizing ART architecture: CORT-X boundary segmentation. *Neural Networks* 2:169–181.

Chittineni, C. B. (1982). Multidimensional edge and line detection by hypersurface fitting using basis functions. *Proceedings of International Symposium on Remotely Sensed Data at LARS*, pp. 245–254, Purdue University, West Lafayette, IN.

Chittineni, C. B. (1983). Edge and line detection in multidimensional noisy imagery data. *IEEE Transactions on Geosciences and Remote Sensing*, 21:163–174

Deekshatulu, B. L., Kulkarni, A. D., and Kashipati, Rao (1985). Quantitative evaluation of enhancement techniques. *Signal Processing* 8:369–375.

Dhawan, A. P., and Dufresne, T. (1990). Low level image processing and edge enhancement using a self organizing neural network. *Proceedings of International Joint Conference on Neural Networks*, San Diego, Vol. I, pp. 503–510.

Duda, R. O., and Hart, P. E. (1973). *Pattern Classification and Scene Analysis*. John Wiley & Sons, New York.

Durbin, R., and Rumelhart, D. E. (1989). Product units: A computationally and biologically plausible extension to back propagation networks. *Neural Computation* 1:133–142.

Farhat, N. H., and Bai, B. (1989). Echo inversion and target shape estimation by neuromorphic processing. *Neural Networks* 2:117–125.

Gonzalez, R. C., and Wintz, P. (1987). *Digital Image Processing*. Addison-Wesley, Reading, MA.

Grossberg, S. (1988). *Neural Networks and Natural Intelligence*. Bradford Books, MIT Press, Cambridge, MA.

Grossberg, S., and Mingolla, E. (1987). Neural dynamics of surface perception: Boundary webs, illuminants, and shape-from-shading. *International Journal of Computer Vison, Graphics and Image Processing* 37:116–165.

Grossberg, S., and Todorovic, D. (1988). A neural network architecture for brightness perception under constant and variable illumination conditions. *Proceedings of International Joint Conference on Neural Networks*, San Diego, Vol. IV, pp. 185–191.

Habibi, A. and Wintz. W. A. (1971). Image coding by linear transformation and block quantization. *IEEE Transactions on Communication Technology* 19:50–62.

Haralick, R. M. (1980). Edge and region analysis for digital image data. *Computer Vision and Graphics and Image Processing* 12:60–73.

Haralick, R. M. (1981). The digital edge. *Proceedings of the IEEE Computer Society Conference on Pattern Recognition and Image Processing*, New York, pp. 285–294.

Hopfield, J. J., and Tank, D. W. (1985). Neural computation of decision in optimization problems. *Biological Cybernetics* 52:141–152.

Hou, H. S., and Andrews, H. C. (1978). Cubic spline for image interpolation and digital filtering. *IEEE Transactions on Acoustics, Speech and Signal Processing* 26:508–516.

Huang, T. S., et al. (1971). Image processing. *Proceedings of IEEE* 59:1586–1609.

Hueckel, M. (1973). A local operator which recognizes edges and lines. *Journal of Association of Computer Machinery* 20:634–647.

Keys, R. G. (1981). Cubic Convolution interpolation for digital image processing. *IEEE Transaction on Acoustics, Speech and Signal Processing* 20:1153–1160.

Kretzmer, E. R. (1952). Statistics of television signals. *Bell System Technical Journal*, July:751–763.

Kulkarni, A. D., and Silvaraman, K. (1984). Interpolation of digital imagery using hyper-surface approximation. *Signal Processing* 7:65–73.

Kulkarni, A. D. (1986). Digital processing of remotely sensed data. In: *Advances in Electronics and Electron Physics*, Vol. 66, P. W. Hawkes (ed.), pp. 309–368, Academic Press, Orlando, FL.

Kulkarni, A. D. (1990a). Neural networks for image restoration. *Proceedings of ACM 18th Annual Computer Science Conference*, Washington, DC., pp. 373–378.

Kulkarni, A. D. (1991). Solving ill-posed problems with artificial neural networks. *Neural Networks* 4:477–484.

Marr, D. (1982). *Vision*. W. H. Freeman and Co., New York.

Morgenthaler, D. G., and Rosenfeld, A. (1981). Multidimensional edge detection by hyper surface fitting. *IEEE Transaction on Pattern Analysis and Machine Intelligence* 3:482–486.

Phillips, D. L. (1962). A technique for the numerical solution of certain integral equations of the first kind. *Journal of Association of Computing Machinery* 9:84–97.

Rosenfeld, A., and Kak, A. (1982). *Digital Image Processing*, Vols. I and II, Academic Press, Orlando, FL.

Sahasrabudhe, S. C., and Kulkarni, A. D. (1977). On solving Fredholm integral equations of first kind. *Journal of Association of Computer Machinery* 24:624–629.

Sahasrabudhe, S. C., and Kulkarni, A. D. (1979). Shift variant image degradation and restoration using SVD. *International Journal of Computer Graphics and Image Processing* 9:203–212.

Seedle, C. (1989). *Edge Detection Using CORT-X Boundary Segmentation. Project Report* (Kulkarni, A. D., Research Advisor), Computer Science Department, University of Texas, Tyler, TX.

Stucki, P. (1979). *Advances in Digital Image Processing*, pp. 177–218. Plenum Press, New York.

Twomey, S., (1963). On numerical solution of Fredholm integral equation of the first kind. *Journal of Association of Computing Machinery* 10:97–101.

Van Allen, E. J., and Kolodzy, P. J. (1988). Application of a boundary counter neural network to illusion and infrared sensor imagery. *Proceedings of International Joint Conference on Neural Network*, San Diego, pp. 193–202.

Yasuoka, Y., and Haralick, R. M. (1983). Peak noise removal by a facet model. *Pattern Recognition* 16:23–29.

Zhou, Y. T., (1988). A novel approach to image restoration based on a neural network. *Proceedings of International Joint Conference on Neural Networks*, San Diego, Vol. 4, pp. 269–276.

3

Feature Extraction

3.1. INTRODUCTION

In the previous chapter we considered early vision processing techniques. This chapter describes techniques used for feature extraction. Pattern recognition systems usually consider a feature space onto which the observation vector is first mapped. The feature vector is then used to decide the class to which the observation vector belongs. The purpose of feature extraction is to reduce data by measuring certain "features" or "properties" that distinguish input patterns. In feature extraction we transform an input observation vector to a feature vector using some orthogonal or nonorthogonal basis functions so that data in the feature space are uncorrelated.

A variety of approaches have been developed for feature extraction. Commonly used feature space techniques include the Fourier transform (FT), moment feature space, chord distribution feature space, the Hough transform, Wigner distribution feature space, orthogonal polynomials, and Gabor functions. Many textbooks and review articles deal with feature space pattern recognition (Duda and Hart, 1973; Tou and Gonzalez, 1974; Casasent, 1985a, b; Lippmann, 1987; Linkser, 1988). Orthogonal transforms such as the Walsh, Walsh Hadamard, or discrete cosine (Ahmed and Rao, 1975; Wintz, 1972) that are used in data compression can also be used for feature extraction.

Once a set of features that distinguish input patterns is obtained, the recognition task reduces to partitioning the feature space. Many feature extraction techniques have been implemented in practice with the help of digital and/or optical systems. The main advantage of digital techniques is the flexibility for nonlinear operations. Optical techniques process pixels in parallel, and the processing speed is limited by the velocity of light. Artificial neural network (ANN) models are robust and fault tolerant; they can be implemented electronically or electrooptically, and they work in parallel. By using ANN models for feature extraction it is possible to combine advantages of both the optical and digital processing.

In this chapter, we discuss ANN models for feature extraction. We also consider the problem of invariant object recognition. We consider invariance with respect to the translational, rotational, and scale differences in input images. The problem of invariance is difficult because of the large number of training samples for which the classifier needs to be trained. To alleviate this, the problem of invariance is often tackled in the feature extraction stage. There are a number of techniques that can be used for invariant feature extraction. The method of feature extraction using moment invariants yields features that are invariant with respect to translation, rotation, and scale differences (Hu, 1962).

We can also extract invariant features using the FT feature space. The two-dimensional FT distribution has some interesting properties: (1) the magnitude of the FT is shift invariant, (2) higher input spatial frequencies correspond to the high-amplitude values further from the origin of the FT plane, and (3) as the input image rotates, the distribution in the FT plane also rotates (Goodman, 1968). These properties of the FT and the similar properties of other transforms can be used for extracting invariant features (Casasent, 1985a, b; Ballard and Brown, 1982). Also, during the extraction of invariant features, significant data reduction is possible. A few well-known methods of feature extraction and their neural network implementations are discussed in the subsequent sections.

3.2. FEATURE EXTRACTION USING MOMENT INVARIANTS

One of the well-known methods for invariant feature extraction is the use of moment invariants. Hu (1962) has defined a set of seven moment-invariant functions that are invariant to translational, scale, and rotational differences in input patterns. The main disadvantage of the moment-invariant technique is that there is no guarantee that the invariant moments, which number exactly seven, form a complete set of descriptors. However, for most practical applications the set of seven invariants is adequate to distinguish between input patterns. The Fourier descriptors form a complete set of features; however, extracted features are usually large in number and are unwieldy to use in classification unless they are grouped together by some grouping criterion. The seven moment invariants are described below.

Let $g(x, y)$ be an image of the size $n \times n$. The $(p + q)$th geometric moment for an image of the size $(2n + 1) \times (2n + 1)$ is given by

$$m_{pq} = \sum_{x=-n}^{n} \sum_{y=-n}^{n} x^p y^q g(x, y) \tag{3.1}$$

for $p, q = 0, 1, 2, 3, \ldots$.

To make these moments invariant to translation, one can define a central moment as

$$m_{pq} = \sum_{x=-n}^{n} \sum_{y=-n}^{n} (x - x')^p (y - y')^q g(x, y) \tag{3.2}$$

where $x' = m_{10}/m_{00}$ and $y' = m_{01}/m_{00}$. The central moments in Eq. 3.2 can be normalized for scale invariance as shown below:

$$\mu_{pq} = m_{pq}^{\gamma}/m_{00} \tag{3.3}$$

where $\gamma = (p + q)/2 + 1$.

Hu (1962) developed the following seven functions of central moments that are invariant to rotational and scale differences.

$$\phi_1 = (\mu_{20} + \mu_{02})$$

$$\phi_2 = (\mu_{20} - \mu_{02})^2 + 4\mu_{11}^2$$

$$\phi_3 = (\mu_{30} - 3\mu_{12})^2 + (3\mu_{21} - \mu_{03})^2$$

$$\phi_4 = (\mu_{30+}\mu_{12})^2 + (\mu_{21} + \mu_{03})^2$$

$$\phi_5 = (\mu_{30} - 3\mu_{12})(\mu_{30} + \mu_{12}) \cdot \left[(\mu_{30} + \mu_{12})^2 - 3(\mu_{21} + \mu_{03})^2 \right]$$

$$+ (3\mu_{21} + \mu_{03})(\mu_{21} + \mu_{03}) \left[3(\mu_{30} + \mu_{12})^2 - (\mu_{12} + \mu_{03})^2 \right]$$

$$\phi_6 = (\mu_{20} - \mu_{02}) \left[(\mu_{30} + \mu_{12})^2 - (\mu_{21} + \mu_{03})^2 \right] + 4\mu_{11}(\mu_{30} + \mu_{12})(\mu_{21} + \mu_{03})$$

$$\phi_7 = (3\mu_{21} - \mu_{03})(\mu_{30} + \mu_{12}) \left[(\mu_{30} + \mu_{12})^2 - 3(\mu_{21} + \mu_{03})^2 \right]$$

$$- (\mu_{30} - 3\mu_{12})(\mu_{12} + \mu_{03}) \left[(3\mu_{30} + \mu_{12})^2 - (\mu_{21} + \mu_{03})^2 \right] \tag{3.4}$$

Kulkarni et al. (1990) have used these moment invariants for aircraft identification. They have considered three types of aircraft: Phantom, F104, and Mirage III. The original images and images with rotations are shown in Figure 3.1. The original and scaled images of the aircraft are shown in Figure 3.2. Their recognition system consists of two stages: the feature extraction stage and the recognition stage. In the feature extraction stage they obtained the moment

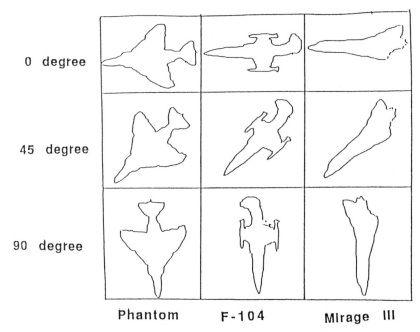

Figure 3.1. *Aircraft images with different rotations. (From Kulkarni et al., 1990, with permission. © 1990 IEEE.)*

invariants that were used as input to the recognition stage. In the recognition stage they used a three-layer feed-forward network with a back-propagation learning algorithm. The moment invariants are shown in Table 3.1.

During training process the images with 0° rotation were used to train the network. In order for the network to stabilize, the training process was iterated 300 times. During the decision-making phase the rotated and scaled aircraft images were used as input images. The model worked well for images with rotational and translational differences. However, the model did not perform well in recognizing objects with different scales. Hu (1962) has shown analytically that moment invariants described by Eq. 3.4 are insensitive to translational, rotational, and scale differences in input images. However, the values of these invariants are small, and they are very sensitive to roundoff errors and/or noise, which makes recognition difficult. One of the solutions to the sensitivity problem is to consider the log values of the moment invariants. Dudani and Breeding (1987) have suggested a different approach to obtain moments that are scale invariant. Moment invariants yield one of the most commonly used methods in practice. Khotanzad and Lu (1987) have used moment invariants as features for character recognition.

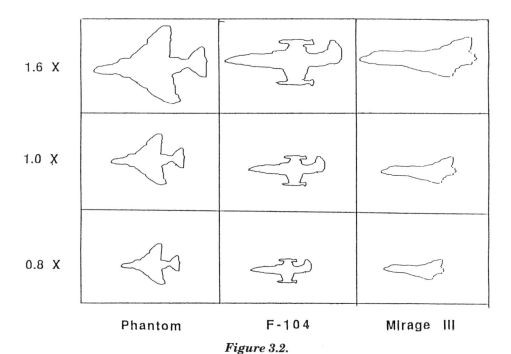

Figure 3.2.

TABLE 3.1. *FEATURES BY MOMENT INVARIANTS*

Transformation	ϕ_1	ϕ_2	ϕ_3	ϕ_4	ϕ_5	ϕ_6
			F104			
0°	0.404	0.114	0.402	0.149	0.0361	0.043
45°	0.435	0.165	0.483	0.219	0.067	0.794
90°	0.404	0.114	0.402	0.149	0.361	0.043
Scale 2 ×	0.4831	0.184	2.265	1.318	2.473	0.516
			Phantom			
0°	0.339	0.073	0.074	0.011	0.001	0.002
45°	0.429	0.121	0.192	0.047	0.004	0.016
90°	0.339	0.073	0.074	0.011	0.001	0.002
Scale 2 ×	0.332	0.066	0.506	0.125	0.031	0.0325
			Mirage III			
0°	0.697	0.445	2.596	1.308	3.913	1.164
45°	0.362	0.683	3.400	2.351	6.632	1.372
90°	0.697	0.445	2.566	1.308	3.913	1.164
Scale 2 ×	0.636	0.366	9.581	6.997	58.10	4.093

3.3. FEATURE EXTRACTION USING ORTHOGONAL TRANSFORMS

In many practical problems the observation vector is obtained by sampling a random process, and it usually consists of a set of correlated random variables. Also, observation vectors are often large in dimension, and they contain redundant information. In order to reduce dimensionality while retaining most of the information, the observation vector can be mapped onto a feature space using orthogonal basis functions such that the transformed data are uncorrelated. The uncorrelated data in the transformed domain can then be ranked according to the degree of significance of their contribution to the information content. Many orthogonal transforms are being used in practice; the best known included the Fourier transform (FT), Walsh Hadamard transform (WHT), Karhunen-Loeve (KL), orthogonal polynomials, and discrete cosine transform (DCT). Textbooks such as those by Ahmed and Rao (1975), Rosenfeld and Kak (1982), and Gonzalez and Wintz (1987) describe these transforms.

Let $\boldsymbol{H}$ be the transform matrix given by

$$\boldsymbol{H}^T = [\,\boldsymbol{\phi}_1, \boldsymbol{\phi}_2, \dots, \boldsymbol{\phi}_n\,] \tag{3.5}$$

where $\boldsymbol{\phi}_i$ are real valued, orthonormal basis vectors; i.e.,

$$\boldsymbol{\phi}_i^T \boldsymbol{\phi}_j = \begin{cases} 1 & \text{for } i = j \\ 0 & \text{for } i \neq j \end{cases} \tag{3.6}$$

Let $\boldsymbol{x}$ be an observation vector; then the transformed vector $\boldsymbol{y}$ is given by

$$\boldsymbol{y} = \boldsymbol{H}\boldsymbol{x} \tag{3.7}$$

where $\boldsymbol{x}^T = (x_1, x_2, \dots, x_n)$ and $\boldsymbol{y}^T = (y_1, y_2, \dots, y_n)$.

From Eq. 3.5 and 3.6, it follows

$$\boldsymbol{H}^T \boldsymbol{H} = \boldsymbol{I} \tag{3.8}$$

Hence, we get

$$\boldsymbol{x} = \boldsymbol{H}^T \boldsymbol{y}$$

$$x_i = \sum_{j=1}^{n} y_j \phi_{ij} \tag{3.9}$$

Often, in order to reduce the dimension, we may retain a subset $\{y_1, y_2, \dots, y_m\}$ of components of $\boldsymbol{y}$, and yet estimate $\boldsymbol{x}$. This can be done by replacing $n - m$ components of $\boldsymbol{y}$ by the preselected b_j to obtain

$$x_i = \sum_{j=1}^{m} y_j \phi_{ij} + \sum_{j=m+1}^{n} b_j \phi_{ij} \tag{3.10}$$

The error in estimation of x is given by

$$\Delta x_i = \sum_{j=m+1}^{n} (y_j - b_j)\phi_{ij} \tag{3.11}$$

The mean squared error is given by

$$\Delta E = E\{(\Delta x)^T (\Delta x)\}$$
$$= \sum_{j=m+1}^{n} E\{(y_j - b_j)^2\} \tag{3.12}$$

The problem of minimizing ΔE is generally called factor analysis or principal component analysis, and the corresponding transform is called the Karhunen-Loeve (KL) transform. Let ϕ_i represent eigenvectors of the covariance matrix Σ_x of an input observation x, and β_i are the corresponding eigenvalues. The minimum mean squared error is given by

$$\Delta E_{\min} = \sum_{i=m+1}^{n} \beta_i \tag{3.13}$$

The KL transform is the optimum one with respect to the mean squared error criterion; however, it involves intensive computations (Ahmed and Rao, 1975; Oja, 1989).

3.4. FOURIER TRANSFORM DOMAIN FEATURE EXTRACTION

The Fourier transform (FT) is a well-known transform technique used in data compression. In order to process digital images we need to consider the discrete Fourier transform (DFT). If $\{x(n)\}$ denotes a sequence $x(n)$, $n = 0, 1, \ldots, N-1$ of N finite valued real or complex numbers, then its discrete Fourier transform is defined as (Rosenfeld and Kak, 1982)

$$c(u) = \frac{1}{N} \sum_{n=0}^{N-1} x(n)e^{-2\pi j un/N} \tag{3.14}$$

for $u = 0, 1, 2, \ldots, N-1$ and $j = \sqrt{-1}$. The exponential functions in Eq. 3.14 are orthogonal. The inverse discrete Fourier transform (IDFT) is defined as

$$x(n) = \sum_{n=0}^{N-1} c(u)e^{2\pi j un/N} \tag{3.15}$$

Equations 3.14 and 3.15 represent the DFT and IDFT for a one-dimensional data sequence. Images are inherently two-dimensional in nature, and we need to consider the two-dimensional Fourier transform. The two-dimensional discrete Fourier transform is given by

$$F(u,v) = \frac{1}{MN} \sum_{m=0}^{M-1} \sum_{n=0}^{N-1} f(m,n)e^{-2\pi j(mu/M + nv/N)} \tag{3.16}$$

for $u = 0, 1, 2, \ldots, M - 1$ and $v = 0, 1, 2, \ldots, N - 1$. The inverse discrete Fourier transform is given by

$$f(m,n) = \sum_{u=0}^{M-1} \sum_{v=0}^{N-1} F(u,v)e^{2\pi j(mu/M + nv/N)} \tag{3.17}$$

for $m = 0, 1, 2, \ldots, M - 1$ and $n = 0, 1, 2, \ldots, N - 1$.

The double summation in Eq 3.16 can be written in a matrix form as

$$\boldsymbol{F_t} = \boldsymbol{PFQ} \tag{3.18}$$

where $\boldsymbol{Q}$ and $\boldsymbol{P}$ are nonsingular orthonormal matrices of the size $M \times M$ and $N \times N$ respectively; $\boldsymbol{F}$ represents the input image matrix, and the elements of matrices $\boldsymbol{P}$ and $\boldsymbol{Q}$ are given by Eq. 31.9 and 3.20, respectively.

$$q_{vn} = \frac{1}{N}e^{-2\pi jnv/N} \tag{3.19}$$

where $v = 0, 1, 2, \ldots, N - 1$ and $n = 0, 1, \ldots, N - 1$.

$$p_{um} = \frac{1}{M}e^{-2\pi jmu/M} \tag{3.20}$$

where $u = 0, 1, \ldots, M - 1$ and $m = 0, 1, \ldots, M - 1$. The inverse Fourier transform is given by

$$\boldsymbol{F} = \boldsymbol{P}^{-1}\boldsymbol{F_t}\boldsymbol{Q}^{-1} \tag{3.21}$$

Feature extraction algorithms using the FT plane have been implemented optically. Some of the properties of the FT (that magnitudes of FT coefficients are shift invariant, high frequencies in input images correspond to large values further from the origin, and with a rotation of the input image the FT distribution also rotates) are used for invariant feature extraction. In order to obtain invariant features, the FT plane is sampled with angular and radial bins. Feature extraction also results in significant data reduction. By sampling the FT plane with wedge-shaped elements, information on rotation can be captured in the extracted features. Similarly, by sampling the FT plane with angular or ring-shaped elements, information on scale can be captured in the extracted

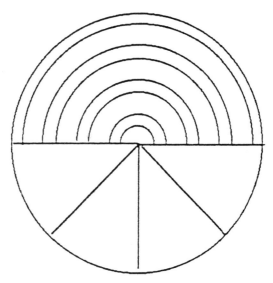

Figure 3.3. *Radial and angular bins.*

features. Since the FT coefficients are symmetrical in the FT plane, it is possible to use half of the FT plane for angular bins and half of the plane for radial bins, as shown in Figure 3.3. The radial bins are given by

$$V_{r_1 r_2} = \iint F^2(u, v)\, du\, dv \qquad (3.22)$$

where the limits of integration are defined by

$$r_1^2 \leq u^2 + v^2 \leq r_2^2 \quad \text{and} \quad 0 \leq u, v \leq n - 1$$

Radial features are insensitive to rotational differences of input images, and they can be used for extracting rotation-invariant image recognition. The angular bins are given by

$$v_{\phi_1 \phi_2} = \iint F^2(u, v)\, du\, dv \qquad (3.23)$$

where the limits of integration are defined by $\phi_1 \leq \tan^{-1}(u/v) \leq \phi_2$ and $0 \leq u, v \leq n - 1$. Angular features are insensitive to coarseness of input images, and they can be used for extracting scale invariant components.

3.5. ANN MODEL FOR FT DOMAIN FEATURE EXTRACTION

ANN models consist of a number of layers, and each of these layers consists of several processing units that may have linear or nonlinear activation functions. Often, in ANN models having units with a linear activation function, information propagation can be described mathematically as a series of vector-matrix multiplications. Each vector-matrix multiplication can be represented as

$$y = Wx \tag{3.24}$$

where x represents the input vector, y represents the output vector, and W is a weight matrix. In biological neural networks, this operation is performed by a large number of neurons operating in parallel.

An electrooptical system is shown in Figure 3.4. The system uses a cylindrical lens with photodetectors for input and output vectors and a photographic film in which the transmittance of each square is proportional to the corresponding weight. On the output side a cylindrical lens focuses a mask onto the corresponding photodetector. ANN models require two types of operations: computation and communication. Computational functions are performed well by electronic systems, although a communication task for a large number of units is performed well by optical systems. A system such as that shown in Figure 3.4 is suitable for parallel operations.

Kulkarni and Byars (1991a, b) have developed an ANN model for feature extraction using the FT plane (Figure 3.5) that consists of seven layers. Layer

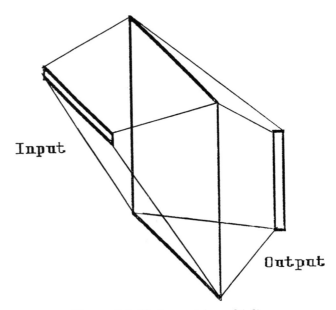

Figure 3.4. *Vector matrix multiplier.*

L_1 is the input layer and represents the input image distribution. Layer L_6 represents the amplitude of the Fourier coefficients in the transformed domain. Layer L_7 represents the output features. Layers L_2 through L_5 are used to obtain the Fourier coefficients. The weights connecting these layers can be obtained as follows.

Equation 3.16 can be rewritten as

$$F(u,v) = \frac{1}{MN} \sum_{m=0}^{M-1} e^{-2\pi mju/M} \sum_{n=0}^{N-1} f(n,m)e^{-2\pi jnv/N} \qquad (3.25)$$

for $u = 0, 1, \ldots, M-1$ and $v = 0, 1, \ldots, N-1$. Substituting

$$e^{-2\pi jmu/M} = \cos(2\pi mu/M) - j\sin(2\pi mu/M)$$

and

$$e^{-2\pi jnv/N} = \cos(2\pi nv/N) - j\sin(2\pi nv/N)$$

we get

$$\begin{aligned}
F(u,v) = \frac{1}{MN} &\left[\sum_{m=0}^{M-1} \cos(2\pi mu/M) \sum_{n=0}^{N-1} f(n,m)\cos(2\pi nv/N) \right. \\
&\left. - \sum_{m=0}^{M-1} \sin(2\pi mu/M) \sum_{n=0}^{N-1} f(m,n)\sin(2\pi nv/N) \right] \\
-j &\left[\sum_{m=0}^{M-1} \cos(2\pi mu/M) \sum_{n=0}^{N-1} f(n,m)\sin(2\pi nv/N) \right. \\
&\left. + \sum_{m=0}^{M-1} \sin(2\pi mu/M) \sum_{n=0}^{N-1} f(m,n)\cos(2\pi nv/N) \right] \qquad (3.26)
\end{aligned}$$

$$= 1/MN[(\boldsymbol{P}_c f \boldsymbol{Q}_c - \boldsymbol{P}_s f \boldsymbol{Q}_s) - j(\boldsymbol{P}_c f \boldsymbol{Q}_s + \boldsymbol{P}_s f \boldsymbol{Q}_c)] \qquad (3.27)$$

where the elements of matrices $\boldsymbol{P}_c$, $\boldsymbol{P}_s$, $\boldsymbol{Q}_c$, and $\boldsymbol{Q}_s$ are given by

$$P_c(u,m) = \cos(2\pi mu/M)$$

$$P_s(u,m) = \sin(2\pi mu/M)$$

for $u = 1, 2, \ldots, M-1$ and $m = 1, 2, \ldots, N-1$.

$$Q_c(v,n) = \cos(2\pi nv/N)$$

$$Q_s(v,n) = \sin(2\pi nv/N)$$

for $v = 1, 2, \ldots, N-1$ and $n = 1, 2, \ldots, N-1$.

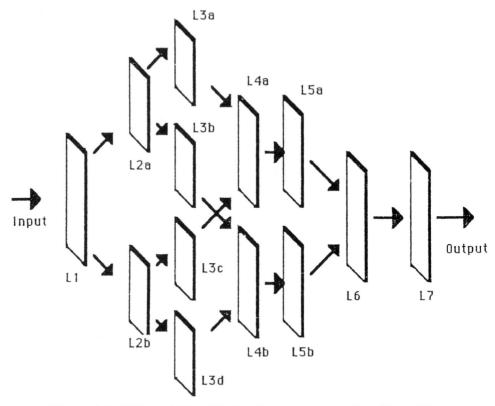

Figure 3.5. *ANN model for FT domain feature extraction. (From Kulkarni and Byars, 1991c, with permission.)*

In Figure 3.5, the weights between layers $L_1 L_{2a}$, and $L_1 L_{2b}$ are the elements of matrices $\boldsymbol{Q}_c$ and $\boldsymbol{Q}_s$, respectively. The weights between the layers $L_{2a} L_{3a}$, $L_{2a} L_{3b}$, $L_{2b} L_{3c}$, and $L_{2b} L_{3d}$ are the elements of matrices $\boldsymbol{Q}_c$, $\boldsymbol{Q}_s$, $\boldsymbol{Q}_s$, and $\boldsymbol{Q}_c$, respectively. Units in layers L_{4a} and L_{4b} correspond to real and imaginary parts of the Fourier coefficients. The units in layers L_{5a} and L_{5b} represent the squares of real and imaginary values of the Fourier coefficients. Layer L_6 represents the amplitudes of the FT coefficients. The units in layer L_7 represent output features. The weights connecting layers L_6 and L_7 correspond to the elements of the angular and radial bins.

Kulkarni and Byars (1991a, b) have developed a software simulation for the ANN model using the FT plane feature extraction technique. They considered two examples. The first used three test patterns representing vertical bars generated using sinusoidal functions. The patterns with rotation of 0°, 45°, and 90°, and their FT distribution planes are shown in Figures 3.6 and 3.7, respec-

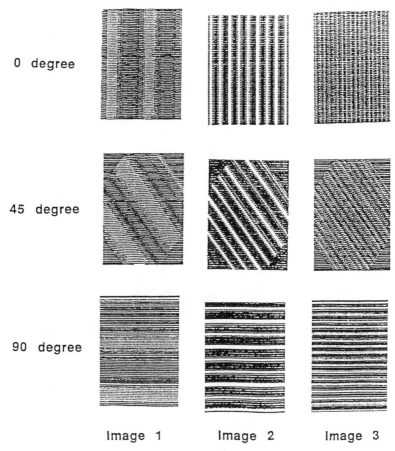

0 degree

45 degree

90 degree

Image 1   Image 2   Image 3

Figure 3.6. *Test patterns. (From Kulkarni and Byars, 1991b, with permission. © 1991 IEEE.)*

tively. In order to extract rotation-invariant features, they used a bin with six rings. The features obtained from a radial bin are shown in Table 3.2. In the second example, they used images of three types of aircraft: Phantom, Mirage III, and F104. The images with 0°, 45°, and 90° of rotations and their FT distribution planes are shown in Figures 3.1 and 3.8, respectively. In order to obtain rotation-invariant features the FT plane was sampled with ring detectors. As in the previous example, they used a bin with six rings. The aircraft images with different scales and their FT distribution planes are shown in Figures 3.2 and 3.9, respectively. To obtain features that are scale invariant, they used a radial bin with eight wedges. The output features are shown in Tables 3.3 and 3.4, respectively. In both the examples the feature vectors were presented to the recognition stage that consisted of a three-layer feed-forward network with a back-propagation learning algorithm.

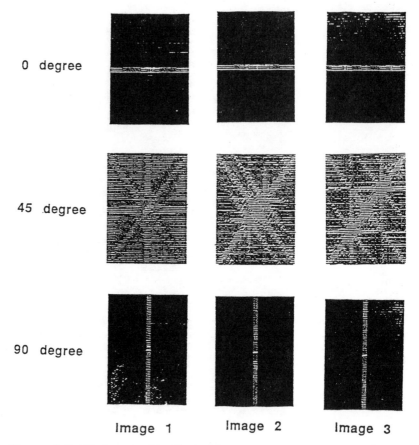

Figure 3.7. *FT domain distribution for patterns in Figure 3.6. (From Kulkarni and Byars, 1991b, with permission. © 1991 IEEE.)*

TABLE 3.2. *FEATURES BY RADIAL BINS (PATTERN)*

Rotation (degrees)	f_1	f_2	f_3	f_4	f_5	f_6
0	0.74	0.07	0.04	0.02	0.01	0.01
45	0.43	0.70	0.37	0.21	0.11	0.08
90	0.80	0.09	0.05	0.03	0.02	0.02
180	0.91	0.17	0.11	0.07	0.51	0.04

The ANN architecture shown in Figure 3.5 can be further simplified using the Radon transform (see below). The Radon transform is defined as (Gindi and Gmitro, 1984)

$$\beta(x', \phi) = \int f(r)\delta(x' - r, \hat{n}) \, d^2r \qquad (3.28)$$

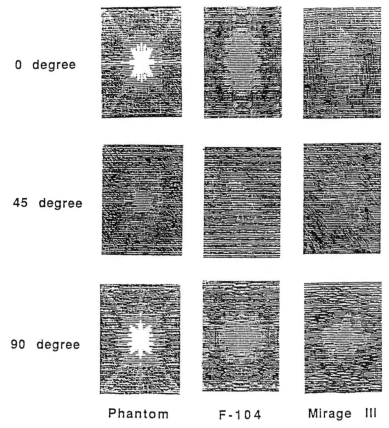

0 degree

45 degree

90 degree

Phantom   F-104   Mirage III

Figure 3.8. *FT distribution for aircraft images in Figure 3.1. (From Kulkarni and Byars, 1991b, with permission. © 1991 IEEE.)*

where $r(x, y)$ is a two-dimensional position vector in the object space, $f(r)$ defines the object, and $\hat{n}$ is the unit vector that makes an angle ϕ with respect to the x axis. It is convenient to think of the Radon transform as a projection of the function $f(x, y)$ onto the axis x', where x' is the axis rotated by angle ϕ from the x axis:

$$\begin{pmatrix} x' \\ y' \end{pmatrix} = \begin{pmatrix} \cos\phi & \sin\phi \\ -\sin\phi & \cos\phi \end{pmatrix} \begin{pmatrix} x \\ y \end{pmatrix} \tag{3.29}$$

For a fixed angle ϕ, $\beta(x', \phi)$ is a one-dimensional function of $x' \cdot \beta(x', \phi)$ is essentially a projection at an angle ϕ, as shown in Figure 3.10. The inverse Radon transform is often used to estimate a two-dimensional (2-D) object from its one-dimensional (1-D) projections.

The inverse Radon transform is well-known from its very successful application in medical computed tomography. The central slice theorem (CST) relates

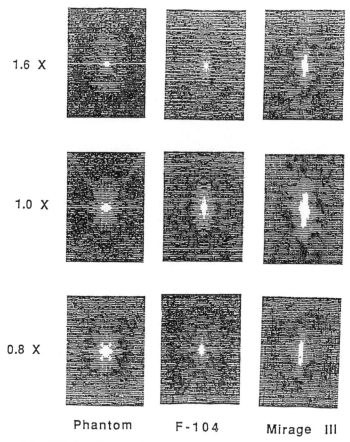

Figure 3.9. *FT distribution for aircraft images in Figure 3.2. (From Kulkarni and Byars, 1991b, with permission. © 1991 IEEE.)*

TABLE 3.3. *FEATURES BY RADIAL BINS (AIRCRAFT IMAGES)*

Rotation (in degrees)	f_1	f_2	f_3	f_4	f_5	f_6
0	0.39	0.23	0.14	0.14	0.82	0.04
45	0.28	0.19	0.18	0.14	0.84	0.04
90	0.39	0.23	0.14	0.14	0.08	0.04
180	0.39	0.23	0.14	0.14	0.08	0.04
0	0.28	0.24	0.13	0.12	0.07	0.04
45	0.27	0.14	0.17	0.12	0.07	0.04
90	0.28	0.24	0.13	0.12	0.07	0.04
180	0.28	0.24	0.13	0.12	0.07	0.04
0	0.39	0.20	0.18	0.18	0.10	0.06
45	0.53	0.25	0.18	0.16	0.10	0.06
90	0.39	0.20	0.18	0.18	0.10	0.06
180	0.39	0.20	0.18	0.18	0.10	0.06

TABLE 3.4. *FEATURES BY ANGULAR BINS (AIRCRAFT IMAGES)*

Scale	f_1	f_2	f_3	f_4	f_5	f_6	f_7	f_8
1.6	0.13	0.10	0.13	0.27	0.12	0.08	0.68	0.99
1.2	0.13	0.10	0.11	0.27	0.12	0.08	0.07	0.10
1.0	0.14	0.10	0.11	0.26	0.13	0.08	0.07	0.11
0.8	0.13	0.10	0.12	0.25	0.13	0.08	0.07	0.11
1.6	0.15	0.07	0.01	0.36	0.10	0.06	0.07	0.09
1.2	0.15	0.07	0.10	0.34	0.10	0.05	0.07	0.11
1.0	0.14	0.07	0.09	0.35	0.11	0.05	0.07	0.10
0.8	0.15	0.07	0.08	0.37	0.11	0.05	0.06	0.10
1.6	0.10	0.11	0.18	0.21	0.12	0.12	0.08	0.09
1.2	0.10	0.12	0.16	0.22	0.12	0.12	0.09	0.08
1.0	0.10	0.12	0.16	0.21	0.12	0.12	0.09	0.09
0.8	0.10	0.12	0.15	0.20	0.12	0.17	0.09	0.09

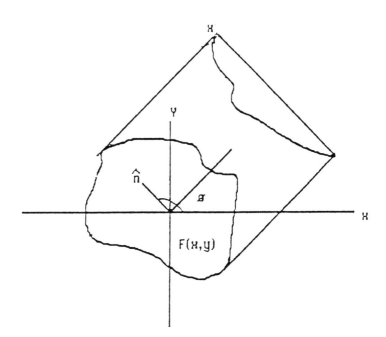

Figure 3.10. *Geometry for the Radon transform.*

the Radon transform of $f(x, y)$ to its Fourier transform. The CST states that the 1-D FT of a projection at an angle ϕ is equal to the 2-D FT of $f(x, y)$ evaluated along a line in the 2-D space collinear to the unit vector $\hat{n}$ that specifies the projection direction. Thus, the Radon transform along with the central slice theorem is used to evaluate the 2-D FT coefficients from 1-D projections of the function $f(x, y)$.

The ANN model for feature extraction using the Radon transform (Figure 3.11) consists of five layers. Layer L_1 is an input layer representing the input

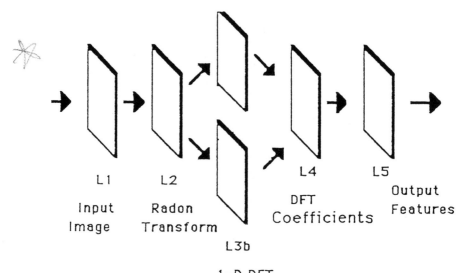

Figure 3.11. *ANN model for feature extraction using the Radon transform. (From Kulkarni and Byars, 1991c, with permission.)*

image distribution. Layer L_2 represents the Radon transform space. Layers L_{3a} and L_{3b} represent real and imaginary parts of the one-dimensional FT coefficients. The weights connecting layers L_2 and L_3 are represented by the elements of the matrices $\boldsymbol{P}_c$ and $\boldsymbol{P}_s$, and are evaluated in the following material (Kulkarni and Byars, 1991c).

Consider the 1-D discrete Fourier transform (DFT) of the function $f(n)$

$$F(u) = \frac{1}{N} \sum_{n=0}^{N-1} f(n) e^{-2\pi jnu/n} \tag{3.30}$$

for $u = 0, 1, 2, \ldots, N - 1$. Equation 3.30 can be represented in a matrix form as

$$\boldsymbol{f}_T = \boldsymbol{P}_c \boldsymbol{f} - j\boldsymbol{Q}_c \boldsymbol{f} \tag{3.31}$$

where $\boldsymbol{f}$ represents the input vector, $\boldsymbol{f}_T$ represents the Fourier coefficients, and the elements of matrices $\boldsymbol{P}_c$ and $\boldsymbol{P}_s$ are given by $P_c(u, n) = 1/N \cos(2\pi nu/N)$ and $P_s(u, n) = 1/N \sin(2\pi nu/N)$ for $u = 1, 2, \ldots, N - 1$. The units in layer L_4 represent amplitudes of the FT coefficients. The rows in layer L_4 correspond to FT coefficients obtained from projection of $f(x, y)$ at angle ϕ_i. Thus, by adding the outputs of units in each row we get radial features. Similarly, by adding outputs of units in each column we get angular features. These features are used as inputs to the recognition stage. Kulkarni and Byars (1991b) have developed a software simulation for the ANN model shown in Figure 3.11. They have successfully used the model for texture recognition and character recognition problems.

3.6. ARTIFICIAL NEURAL NETWORK MODEL USING WHT DOMAIN FEATURE EXTRACTION

In the previous section we developed an ANN architecture using the FT transform. It is also possible to develop an ANN model using other transforms such as the Walsh–Hadamard transform (WHT) or the discrete cosine transform (DCT). A possible ANN architecture using the WHT is discussed in this section. The Walsh representation of signals is analogous to the Fourier representation, and the Walsh–Hadamard transform is analogous to the DFT. A set of the first eight Walsh functions is shown in Figure 3.12 (Ahmed and Rao, 1975). The WHT can be expressed in terms of Hadamard matrices $\boldsymbol{H}(n)$. These matrices can be generated using the following recursive relations:

$$\boldsymbol{H}(n) = \begin{pmatrix} \boldsymbol{H}(n-1) & \boldsymbol{H}(n-1) \\ \boldsymbol{H}(n-1) & -\boldsymbol{H}(n-1) \end{pmatrix} \tag{3.32}$$

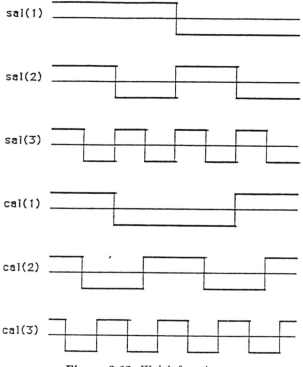

Figure 3.12. *Walsh functions.*

where $n = 1, 2, \ldots, N$ and $\boldsymbol{H}(0) = 1$.

$$\boldsymbol{H}(1) = \begin{pmatrix} 1 & 1 \\ 1 & -1 \end{pmatrix}$$

$$\boldsymbol{H}(2) = \begin{pmatrix} 1 & 1 & 1 & 1 \\ 1 & -1 & 1 & -1 \\ 1 & 1 & -1 & -1 \\ 1 & -1 & -1 & 1 \end{pmatrix}$$

The rows and columns of the Hadamard matrix are mutually orthogonal. It can be easily shown that the inverse of the Hadamard matrix $\boldsymbol{H}(n)$ is given by

$$\boldsymbol{H}^{-1}(n) = \frac{1}{N}\boldsymbol{H}(n) \tag{3.33}$$

where N is the size of the matrix. The WHT transform for two-dimensional discrete data is given by

$$\boldsymbol{F}_{T_{m,n}} = \boldsymbol{H}_{m,m}\boldsymbol{F}_{m,n}\boldsymbol{H}_{n,n} \tag{3.34}$$

and the corresponding inverse transform is given by

$$\boldsymbol{F}_{m,n} = \frac{1}{MN}[\boldsymbol{H}_{m,m}\boldsymbol{F}_{T_{m,n}}\boldsymbol{H}_{n,n}] \tag{3.35}$$

where M and N represent the number of rows and columns in matrix $\boldsymbol{H}$. Similar to the FT, properties of the WHT can be used to extract invariant features. The angular bins can be used to capture information invariant to rotation, and the radial bins can be used to capture information invariant to scale. Unlike the FT, in the WHT plane, wedge and ring detectors must be centered around the top left corner of the WHT plane, as shown in Figures 3.13 and 3.14.

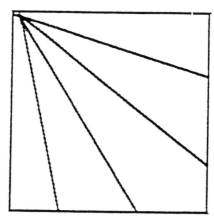

Figure 3.13. *Radial bins for the WHT plane.*

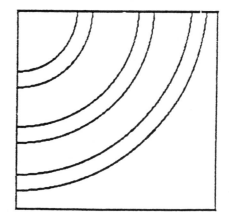

Figure 3.14. *Angular bins for the WHT plane.*

The ANN model for feature extraction using the WHT feature space (Figure 3.15 consists of four layers. The units in layer L_1 represent the input image distribution. The weights between layers L_1L_2, and L_2L_3 correspond to the matrices $\boldsymbol{H}_{n,n}$ and $\boldsymbol{H}_{m,m}$, respectively. The units of layers L_{4a} and L_{4b} represent the output features. The weights between layers L_3 and L_{4a}, and between L_3 and L_{4b} are chosen such that outputs from the units in a given wedge or ring are summed by units in layers L_{4a} and L_{4b}. The units in layer L_{4a} correspond to the radial bins and the units in the layer L_{4b} correspond to the angular bins.

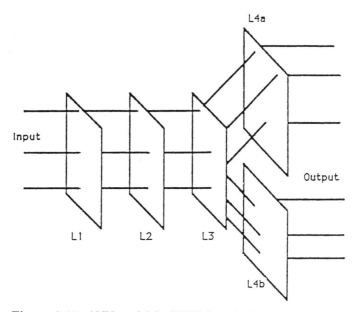

Figure 3.15. *ANN model for WHT domain feature extraction.*

3.7. INVARIANT FEATURE EXTRACTION USING ADALINE

Widrow et al. (1988) have suggested a pattern recognition system consisting of an "invariance net" and a trainable classifier. The invariance net is designed to produce a set of outputs that are insensitive to translation, rotation, scale change, perspective change, etc. of the retinal input pattern. The outputs of the invariance net are then scrambled. When these outputs are fed to a trainable classifier, the final outputs are descrambled, and the original patterns are produced in the standard position, orientation, scale, etc. The entire system is a layered network of adaptive linear neurons (ADALINEs) (Widrow and Winter, 1988). The basic building block of this network is the adaptive linear neuron (ADALINE), as shown in Figure 3.16. The output y_k in this case is given by

$$y_k = \sum_{j=0}^{N} w_{jk} x_{jk} \qquad (3.36)$$

where $\boldsymbol{w}_k = [w_{0k}, w_{1k}, \ldots, w_{nk}]^T$ is the weight vector and $\boldsymbol{x}_k = [x_{0k}, x_{1k}, x_{2k}, \ldots, x_{nk}]^T$ is an input vector. The bias weight w_{0k} is connected to a constant input $x_{0k} = 1$ and controls the threshold level. Decisions are made by a two-level

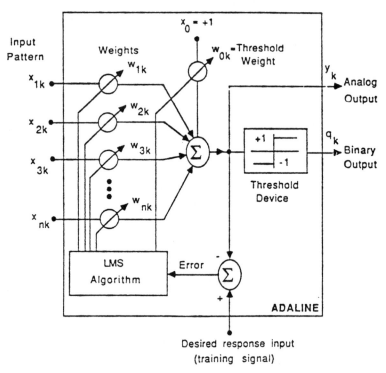

Figure 3.16. *Adaptive linear (ADALINE) neuron. (From Widrow et al., 1988, with permission. © 1988 IEEE.)*

quantizer. The binary $+1$ output is $q_k = \text{sgn}(y_i)$. An adaptive algorithm automatically adjusts the weights so that the actual output responses are as close as possible to the desired output responses. This is done using a least-squares (LMS) algorithm, often called the Widrow-Hoff Delata rule (Rumelhart et al., 1986).

The ADALINES can be connected to ANN logic devices to provide an output. Systems of this kind are called MADALINES (many ADALINES). A multilayer network can be built using ADALINES to extract features that are translation, rotation, and scale invariant. The architecture for a translation feature extraction network is shown in Figure 3.17. In the first column of the network, the weights between layers IP and L_{11} are given by matrix $\boldsymbol{W}_1$. The weights connecting layers IP and L_{21} are given by T_{D1} ($\boldsymbol{W}_1$), where the operator T_{D1} ($\boldsymbol{W}_1$) represents "translation down one." This set of weights is the same as $\boldsymbol{W}_1$ except that the weights are translated down en masse by a unit distance. The weights between layers IP and L_{31} are given by $T_{D2}(\boldsymbol{W})$, where operator T_{D2} represents translation down by two units. As the input pattern moves up and

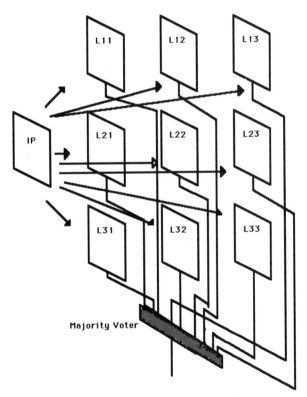

Figure 3.17. *Network for translation-invariant feature extraction.*

down, depending on the position of the input pattern, one of the three layers in the first column will produce the maximum output. Several such columns can be used to obtain invariance with respect to the left-right shift in input patterns. The pattern of weights for the whole layer is given by

$$
\begin{pmatrix}
W_1 & T_{R1}(W_1) & T_{R2}(W_1) \\
T_{D1}(W_1) & T_{R1}T_{D1}(W_1) & T_{R2}T_{D1}(W_1) \\
T_{D2}(W_1) & T_{R1}T_{D2}(W_1) & T_{R2}T_{D2}(W_1)
\end{pmatrix}
\tag{3.37}
$$

where the operator T_{R1} represents "translation one right." As the input pattern moves left and right, depending on the position of the input pattern, one of the three layers of the row (the row is decided by up-and-down movement of the input pattern) will produce the maximum output. Thus, the output of the network is insensitive to translational differences.

In order to obtain an output that is insensitive to rotational differences, one can use several slabs similar to that shown in Figure 3.17. The weight matrices of these slabs are similar to the weight matrices of the first slab except that they are rotated en masse. For example, the array of weight matrices for the second slab can be represented as

$$
\begin{pmatrix}
T_{RC1}(W_1) & T_{R1}T_{RC1}(W_1) & T_{R2}T_{RC1}(W_1) & T_{R3}T_{RC1}(W_1) \\
T_{D1}T_{RC1}(W_1) & T_{R1}T_{D1}T_{RC1}(W_1) & T_{R2}T_{D1}T_{RC1}(W_1) & T_{R3}T_{D1}T_{RC1}(W_1) \\
T_{D2}T_{RC1}(W_1) & T_{R1}T_{D2}T_{RC1}(W_1) & T_{R2}T_{D2}T_{RC1}(W_1) & T_{R3}T_{D2}T_{RC1}(W_1) \\
T_{D3}T_{RC1}(W_1) & T_{R1}T_{D3}T_{RC1}(W_1) & T_{R2}T_{D3}T_{RC1}(W_1) & T_{R3}T_{D3}T_{RC1}(W_1)
\end{pmatrix}
$$

$$\tag{3.38}$$

The same principles can be used to design invariance nets to be insensitive to scale or pattern size. A point of expansion is specified on the retina so that input patterns can be expanded or contracted with respect to this point, and two ADALINEs can be trained to give similar responses to patterns of similar forms, if the weight matrix of one were expanded (or contracted) relative to the other about the point of expansion. The amplitude of the weights must be scaled in the inverse proportion to the square of the linear dimension of the retinal pattern. As many more slabs are added, the invariance net can be built around this idea to be sensitive to pattern size as well as translation and rotation. Widrow et al. (1988) have developed a computer simulation of the network with 25 ADALINEs on each slab. They trained the network with 36 patterns, each represented by a 5×5 grid. The main disadvantage of this architecture is that the number of weights in the invariant network becomes excessively high for smaller translational, angular, and scale increments.

3.8. SUMMARY

Feature extraction corresponds to intermediate-level processing. The main purpose of feature extraction is to reduce data by measuring certain "properties" that distinguish input patterns. The problem of invariant object recognition is also tackled in a feature extraction stage. Conventional methods, as well as ANN models for feature extraction, are discussed in this chapter. We discussed methods such as the moment invariants, and FT domain feature extraction. We also introduced the architecture for an ANN model for feature extraction using the FT plane. The model was further simplified using the Radon transform. As an illustration, aircraft images were analyzed using the model. The ANN model for invariant feature extraction using ADALINEs was also discussed.

REFERENCES

Ahmed, N., and Rao, K. R. (1975). *Orthogonal Transforms for Digital Signal Processing*. Springer-Verlag, Berlin.

Ballard, D. H., and Brown, C. M. (1982). *Computer Vision*. Prentice Hall, Engelwood Cliffs, NJ.

Casasent, D. (1985a). Hybrid optical/digital image pattern recognition: A review. *Proceedings of SPIE*, 528:64–82.

Casasent, D. (1985b). Coherent optical pattern recognition: A review. *Optical Engineering*, 24:26–32.

Duda, R. O., and Hart, P. E. (1973). *Pattern Classification and Scene Analysis*. John Wiley & Sons, New York.

Dudani, S. A., and Breeding, K. J. (1987). Aircraft identification by moment invariants. *IEEE Transactions on Computers* C-36:39–45.

Gindi, G. R., and Gmitro, A. F. (1984). Optical feature extraction via Random transform. *Optical Engineering* 23:499–506.

Gonzales, R. C., and Wintz, P. (1987). *Digital Image Processing*. Addison-Wesley, Reading, MA.

Goodman, J. W. (1968). *Introduction to Fourier Optics*. McGraw Hill, New York.

Hu, M. K. (1962). Visual pattern recognition by moment invariants. *IRE Transactions on Information Theory* IT-8:28–32.

Khotanzad, A., and Lu, J. H. (1987). Distorted invariant character recognition by multi-layer perceptron and backpropagation learning, *Proceedings of Joint International Conference on Neural Networks*, San Diego, Vol. I:625–632.

Kulkarni, A. D., et al. (1990). Neural networks for invariant object recognition. In: *Proceedings of Symposium on Applied Computing*, Fayetteville, Arkansas, pp. 28–32.

Kulkarni, A. D., and Byars, P. (1991a). Artificial neural network models for image understanding. In: *Proceedings of SPIE Conference on Image Processing Algorithms and Techniques II*, San Jose, CA, 1452:512–522.

Kulkarni, A. D., and Byars, P. (1991b). Neural nets for invariant object recognition. In: *Proceedings of the Symposium on Applied Computing*. Kansas City, MO, pp. 336–344.

Kulkarni, A. D., and Byars, P. (1991c). Artificial neural network models for texture classification via the Radon transform. In: *Proceedings of SPIE Conference on Intelligent*

Robots and Computer Vision X: Neural, Biological and 3-D methods, Boston, MA, 1608:518–525.

Linsker, R. (1988). Self organization in perceptual network. *Computer* 21:11–22.

Lippmann, R. P. (1987). An introduction to computing with neural nets. In: *IEEE Transactions on Acoustics, Speech, and Signal Processing* 32:4–22.

Oja, E., (1989). Neural networks, principal components and subspaces. *International Journal of Neural Systems*, 1:61–68.

Rosenfeld, A., and Kak, A. (1982). *Digital Image Processing*, Vols. I and II. Academic Press, Orlando, FL.

Rumelhart, D. E., et al. (1986). *Parallel Distributed Processing*, Vol. I. MIT Press, Cambridge, MA.

Tou, J. T., and Gonzalez, R. C. (1974). *Pattern Recognition Principles: Trainable Pattern Classifiers—the Deterministic Approach*. Addison-Wesley, Reading, MA.

Widrow, B., and Winter, R. (1988). Neural nets for adaptive filtering and adaptive pattern recognition. *Computer*, 21:25–39.

Widrow, B. et al. (1988). Layered neural nets for pattern recognition. *IEEE Transactions on Acoustics Speech and Signal Processing* 26:1109–1118.

Wintz, P. A. (1972). Transform picture coding. *Proceedings of the Institute of Electrical and Electronics Engineering* 60:809–830.

4

Texture Analysis

4.1. INTRODUCTION

Texture is generally recognized as being fundamental to perception. A taxonomy of problems encountered within the context of texture analysis could be that of classification, description, and segmentation. Machine analysis and recognition of texture patterns have applications in radiography, and aerial and satellite photography, among other areas.

There is no precise definition or characterization of texture available in practice. Texture has been described in a variety of ways. Intuitively, texture descriptors provide measures of properties such as smoothness, coarseness, and regularity. One way to describe texture is to consider it as being composed of elements of texture primitives. Texture can also be defined as a mutual relationship among intensity values of neighboring pixels repeated over an area larger than the size of the relationship.

The task of extracting texture features from the input image is critical. If one could model and quantify the process by which the human recognizes texture, one could construct a highly successful recognition system. Unfortunately, the process by which we recognize texture is not really understood, and researchers are left to consider some ad hoc techniques such as statistical, structural, and spectral methods, as well as artificial neural network (ANN) models. Human observers are capable of performing some image segmentation and discrimination tasks under conditions (such as brief exposure of a test image) that prevent detailed scrutiny of the image. This ability is referred to as "effortless" or "preattentive" visual discrimination. In a sense two images (which do not portray particular objects or forms) are said to have the same "texture" if they are not effortlessly discriminable to a human observer.

Many texture feature extraction and recognition algorithms are available in practice (Haralick, 1967; Haralick et al., 1973; Weszka et al., 1976; Ehrich and Foith, 1978; O'Toole and Stark, 1980; Rosenfeld and Kak, 1982; Ballard and Brown, 1982; Coggins and Jain, 1985; Daugman, 1988a, b, 1989). Conventional texture recognition algorithms can be grouped into three classes: structural, statistical, and spectral. Statistical approaches yield characterizations of textures as smooth, coarse, grainy, and so on. Statistical algorithms are based on the relationship between intensity values of pixels; measures include the entropy, contrast, and correlation based on the gray level cooccurrence matrix. Structural algorithms are based on the image primitives; they regard the primitive as a forming element to generate repeating patterns and describe rules for generating them.

The notion of a primitive is central to texture analysis. A *texel* is (loosely) a visual primitive with certain invariant properties. Texels occur repeatedly in different positions, deformations, or orientations inside a given area. Texture primitives may be pixels or aggregates of pixels. One way of describing rules that govern texture is through a grammar. Structural approaches deal with the grammar rules to generate patterns by applying these rules to a small number of symbols. Spectral techniques are based on properties of the Fourier spectrum and are used primarily to detect global periodicity in the image by identifying high-energy narrow peaks in the spectrum. Statistical and structural measures lack good neurophysiological support (Rao and Vemuri, 1989). Recently a few ANN architectures for texture analysis have been proposed (Clark et al., 1987; Daugman, 1988a, b; Visa, 1990; Kulkarni and Byars, 1992). ANN models as well as statistical methods for texture analysis are discussed in this chapter.

4.2. STATISTICAL METHODS

In statistical methods, we describe features using a spatial gray level dependency (SGLD) matrix. For a two-dimensional image $f(x, y)$ with N discrete gray values, we define the spatial gray level dependency matrix $\boldsymbol{P}(d, \phi)$ for each d and ϕ. The element p_{ij} is defined as the relative number of times a gray level pair (i, j) occurs when pixels separated by the distance d along the angle ϕ are compared. Each element is finally normalized by the total number of occurrences giving the cooccurrence matrix $\boldsymbol{P}$. A spatial gray level dependency matrix is also called a cooccurrence matrix, and it is given by

$$\mathbf{P}(d, \phi) = \begin{vmatrix} p_{00} & p_{01} \cdots & p_{0, N-1} \\ p_{10} & p_{11} \cdots & p_{1, N-1} \\ p_{N-1, 0} & P_{N-1, 1} \cdots & P_{N-1, N-1} \end{vmatrix} \qquad (4.1)$$

where p_{ij} is given by

$$P_{ij} = \frac{\text{number of pixel pairs with intensity } (i, j)}{\text{total number of pairs considered}}$$

Commonly used features that are obtained from the cooccurrence matrix are the energy, entropy, correlation, inertia, and local homogeneity (Haralick et al., 1973). These are given by the following expressions.

1. Angular second moment (a measure of picture homogeneity)

$$\phi_1 = \sum_{i=0}^{N-1} \sum_{j=0}^{N-1} p_{ij}^2 \tag{4.2}$$

2. Contrast (measure of amount of intensity variation)

$$\phi_2 = \sum_{i=0}^{N-1} \sum_{j=0}^{N-1} (i - j)^2 p_{ij} \tag{4.3}$$

3. Correlation (a measure of gray level dependencies)

$$\phi_3 = \sum_{i=0}^{N-1} \sum_{j=0}^{N-1} (1 - \mu_x)(1 - \mu_y) p_{ij}/\sigma_x \sigma_y \tag{4.4}$$

where

$$\mu_x = \sum_{i=0}^{N-1} \sum_{j=0}^{N-1} p_{ij}$$

$$\mu_y = \sum_{i=0}^{N-1} \sum_{j=0}^{N-1} p_{ij}$$

$$\sigma_x^2 = \sum_{i=0}^{N-1} \sum_{j=0}^{N-1} p_{ij}(i - \mu_x)^2$$

$$\sigma_y^2 = \sum_{i=0}^{N-1} \sum_{j=0}^{N-1} p_{ij}(j - \mu_y)^2$$

4. Entropy (another homogeneity measure)

$$\phi_4 = -\sum_{i=0}^{N-1} \sum_{j=0}^{N-1} p_{ij}\log(p_{ij} + \varepsilon) \tag{4.5}$$

where ε is a small positive constant to avoid overflow when p_{ij} equals zero. The basic idea here is to characterize the "content" of the cooccurrence matrix via these descriptors. Haralick et al. (1973) have suggested a set of 28 texture features based on the cooccurrence matrix. These features characterize texture patterns. The angular moment feature (ϕ_1) is a measure of the homogeneity of the image. The contrast feature (ϕ_2) is a difference moment and is a measure of the amount of local gray tone variation present in the image. The correlation feature (ϕ_3) is a measure of gray tone linear dependencies in the image. These features have been used successfully in many image-processing applications.

Based on the above measures, Visa (1990) has developed a system for texture classification and recognition that consists of two stages: the feature extraction stage and the recognition stage. In the feature extraction stage, Visa (1990) has used features such as energy, entropy, correlation, homogeneity, and inertia. The recognition stage in the model consists of a self-organizing network that produces Kohonen's feature maps (Kohonen, 1988). These feature maps can be used directly for texture recognition.

4.3. SPECTRAL APPROACHES

These approaches are based on properties of the Fourier transform. In the late 1960s, researchers found that the threshold visibility of sinusoidal gratings depends on the spatial frequency of the gratings (Cambell and Maffei, 1970; Cambell and Robson, 1968) . The potential power of Fourier analysis as a tool for studying human vision was noted immediately. The Fourier spectrum is ideally suited for describing the directionality of periodic or almost periodic 2-D patterns in the image. These global texture patterns are distinguishable as concentrations of high-energy peaks in the spectrum.

Many spatial frequency-filtering techniques have been developed in practice. Bajcsy and Lieberman (1976) have used spectrograms for texture segmentation. Spectrograms are represented by square magnitudes of the finite support Fourier transform coefficients. The difference-of-Gaussians (DOG) representation based on 2-D band-pass filters has been used as a model of a human vision system (Marr, 1982). Coggins and Jain (1985) have used radial and angular bins in the logarithmic Fourier transform (FT) domain for extracting texture feature. Beck et al. (1987) have investigated texture segregation in a three-part (tripartite) pattern in which each part contains equal numbers of two different squares that are arranged in vertical strips in the top and bottom parts and in a checkerboard in the central part. Their experiment supports the hypothesis that tripartite segregation is primarily a function of spatial frequency components and not the grouping process. Reed and Wechsler (1990) have suggested a system for texture segmentation using the Wigner distribution. A few well-known spatial filtering techniques such as the spectrogram, difference-of-Gaussians (DOG) representation, and Wigner distribution are discussed below.

Cambell and Robson (1968) carried out some adaptation experiments. They found that the sensitivity of subjects to a high-contrast grating was temporarily reduced after exposure to such gratings, and this desensitization was specific to the orientation and spatial frequency of gratings. They concluded that the visual pathway included a set of channels that are orientation and spatial frequency selective. Based on their observation, Wilson and Giese (1977) and Wilson and Bergen (1979) developed a model using the difference-of-Gaussians (DOG) filters. The basic idea in the method is that at each point in the visual field there are four masks of filters. The spatial receptive fields of these filters have approximately the shape of a DOG function. These channels are labeled N, S, T, and U in order of increasing size. The DOG representation expresses the image as the sum of the outputs of a bank of isotropic 2-D bandpass filters. The impulse response of DOG filters is given by

$$h(x, y) = h_1(x, y) - h_2(x, y)$$

$$= A \exp(-a_1 x^2 - a_2 y^2) - B \exp(-b_1 x^2 - b_2 y^2) \qquad (4.6)$$

Here signal representations consist of a number of filtered versions of the original image. The DOG representations also are used in the multiresolution or pyramid representation of an image.

The two-dimensional spectrogram of an image can be defined as

$$\boldsymbol{F}_{x,y}(u, v) = \iint F_{x,y}(x', y')e^{-jux'-jvy'} \, dx' \, dy' \qquad (4.7)$$

where $F_{x,y}(x', y') = f(x', y')h(x - x', y - y')$, $f(x', y')$ is the original image, and $h(x - x', y - y')$ is the window centered at (x, y). The spectrogram is simply the squared magnitude of $\boldsymbol{F}_{x,y}(u, v)$

$$S_f(x, y, u, v) = |\boldsymbol{F}_{x,y}(u, v)|^2 \qquad (4.8)$$

The squared magnitude of the finite support Fourier transform has been used by Bajcsy and Lieberman (1976) to extract texture features. Ginsburg and Coggins (1981) suggested transfer functions for spatial frequency channels defined by the Gaussian function on the log scale. Figure 4.1 shows two representations of spatial frequency filters in the Fourier transform (FT) domain plane. Coggins and Jain (1985) used filtered images with similar filter functions for texture segmentation. They used 11 channels (four orientation channels and seven spatial frequency channels) for filtering. They obtained a feature vector with 11 features at each pixel and used a clustering technique to label pixels.

A texture segmentation system based on the Wigner distribution (WD) has been proposed by Reed and Wechsler (1990). The system consists of four stages: the preprocessing stage, the image representation stage, the data reduction stage, and the boundary detection stage, as shown in Figure 4.2. The preprocessing stage serves as an antialiasing filter. The image representation stage

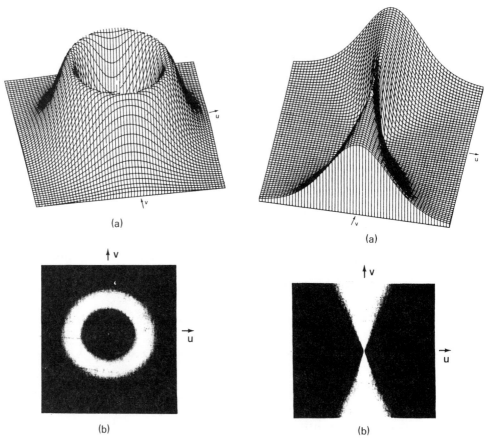

Figure 4.1. *Spatial frequency filters. (From Coggins and Jain, 1985, with permission.)*

uses the pseudo-Wigner distribution (PWD). The Wigner distribution was originally suggested to characterize the quantum mechanical duality between the position and the momentum of a particle (Wigner, 1932). The use of this distribution for 2-D and 3-D image processing was first proposed by Jacobson and Wechsler (1988). For discrete images the 2-D PWD is defined as

$$P_W(m, n, p, q) = 4 \sum_{k=-N_2+1}^{N_2-1} \sum_{1=-N_1+1}^{N_1-1} h_{N_1 N_2}(k, l) \sum_{r=-M_1+1}^{M_2-1} \sum_{s=-M_1+1}^{M_1-1} g_{M_1, M_2}(r, s)$$

$$\times f(m + r + k, n + s + l) f^*(m + r - k, n + s - l)$$

$$\times \exp[-j(2\pi kp/P + 2\pi lq/Q)] \tag{4.9}$$

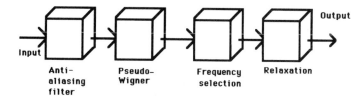

Figure 4.2. *Reed and Wechsler segmentation system.*

where

$$p = 0, \pm 1, \cdots, \pm (N_2 - 1)$$

$$q = 0, \pm 1, \cdots, \pm (N_1 - 1)$$

$$P = 2N_2 - 1$$

$$Q = 2N_1 - 1$$

and m and n are integers. In Eq. 4.9, the asterisk indicates the complex conjugate. The functions $h_{N_1, N_2}(k, l)$ and $g_{M_1, M_2}(r, s)$ are window functions.

A property of the 2-D Wigner distribution that is of particular interest in image-processing applications is that it is strictly a real-valued function. The third stage in the model is the data reduction stage. The result of applying PWD to an image is representation of the frequency content at each pixel. Each pixel is represented by a 2-D array representing its frequency content. For an $N \times N$ image and a main window of size $N_1 \times N_2$, we get $2N_1 \times 2N_2 \times N \times N$ elements. One method to reduce these data is to save only the frequency contents at frequencies containing the most energy. In the fourth stage a relaxation method has been used for boundary segmentation. The results of texture segmentation are shown in Figure 4.3a through 4.3d. Figure 4.3a shows the original image. The image after antialiasing filtering is shown in Figure 4.3b. The primary frequency plane of the PWD and the result of the relaxation stage are shown in Figures 4.3c and 4.3d, respectively.

O'Toole and Stark (1980) have suggested yet another method for texture feature extraction. They used the Hotelling trace transformation to extract features for texture recognition. Here, the mapping of an observation vector x to the feature vector y is given by

$$y = Hx \tag{4.10}$$

The transformation matrix H can be obtained from class scatter matrices in such a way as to maximize the class separability measure J_1 given by

$$J_1 = \text{tr}(S_2^{-1} S_1) \tag{4.11}$$

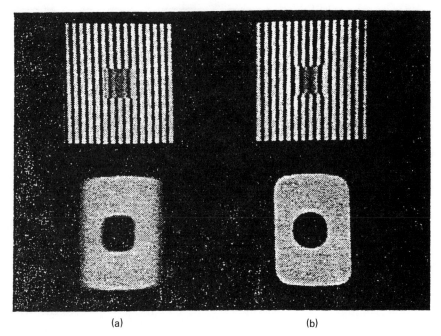

(a)   (b)

Figure 4.3. *Segmentation of synthesized textures. (From Reed and Wechsler, 1990, with permission. © 1990 IEEE.)*

where $\boldsymbol{S}_1$ is the between-class scatter matrix, a measure of difference in class means, and is given by

$$\boldsymbol{S}_1 = \sum P_i (\boldsymbol{x}_i - \boldsymbol{x}_0)(\boldsymbol{x}_i - \boldsymbol{x}_0)^T \qquad (4.12)$$

and $\boldsymbol{S}_2$, the pooled covariance matrix, is given by

$$\boldsymbol{S}_2 = P_i \boldsymbol{D}_i \qquad (4.13)$$

where P_i is the a priori probability of class i, $\boldsymbol{x}_i$ is a mean vector for class i, $\boldsymbol{x}_0$ is the vector representing pooled mean, and $\boldsymbol{D}_i$ is a class covariance matrix, elements of which are given by

$$d_{lk} = \sum_{n_1} (x_k - x_{0k})(x_l - x_{0l}) \qquad (4.14)$$

for $k = 1, 2, \ldots, n_2$, $l = 1, 2, \ldots, n_2$, where n_2 represents the number of elements in the feature vector, and n_1 is the number of samples in class i. In Eq. 4.14, x_k and x_l represent elements of the feature vector $\boldsymbol{x}$, and $\boldsymbol{x}_0$ represents the corresponding mean vector.

The optimum transformation H with respect to J_1 is then given by the first m eigenvectors of $S_2^{-1} S_1$.

$$H = (\phi_1 \phi_2, \ldots, \phi_m)^T$$

where ϕ_i is the ith eigenvector of the matrix $S_2^{-1} S_1$, and λ_i are the corresponding eigenvalues ordered so that

$$\lambda_1 \geq \lambda_2 \geq \lambda_3 \cdots \geq \lambda_m$$

The transform yields an m-dimensional feature space determined by the m largest eigenvectors. O'Toole and Stark (1980) have used these features along with the nearest classifier stage for texture recognition. They also have used features obtained by Foley–Sammon discriminant vectors. Foley and Sammon (1975) have proposed selecting a discriminant vector ϕ that maximizes the Fisher ratio. The Fisher ratio $r(\phi)$ is the ratio of the projected class mean difference to the sum of the within-class scatter matrix along the discriminant vector ϕ. It is given by

$$r(\phi) = \left| \phi^T \sum (x_i - x_0) \right|^2 / \phi^T \left(\sum D_i \right) \phi \tag{4.15}$$

where D_i is the covariance matrix for class i. In finding the transformation to the m-dimensional feature space, they have suggested an orthogonal set of vectors $\phi_1, \phi_2, \ldots, \phi_m$ so that

$$r(\phi_1) \geq r(\phi_2) \geq \cdots \geq r(\phi_m) \tag{4.16}$$

The transformation matrix H is then given by

$$H = (\phi_1 \phi_2, \ldots, \phi_m)^T \tag{4.17}$$

The procedure for computing the discriminant vectors is provided by Foley and Sammon (1975).

4.4. ARTIFICIAL NEURAL NETWORK MODELS FOR TEXTURE ANALYSIS

Recently many ANN models have been suggested for texture recognition (Clark et al., 1987; Daugman, 1988a, b, 1989; Rao and Vemuri, 1989; Kulkarni and Byars, 1991; Visa, 1990). A generic model for segmenting images using texture requires the identification of those features that both define texture and allow discrimination between different textures. A class of 2-D filters based on the Gabor functions has been suggested (Clark et al., 1987; Daugman, 1988b). Rao and Vemuri (1989) have suggested a neural network architecture for texture segmentation and labeling. Their model consists of two major components: the feature extraction network and the texture discrimination network. The feature extraction network is a multilayered hierarchical network governed by Grossberg's boundary counter (BC) system (Grossberg and Mingolla, 1988). The texture discrimination network is based on the adaptive learning algorithm by Kohonen (1988). ANN models based on FT domain feature extraction (Kulkarni and Byars, 1991) can also be used for texture feature extraction.

The family of 2-D Gabor elementary functions has been used for many early vision tasks. The Gabor filters are optimal in several senses: they have tunable orientation bandwidths, they can be defined to operate over a range of spatial frequency channels, and they obey the uncertainty principle in two dimensions. Moreover, the receptive fields of neurons in the visual cortex are known to have shapes that approximate 2-D Gabor filters. The parameters in the 2-D Gabor family of elementary functions directly capture the chief neurophysiological properties such as localization in visual space, spatial dimensions, and preorientation. The family of 2-D elementary functions constitutes a generalization of the 1-D elementary functions proposed in 1946 by Gabor. An image can be represented as the sum of outputs of a bank of 2-D Gabor-filtered images with the impulse response $h(x, y)$ given by

$$h(x, y) = \exp\left\{-\pi\left[(x - x_0)^2/\alpha^2 + (y - y_0)^2/\beta^2\right]\right\}$$

$$\times \exp\{-2\pi i[u_0(x - x_0) + v_0(y - y_0)]\} \qquad (4.18)$$

The frequency response of the above filter is given by

$$H(u, v) = \exp\left\{-\pi\left[(u - u_0)^2/\alpha^2 + (v - v_0)^2/\beta^2\right]\right\}$$

$$\times \exp\{-2\pi i[x_0(u - u_0) + y_0(v - v_0)]\} \qquad (4.19)$$

Because the above class of filters is orientation-sensitive, the resulting representation is a 4-D representation. Daugman (1988b) has shown that this class of filters achieves lower limits imposed by the 2-D uncertainty inequalities

$$\Delta x \, \Delta u \geq 1/4\pi$$

$$\Delta y \, \Delta v \geq 1/4\pi$$

He has also shown that the 2-D Gabor functions agree with the 2-D receptive field profiles measured for simple cells in the cat cortex (Figure 4.4). In the case of digital images that are two-dimensional in nature, the 2-D Gabor elementary functions can be parameterized for an invariant Gaussian window that is positioned on fully overlapping lattice locations.

$$\{x_m, y_n\} = \{mM, nN\}$$

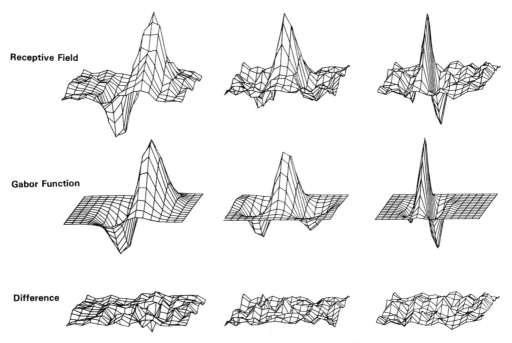

Receptive Field

Gabor Function

Difference

Figure 4.4. *2-D receptive fields and Gabor functions. (From Daugman, 1988b, with permission. © 1988 IEEE.)*

for integers (m, n) and corresponding lattice dimensions (M, N). The 2-D elementary functions are given by

$$g_{mnrs}(x, y) = \exp\left\{-\pi\alpha^2\left[(x - mM)^2 + (y - nN)^2\right]\right\}$$

$$\times \exp\{-2\pi i[rx/M + sy/N]\} \tag{4.20}$$

Let $f(x, y)$ be an image to be represented in some optimal sense by being projected onto a set of vectors $g_i(x, y)$ such that

$$f'(x, y) = \sum_{i=1}^{n} a_i g_i(x, y) \tag{4.21}$$

where error ε in $f(x, y)$ is given by

$$\varepsilon = \sum_{x, y} [f(x, y) - f'(x, y)]2$$

If the elementary functions $\{g_i(x, y)\}$ form a complete orthogonal set, then the representation $f'(x, y)$ is exact. If the elementary functions do not form an orthogonal set, then in general the representation $f'(x, y)$ will be inexact, and the desired set of coefficients a_i must be determined by minimizing the squared error. The error function ε will be minimized only when its partial derivatives with respect to all n coefficients $\{a_i\}$ equal zero; i.e.,

$$\partial\varepsilon/\partial a_i = -2\sum_{x,y} f(x,y)g_i(x,y) + 2\sum \left\{ \left[2\left(\sum_{k=1}^{n} a_k g_k(x,y) \right) \right] g_i(x,y) \right\} = 0$$

(4.22)

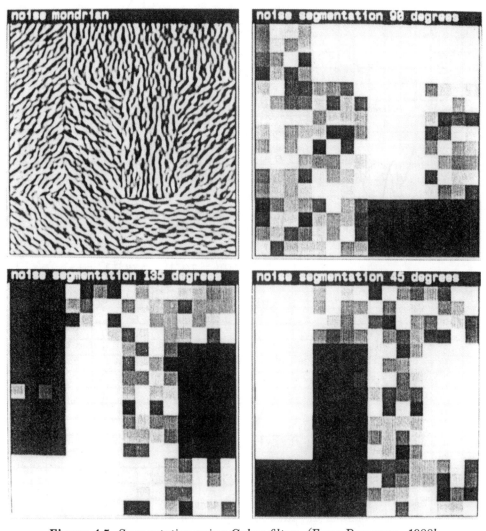

Figure 4.5. *Segmentation using Gabor filters. (From Daugman, 1988b, with permission. © 1988 IEEE.)*

To satisfy this condition for each of the a_i, Eq. 4.22 generates a system of n simultaneous equations in n unknowns:

$$\sum_{x,y} f(x,y)g_i(x,y) = \sum_{x,y} \left\{ \left[\sum_{k=1} a_k g_k(x,y) \right] g_i(x,y) \right\} \qquad (4.23)$$

The system of equations can be solved in principle by algebraic means to find the set of optimal coefficients. However, it becomes difficult in practice to solve this huge system of equations. Daugman (1988a, b, 1989) has suggested a neural network architecture to solve the system of equations. The Gabor coefficients can be used for texture segmentation. By examining the distributions of the spatially localized 2-D Gabor coefficients, it is possible to achieve image segmentation. Figure 4.5a shows that the input image consists of a collage of

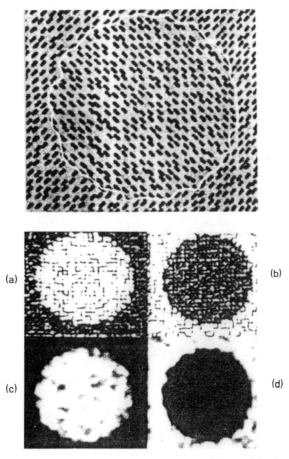

(a)

(b)

(c)

(d)

Figure 4.6. *Segmentation using Gabor filters. (From Clark et al., 1987, with permission. © 1987 IEEE.)*

anisotropically filtered white noise fields. The segmented image obtained by clustering local Gabor coefficients is shown in Figures 4.5b–d.

Clark et al. (1987) have also used the 2-D Gabor filters for texture segmentation. They considered Gabor filters given by Eq. 4.18. As an illustration, they considered a synthetic image and have shown that the regions can be easily segmented by using only two Gabor filters centered at a radial frequency corresponding to the periodicity of the line segments and oriented at angles about $\pi/4$ and $-\pi/4$ radians. The filters used had unity aspect ratio and a bandwidth of 1.3 octaves. The resulting segmentation is shown in Figure 4.6.

The ANN model for feature extraction using the FT domain features has been discussed in Chapter 3. The model uses angular and radial bins. Texture patterns can be distinguished by either directivity or coarseness. It can be seen that features corresponding to radial bins are sensitive to coarseness of texture patterns. These features can be used to distinguish texture patterns based on their coarseness and fineness of details. The features corresponding to angular bins are sensitive to directivity patterns of the input image. These features can

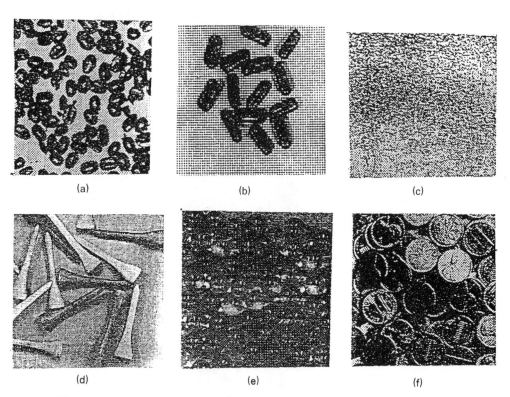

(a)   (b)   (c)

(d)   (e)   (f)

Figure 4.7. *Texture patterns. (From Kulkarni and Byars, 1991a, with permission.)*

be used to distinguish texture patterns based on their directivity pattern. Kulkarni and Byars (1992) have used these properties in their ANN model. They used the Radon transform to calculate 2-D FT coefficients. Use of the Radon transform (Gindi and Gmitro, 1984) simplifies the architecture significantly.

As an illustration, they used the 10 texture patterns shown in Figure 4.7, each represented by a 64 × 64 image. In order to obtain the Radon transform they used six projections at 0°, 15°, 30°, 45°, 60° and 75°, and eight samples for each projection; this resulted in eight angular features. Software was developed to simulate the model. The features obtained are shown in Figure 4.8. In the recognition stage they used a three-layer BP network as a classifier. There were 14 units in the input layer, 29 in the hidden layer, and 10 in the output layer. The 14 units in the input layer correspond to the 14 angular and radial features. The 10 units in the output layer represent the 10 texture patterns. The BP network was initially trained using these features. The training set data were then reclassified to check the classification accuracy.

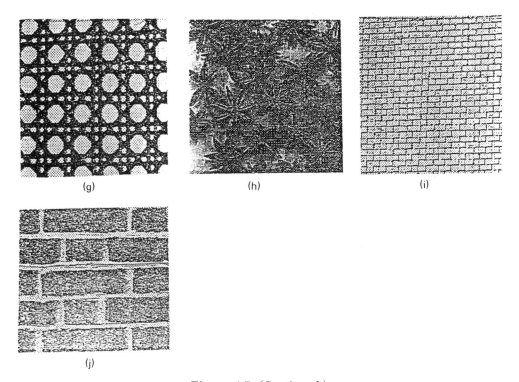

(g) (h) (i)

(j)

Figure 4.7. *(Continued.)*

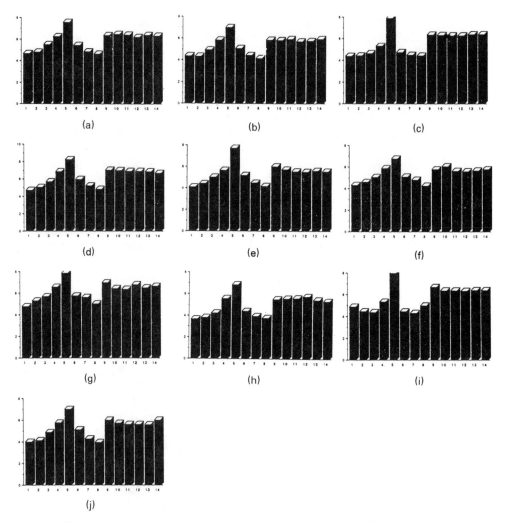

Figure 4.8. *Feature vector for patterns in Figure 4.7. (From Kulkarni and Byars, 1991a, with permission.)*

4.5. SUMMARY

Texture is generally recognized as fundamental to perception, although there is no precise definition of texture in practice. Conventional methods as well as ANN models for texture segmentation are described in this chapter. Statistical methods of texture feature extraction are based on cooccurrence matrices. Structural methods use primitives to define texture patterns, and spectral methods are based on the properties of the Fourier transform. ANN models based on angular and radial bins in the FT plane are described in this chapter. The features extracted here distinguish texture patterns by their directivity and coarseness. Gabor functions are also used in texture recognition. These functions correlate with the profile of receptive fields in the vision system. The Gabor functions are orientation sensitive and are local. A few illustrative examples of texture segmentation using the Gabor functions are also provided.

REFERENCES

Bajcsy, R., and Lieberman, L. (1976). Texture gradient as a depth clue. *Computer Graphics and Image Processing* 1:52–67.

Ballard, D. H., and Brown, C. M. (1982). *Computer Vision*. Prentice Hall, Engelwood Cliffs, NJ.

Beck, J., et al. (1987). Spatial frequency channels and perceptual grouping. *Computer Vision, Graphics and Image Processing* 37:299–325.

Cambell, F. W., and Robson, J. G. (1968). Application of Fourier analysis to the visibility gratings. *Journal of Physiology* 197:551–566.

Cambell, F. W., and Maffei, L. (1970). Electro-physiological evidence for existence of orientation and size detectors in human visual systems. *Journal of Physiology* 207: 635–652.

Coggins, J. M., and Jain, A. K. (1985). A spatial filtering approach to texture analysis. *Pattern Recognition Letters* 3:195–203.

Clark, M., et al. (1987). Texture segmentation using a class of narrow-band filters. *Proceedings of International Conference on Acoustics, Speech, and Signal Processing*, April, pp. 14.6.1–14.6.4.

Daugman, J. G. (1988a). Relaxation neural network for nonorthogonal image transforms. *Proceedings of International Joint Conference on Neural Networks, San Diego*, Vol. I, pp. 547–560.

Daugman, J. G. (1988b). Complete discrete 2-D Gabor transforms by neural networks for image analysis and compression. *IEEE Transactions on Acoustics, Speech and Signal Processing* 36:1169–1179.

Daugman, J. G. (1989). Network for image analysis: Motion and texture. *Proceedings of International Joint Conference on Neural Networks*, Washington DC, Vol. I, pp. 189–193.

Ehrich, R. W., and Foith, J. P. (1978). *A view of texture topology and texture description. Computer Graphics and Image Processing* 8:174–202.

Foley, D. H., and Sammon, J. W. (1975). *IEEE Transactions on Computers* 24:

Gabor, D. (1946). Theory of communication. *Journal of Institute of Electrical* 93:429–457.

Gindi, G. R., and Gmitro, A. F. (1984). Optical feature extract transform. *Optical Engineering* 23:499–506.

Ginsburg A. P., and Coggins, J. M. (1981). Texture analysis ties of the human visual system. *Proceedings of International and Society, Atlanta*, pp. 112–117.

Grossberg, S., and Mingolla, E. (1988). A neural vision: Multiple scale segmentation and r *Joint Conference on Neural Networks, S*

Haralick, R. M. (1967). Statistical *Institute of Electrical and Electr*

Haralick R. M., et al. (1973). Texture features for image classification. *IEEE Transactions on System, Man and Cybernetics* 3:610–620.

Jacobson, L., and Wechsler, H. (1988). Joint spatial/spatial frequency representation. *Signal Processing* 14:37–68.

Kohonen, T. (1988). *Self Organization and Associative Memory*. Springer-Verlag, Berlin.

Kulkarni, A. D., and Byars, P. (1991). Artificial neural network models for image understanding. *Proceedings of SPIE Conference on Image Processing Algorithms and Techniques II* 1452:512–522.

Kulkarni, A. D., and Byars, P. (1992). Artificial neural network models for texture classification via the Radon transform. *Proceedings of Symposium on Applied Computing, Kansas City*, Vol. II, pp. 659–664.

Marr, D. (1982). *Vision*. W. H. Freeman, New York.

O'Toole, R. K., and Stark, H. (1980). Comparative study of optical vs. all digital techniques in textural pattern recognition. *Applied Optics* 19:2496–2506.

Rao, N., and Vemuri, V. (1989). A neural network architecture for texture segmentation and labelling. *Proceedings of International Joint Conference on Neural Networks, Washington, DC*, Vol. I, pp. 127–133.

Reed, T. R., and Wechsler, H. (1990). Segmentation of textured images and Gestalt organization using spatial/spatial-frequency representations. *IEEE Transactions on Pattern Analysis and Machine Intelligence* 12:1–12 .

Rosenfeld, A., and Kak, A. (1982). *Digital Image Processing*, Vol. I. Academic Press, Orlando, FL.

Visa, A. (1990). A texture classifier based on neural network principles. *Proceedings of International Joint Conference on Neural Networks, San Diego*, Vol. I, pp. 491–496.

Weszka, J. C., et ⸍ ⁾76). A comparative study of texture measures for terrain classification. *JF⸍   tions on Systems, Man and Cybernetics* 6:269–285.

Wigner ⸍   uantum correction for thermodynamic equilibrium. *Physics Rev⸍*

⸍ R. (1979). A four mechanism model for spatial vision.

⸍. (1977). Threshold visibility for frequency gradient
1190.

5

Supervised Classifiers

5.1. INTRODUCTION

Conventional classification techniques can be grouped into two categories: decision theoretic (or statistical) and syntactic. In the statistical approach, a set of features is extracted from the input pattern, and the classification is carried out by partitioning the feature space. In statistical pattern recognition the problem of decision making is posed in probabilistic terms. Here we are not concerned with whether the classifier makes a wrong decision, but we are concerned with the probability of a wrong decision. Textbooks such as those by Duda and Hart (1973), Chen (1973), Ullman (1973), and Tou and Gonzalez (1974) deal primarily with statistical aspects of decision making.

Features in the feature space and their statistical properties are often important in decision making. However, sometimes structural relationships among the features contain critically important information. Syntactic or structural pattern recognition methods deal with extracting this information. Such methods are built on earlier work in mathematical linguistics. In the syntactic approach, each pattern class is characterized by several subpatterns and their relationships. Textbooks such as those by Fu (1977) and Gonzalez and Thompson (1978) deal with syntactic methods.

Another way of grouping pattern recognition techniques is into supervised and unsupervised methods. In the case of supervised methods, a certain number of training samples are available for each class, and these are used to train the classifier. In the case of unsupervised methods, training samples are not available. Decision theoretic methods can again be divided into parametric and nonparametric methods. In parametric methods, each pattern class is characterized by a statistical distribution that depends in turn on a certain number of parameters. Nonparametric methods do not assume any such distribution.

It has been established that neural networks are a powerful and reasonable alternative to traditional classifiers. ANN models have been used successfully in many pattern recognition applications. The main advantages of neural networks over traditional classifiers are: (1) they provide high computation rates because of massive parallelism, (2) they are adaptive, and (3) they provide a greater degree of robustness or fault tolerance. Textbooks such as those by Pao (1989), Rumelhart et al. (1986), Hecht-Nielsen (1990), and Wasserman (1989) deal with neural network classifiers. Lippmann (1987), in his excellent review article, has compared conventional classifiers with neural net classifiers. He has given a taxonomy of six neural net classifiers: the perceptron, back-propagation networks, the Hamming network, Hopfield nets, and the Boltzman machine. Conventional classifiers along with neural net classifiers for supervised classification are discussed in this chapter.

5.2. CONVENTIONAL CLASSIFIERS

Pattern classification essentially partitions the feature space with decision boundaries. In statistical methods input samples are characterized by their probability density function. The classification problem is often difficult because samples of various classes overlap in the feature space. Typical probability density functions for a two-category problem are shown in Figure 5.1. Here, the probabilistic decision is made based on a threshold: if the observation value x is less than the threshold T, the sample is assigned to class ω_1; if x is greater than T, the sample is assigned to class ω_2; if x is equal to T, the sample can be assigned to either class. In a multidimensional feature space the problem of partitioning the feature space is more complex.

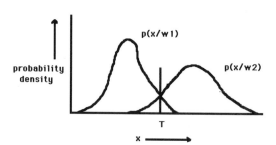

Figure 5.1. Probability density functions.

There are many different ways to represent pattern classifiers. One way is in terms of a set of discriminant functions $g_i(x)$. The classifier is said to assign a feature vector x to class ω_i if $g_i(x) > g_j(x)$ for $j \neq i$. Here, the classifier is viewed as a machine that computes m discriminant functions and selects the category corresponding to the largest discriminant. The simplest form of discriminant functions is the linear discriminant function. Let $x = (x_1, x_2, \ldots, x_n)^T$ be the observation vector, and $\omega_1, \omega_2, \ldots, \omega_m$ be the m classes. The problem is to assign x to a proper class ω_i. A discriminant function is a linear combination of components of x and, in a multidimensional case is given by

$$g(x) = w^T x + w_0 \tag{5.1}$$

where w^T is the weight vector and w_0 is the threshold weight. The two-category linear classifier is simple: if $g(x) > 0$, assign x to ω_1; if $g(x) < 0$, assign x to ω_2; if $g(x) = 0$, x can be assigned to either class. In a multidimensional case, the classifier divides the feature space into m regions, as shown in Figure 5.2. The boundary between the two regions is a portion of the hyperplane defined by

$$g_i(x) - g_j(x) = 0$$

or

$$(w_i - w_j)^T x + (w_{i0} - w_{j0}) = 0 \tag{5.2}$$

A sample vector x is assigned to a class ω_i if $g_i(x) > g_j(x)$ for all $j, i \neq j$.

Often, partitioning the feature space by using discriminant functions may not be possible; in such a case the minimum-distance classifier can be used. In minimum-distance classifiers, Euclidean distances between the sample points in the feature space are used for classification. Here, the reference vectors are used as training samples. Let $r_1, r_2, \ldots, r_m$ represent the reference vectors for m classes. For each input observation x the classifier calculates $\|x - r_i\|$ for $i = 1, 2, \ldots, m$. The classifier then assigns the input sample x to the class ω_i for

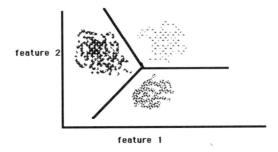

feature 2

feature 1

Figure 5.2. *Linear discriminant functions.*

which the distance $\|\boldsymbol{x} - \boldsymbol{r}_i\|$ is the minimum. The Euclidean distance $\|\boldsymbol{x} - \boldsymbol{r}_i\|$ is given by

$$\|\boldsymbol{x} - \boldsymbol{r}_i\| = \left[(\boldsymbol{x} - \boldsymbol{r}_i)^T(\boldsymbol{x} - \boldsymbol{r}_i)\right]^{1/2} \tag{5.3}$$

Another commonly used approach is the maximum-likelihood classifier. Here, we assume a multivariate normal distribution. The probability density value associated with the statement that observation vector $\boldsymbol{x}_i$ belongs to class k is given by

$$p(\boldsymbol{x}_i/\omega_k) = (2\pi)^{-n/2}\left|\sum_k\right|^{-1/2}\exp\left[-\left(\frac{1}{2}\right)(\boldsymbol{x}_i - \mu_k)^T\sum_{k^{-1}}(\boldsymbol{x}_i - \mu_k)\right] \tag{5.4}$$

where n is the number of measurement variables associated with the observation vector $\boldsymbol{x}_i$; $p(\boldsymbol{x}_i/\omega_k)$ is the probability density value associated with the observation vector $\boldsymbol{x}_i$, as evaluated for class k, Σ_k is the covariance matrix for class k, and μ_k is the mean vector for class k.

In the maximum-likelihood classification, for each observation vector we calculate the probability that an observation vector belongs to each of the classes. The individual observation vector is then assigned to the class for which the probability is the greatest. In practice, the mean vector and covariance matrix are calculated from the observed samples or training sets that are of finite size. With finite size samples, Eq. 5.4 can be rewritten as

$$\ln[\,p(\boldsymbol{x}_i/\omega_k)] = -\frac{n}{2}\ln(2\pi) - \frac{n}{2}\boldsymbol{D}_k - \frac{1}{2}(\boldsymbol{x}_i - \boldsymbol{m}_k)^T\boldsymbol{D}_k^{-1}(\boldsymbol{x}_i - \boldsymbol{m}_k) \tag{5.5}$$

where $\boldsymbol{D}_k$ is the covariance matrix associated with class k, taken as an estimator of Σ_k; and $\boldsymbol{m}_k$ is the mean vector associated with class k, taken as the estimator of μ_k. Since the log of the probability distribution function is a monotonically increasing function, decisions can be made by comparing the values for each class. A simplified decision rule can be obtained by eliminating the constants:

$$F_k(\boldsymbol{x}_i) = \ln\boldsymbol{D}_k + (\boldsymbol{x}_i - \boldsymbol{m}_k)^T\boldsymbol{D}_k^{-1}(\boldsymbol{x}_i - \boldsymbol{m}_k) \tag{5.6}$$

Here, the observation vector $\boldsymbol{x}_i$ is assigned to class k for which the function F_k is the minimum.

Prior probabilities can be incorporated in the classification using the law of conditional probability. If $P(\omega_k)$ is the probability that an observation belongs to class ω_k, and $P(\boldsymbol{x}_i)$ is the probability of occurrence of measurement vector $\boldsymbol{x}_i$, then the conditional probability $P(\omega_k/\boldsymbol{x}_i)$ that an observation $\boldsymbol{x}_i$ belongs to class ω_k is given by

$$P(\omega_k/\boldsymbol{x}_i) = P(\omega_k, \boldsymbol{x}_i)/P(\boldsymbol{x}_i) \tag{5.7}$$

where $P(\omega_k, \boldsymbol{x}_i)$ is the joint probability. Similarly, we get

$$P(\boldsymbol{x}_i/\omega_k) = P(\omega_k, \boldsymbol{x}_i)/P(\omega_k) \tag{5.8}$$

With Eq. 5.7 and 5.8, the decision rule can be modified as:

$$F_k(\boldsymbol{x}_i) = \ln|\boldsymbol{D}_k| + (\boldsymbol{x}_i - \boldsymbol{m}_k)^T \boldsymbol{D}_k^{-1}(\boldsymbol{x}_i - \boldsymbol{m}_k) - 2\ln P(\omega_k) \tag{5.9}$$

In the maximum-likelihood classifier the function $F_k(\boldsymbol{x}_i)$ is evaluated for all possible classes for each $\boldsymbol{x}_i$; hence, it is computationally intensive. To alleviate this problem, tree classifiers are often preferred over single-stage classifiers. Tree classifiers are also known as multilevel classifiers. Here, the classification is performed at various levels. A typical tree classifier is shown in Figure 5.3. At the first level, the classes are grouped into m_1 groups using only n_1 features such that $m_1 < m$ and $n_1 < n$, where m represents the total number of classes and n represents the total number of features. The n_1 features are selected to maximize the separability for the m_1 classes. The same procedure is repeated at subsequent nonterminal nodes until each of the m classes is identified. There are three major tasks in designing a tree classifier: (1) to set up the structure of an optimum tree, (2) to choose the most effective subset of features at each nonterminal node, and (3) to choose the decision rule at each nonterminal node. During the design of a tree classifier, one would like to obtain the optimum tree classifier in the sense of achieving the highest possible classification accuracy while using the least possible computational time. A binary tree classifier can be considered a special case of a tree classifier. Kulkarni (1983) has used a binary tree classifier for multispectral image analysis.

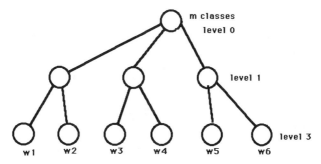

Figure 5.3. *Tree classifier.*

5.3. ANN MODELS AS CLASSIFIERS

It has been well established that ANN models are a powerful and reasonable alternative to conventional classifiers. Studies comparing neural network classifiers and conventional classifiers are available (Huang and Lippmann, 1988). Potential benefits of neural network classifiers extend beyond the high computation rates provided by massive parallelism. Neural network classifiers provide a greater degree of robustness and fault tolerance. ANN models with various learning algorithms can be used as supervised and unsupervised classifiers.

The use of neural networks for pattern classification may be traced back to the perceptron models originated by Rosenblatt (1958, 1962) in the 1950s. The perceptron models used the concept of the reward and punishment. In the late 1960s, progress in neural network models was slowed down by the limited capabilities of early single-layer perceptron models (Minsky and Papert, 1969). Today a number of well-developed theories and learning algorithms for ANN models are available. These include a multilayer perceptron, back-propagation learning, Boltzman machines, the Hamming net, the Hopfield net, the neocognitron, etc. (Hopfield and Tank, 1985; Rumelhart et al., 1986; Lippmann, 1987; Fukushima, 1988; Caudill, 1988; Oja, 1989).

A block diagram of a neural network classifier is presented in Figure 5.4. Here, an input vector is fed in parallel to the first stage. The first stage computes matching scores. These scores are fed in parallel to the next stage over m analog input lines. The maximum of these values is selected and enhanced. The second stage has one output for each of the m classes. In the simplest classification system the output lines directly label output class identities. In more complex systems, if the correct output is provided, then the output information is fed back to the first stage of the classifier to adapt weights according to some learning algorithm.

A perceptron model shown in Figure 5.5 recognizes simple patterns. The model can be trained and can make decisions. During the training phase pairs

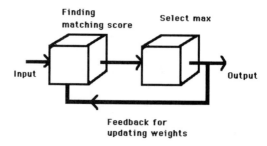

Figure 5.4. *Neural network classifier (block diagram).*

output

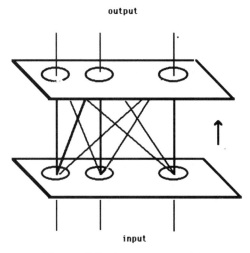

input

Figure 5.5. *Perceptron model.*

of input and output vectors are used to train the network. With each input vector the actual output is compared with the desired output, and the error between the actual and desired outputs is used to update the weights. The algorithm can be described in the following steps:

1. Initialize the weights using small random values.
2. Present an input vector **x** and obtain the actual outputs as shown below:

$$y_i = Fn\left(\sum_{j=1}^{m} w_{ij} x_j \right) \tag{5.10}$$

where $Fn(\cdot)$ represents a Sigmoid transfer function.
3. Change in weight w_{ij} is given by

$$\Delta w_{ij} = \beta [y_j - d_j] x_i \tag{5.11}$$

where dj represents the desired output and β is the learning constant.
4. Update the weights as

$$w_{ij}(t + 1) = w_{ij}(t) + \Delta w_{ij} \tag{5.12}$$

Repeat steps 2 through 4 for all samples in the training set until the error between the actual and desired outputs becomes smaller than some desirable value $\varepsilon_{\min}$ or iterations reach some maximum number $N_{\max}$.

A perceptron model such as shown in Figure 5.5 can be used only when the classes are linearly separable. For more complex decision boundaries we need a multilayer perceptron model. The behavior of a multilayer network with nonlinear units is complex. A multilayer network can be trained with a back-propagation learning algorithm, which is thoroughly discussed in the definitive work by Rumelhart et al. (1986). Learning via back-propagation involves the presentation of pairs of input and output vectors. The actual output for a given vector is compared with the desired or target output. If there is no difference, no weights are changed; otherwise, the weights are adjusted to reduce the difference. This learning method essentially uses a gradient search technique to minimize the cost function that is equal to the mean square difference between the desired and actual outputs. The network is initialized by setting random weights and thresholds, and the weights are updated with each iteration to minimize the mean squared error.

A fundamental building block in a back-propagation network is the artificial neuron, as shown in Figure 5.6. The input to the neuron is obtained as the weighted sum given by

$$net = \sum_{i=1}^{n} O_i w_i \tag{5.13}$$

In Figure 5.6, F is the activation function, which has a sigmoid form. The sigmoid function is often used because it has a simple derivative. With a sigmoid activation function, the output of the neuron is given by

$$out = F(net) \tag{5.14}$$

$$= 1/(1 + e^{-net}) \tag{5.15}$$

It can be seen that

$$\frac{\partial F(net)}{\partial net} = \frac{e^{-net}}{(1 + e^{-net})^2}$$

$$= \left(\frac{1}{1 + e^{-net}}\right)\left(\frac{e^{-net}}{1 + e^{-net}}\right)$$

$$= out(1 - out)$$

$$= F(net)[1 - F(net)] \tag{5.16}$$

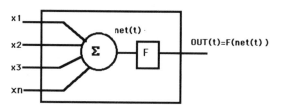

Figure 5.6. Artificial neuron.

The activation function is also called the squashing function. Any other function that is differentiable everywhere can also be used in the back-propagation algorithm. A simple feed-forward three-layer network is shown in Figure 5.7. The units in layer L_1 serve only as distribution points; they perform no input summations. Each neuron in layers L_2 and L_3 produces *net* and *out* signals as shown in Eq. 5.13 and 5.14. The back-propagation learning algorithm for a three-layer network is discussed below. The algorithm can be extended to a network with more than three layers.

Step 1: Initialize the weights. The weights between layers L_1L_2 and L_2L_3 are initialized to small random values so that the network is not saturated by large values of weights.

Step 2: Present a continuous-valued input vector $\boldsymbol{x} = (x_1, x_2, \ldots, x_n)^T$ to layer L_1 and obtain the output vector $\boldsymbol{y} = (y_1, y_2, \ldots, y_m)^T$ at layer L_3. In order to obtain the output vector $\boldsymbol{y}$, calculation is done layer by layer starting from layer L_2. The net value of each neuron in layer L_2 is calculated as the weighted sum of its inputs. The net input is then passed through the activation function F to produce *out* values for each neuron in layer L_2. The outputs of neurons in layer L_2 serve as inputs to neurons in layer L_3. The process is repeated to obtain the output vector $\boldsymbol{y}$ at layer L_3.

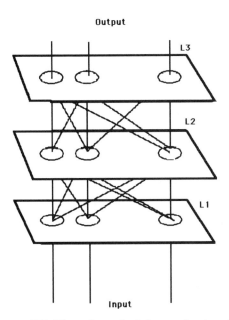

Output

Figure 5.7. *Three-layer feed-forward network.*

Step 3: Calculate change in weights. In order to do this, the output vector y is compared with the desired output vector or the target vector d, and the error between the two vectors is obtained. The error is then propagated backward to obtain the change in weights Δw_{ij} that is used to update the weights. Δw_{ij} for weights between layers $L_2 L_3$ is given by

$$\Delta w_{ij} = \alpha O_j \delta_i \qquad (5.17)$$

where α is a training rate coefficient (typically 0.01 to 1.0), O_j is the output of neuron j in layer L_2, and δ_i is given by

$$\delta_i = [\partial F(net_i)/\partial net_i](d_i - O_i)$$
$$= O_i(1 - O_i)(d_i - O_i) \qquad (5.18)$$

In Eq. 5.15, O_i represents the actual output of neuron i in layer L_3, and d_i represents the target or the desired output at neuron i in layer L_3. Layer L_2 has no target vector, so Eq. 5.18 can not be used for layer L_2. The back-propagation algorithm trains the hidden layers by propagating the output error back through layer by layer, adjusting weights at each layer. The change in weights between layers $L_1 L_2$ can be obtained as

$$\Delta w_{ij} = \beta O_j \delta_{Hi} \qquad (5.19)$$

where β is a training rate coefficient for layer L_2 (typically 0.01 to 1.0), O_j is the output of neuron j in layer L_1, and

$$\delta_{Hi} = O_i(1 - O_i)\sum_k \delta_k w_{ik} \qquad (5.20)$$

In Eq. 5.20, O_i is the output of neuron i in layer L_2, and the summation term represents the weighted sum of all δ values corresponding to neurons in layer L_3 that are obtained by using Eq. 5.18.

Step 4: Update the weights:

$$w_{ij}(n + 1) = w_{ij}(n) + \Delta w_{ij} \qquad (5.21)$$

where $w_{ij}(n + 1)$ represents the value of the weight at iteration $n + 1$ (after adjustment), and $w_{ij}(n)$ represents the value of the weight at iteration n.

Step 5: Obtain the error ε for neurons in layer L_3.

$$\varepsilon = \sum_i (O_i - d_i)^2 \qquad (5.22)$$

If the error ε is greater than some minimum ε_{min}, then repeat steps 2 through 4; otherwise terminate the training process.

The back-propagation algorithm implements the gradient by minimizing the summed squared error. For models with two layers the model is guaranteed to find the best set of weights. With a multiple-layer model there is a danger of getting stuck in a local minimum. However, the fatal problem of local minima is irrelevant for a wide variety of tasks. The back-propagation algorithm has been tested with a number of deterministic problems and has been widely used in many pattern recognition problems. ANN models with the BP learning algorithm have been used to analyze satellite images. The data are obtained from a sensor called the thematic mapper (TM) (Kulkarni et al., 1991; Kulkarni, 1991), which is a multispectral scanner that captures data in seven spectral bands. Conventional methods for multispectral image analysis include a maximum-likelihood classifier, a minimum-distance classifier, and various clustering techniques. The TM collects images of a 185-km-wide swath. It has seven spectral bands, one of which is a thermal band. The resolution of a nonthermal band is 30 m × 30 m (Kulkarni, 1986). After a TM image has been properly processed and resampled, each pixel can be characterized by seven numbers, corresponding to the pixel's intensity as measured in each of the seven bands. Assigning pixels to various categories is a computationally intensive process. A TM scene usually has a size of 5300 pixels × 4000 scan lines. In the illustrative example, Kulkarni et al. (1991) have selected a scene (#y4018116055) of January 1983. The scene represents Mississippi river bottom land. The original image for spectral band 5 is shown in Figure 5.8. They used a back-propagation network

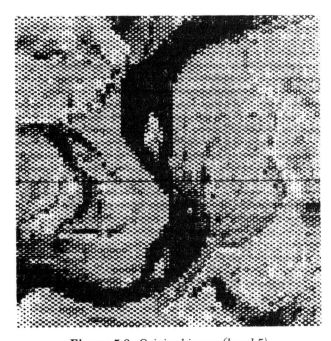

Figure 5.8. *Original image (band 5).*

with three layers: the input layer, hidden layer, and output layer. They used seven, 16, and four units in the input, hidden, and output layers, respectively. The seven units in the input layer represent seven spectral band values. The four units in the output layer represent four categories of objects. During the training phase, four training areas of the size 10 scans × 10 pixels were used. They had to iterate the training set data 900 times to ensure that the weights were stabilized. The learning process consumed 35.6 seconds of CPU on a CRAY X-MP machine. A similar ANN model was also developed on an IBM PS/2 system. The learning process with the same training set data consumed 88,155 seconds (24.48 hours) of processing time. The classified output is shown in Figure 5.9. The training set data was reclassified to check the accuracy and were found to be classified with a 99% accuracy.

A Hopfield network (Figure 5.10) can also be used as a classifier. These networks are essentially used with binary inputs. In order to use a Hopfield network as a classifier for images with gray values, one needs to encode gray levels into binary numbers. In a Hopfield network, weights are initialized using training samples for all classes. In the decision-making phase the unknown pattern is imposed on the net at time $t = t_0$. Following this initialization, the net iterates in discrete time steps using the given formula. The network is considered to have converged when the outputs no longer change on successive

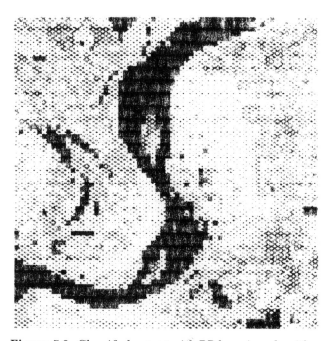

Figure 5.9. *Classified output with BP learning algorithm.*

Output

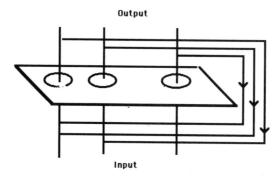

Input

Figure 5.10. *Hopfield network.*

iterations. The pattern specified by the node outputs after the convergence is the network output.

When the Hopfield net is used as a classifier, the output after the convergence must be compared to the M exemplars to determine if it matches an exemplar exactly. If it does, the output is that class whose exemplar matched the output pattern. If it does not, then a "no-match" result occurs. The learning algorithm for the Hopfield network can be described as follows, (Lippmann, 1987):

Step 1: Initialize connection weights as

$$t_{ij} = \sum_{k=0}^{m-1} x_{ik} x_{jk} \qquad \text{for } i \neq j \tag{5.23}$$

where $0 \leq i, j \leq m - 1$, t_{ij} is the connection weight from node i to node j, and x_{ik} can be $+1$ or -1 if element i is an exemplar of class k.

Step 2: Present an unknown input pattern

$$\mu_i(t) = x_i \qquad \text{for } 0 \leq i \leq n - 1 \tag{5.24}$$

where $\mu_i(t)$ is the output of node i at time t, and x_i is element i of the input pattern.

Step 3: Iterate until convergence; i.e.,

$$\mu_i(t + 1) = F\left[\sum_{i=1}^{N-1} t_{ij} \mu_j(t) \right] \qquad \text{for } 0 \leq j \leq m - 1 \tag{5.25}$$

A Hamming network is similar to a Hopfield network and can be used as a supervised classifier. The Hamming net calculates the Hamming distance to the exemplar for each class and selects the class with the minimum Hamming distance. The Hamming distance is the number of bits in the input that do not match the corresponding exemplar bits. The Hamming network (Figure 5.11) consists of four layers. Layer L_1 represents the input layer. Layer L_2 calculates the matching scores. The weights between layers L_1 and L_2 are similar to the corresponding values of elements of the input exemplar. The number of units in the input layer represents the number of elements in the input vector. The number of units in layers L_2, L_3 and L_4 is equal to the number of output categories. Units in layer L_3 are connected by feedback connections similar to a Hopfield network. Weights connecting units between layers L_1L_2 are represented as elements w_{ij} of matrix $\boldsymbol{W}$, and the feedback connections in layer L_3 are represented by elements t_{ij} of matrix $\boldsymbol{T}$. Feature vectors for each class are encoded into the weight matrix. For any given input the corresponding matching scores are calculated. The output of layer L_2 is fed to layer L_3. The input pattern is then removed. Layer L_3 iterates until the output of only one node is positive. Layer L_4 is the output layer. The final output is obtained at layer L_4. Each unit in layer L_4 represents a category. The input vector is assigned to a class depending on which of the units in the output layer shows the maximum output value. Lippmann (1987) has pointed out a number of advantages of the Hamming network over the Hopfield net. The Hamming net implements the optimum minimum error classifier when bit errors are random and independent.

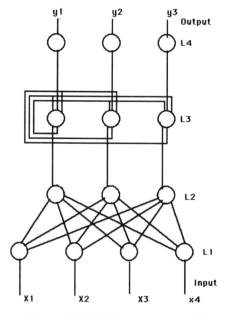

Figure 5.11. *Hamming network.*

5.4. SUMMARY

Conventional classification techniques include statistical and syntactic methods. In this chapter statistical methods such as the maximum-likelihood, nearest-neighbor, and minimum-distance classifications have been discussed. Neural networks represent a powerful alternative to conventional methods. ANN models such as the perceptron, back-propagation, Hopfield net, and Hamming net were also discussed in the chapter.

REFERENCES

Caudill, M. (1988). Neural network primers, Part IV. *AI Experts* August:61–67.

Chen, C. H. (1973). *Statistical Pattern Recognition*. Hayden, Washington, DC.

Duda, R. O., and Hart, P. E. (1973). *Pattern Classification and Scene Analysis*. John Wiley & Sons, New York.

Fu, K. S. (1977). *Syntactic Methods in Pattern Recognition: Applications*. Springer Verlag, New York.

Fukushima, K. (1988). Neural networks for visual pattern recognition. *Computer* March:65–74.

Gonzalez, R. C., and Thompson, M. G. (1978). *Syntactic Methods in Pattern Recognition*. Addison-Wesley, Reading, MA.

Hecht-Nielsen, R. (1990). *Neurocomputing*. Addison-Wesley, Reading, MA.

Hopfield, J. J., and Tank, D. W. (1985). Neural computation of decision in optimization problems. *Biological Cybernetics* 52:141–152.

Huang, W. Y., and Lippmann, R. P. (1988). Comparison between neural net and conventional classifiers. *Proceedings of Joint International Conference on Neural Networks, San Diego*, Vol. IV, pp. 485–493.

Kulkarni, A. D. (1983). Categorization of multi-spectral data using binary tree classifier. *Proceedings of Seventeenth International Symposium on Remote Sensing of Environment, Ann Arbor, MI*, pp. 609–612.

Kulkarni, A. D. (1986). Digital Processing of Remotely Sensed Data. *In Advances in Electronics and Electron Physics*, Vol. 66, P. W. Hawkes (ed.), pp. 309–368. Academic Press, Orlando FL.

Kulkarni, A. D., et al. (1991). Multispectral image analysis using artificial neural network system on a Cray X-MP. *Proceedings of the Symposium on Applied Computing, Kansas City, MO*, p. 345.

Kulkarni, A. D. (1991). Neural networks for pattern recognition. In: *Progress in Neural Networks*, Vol. I, O. Omidvar (ed.), pp. 197–219, Ablex, New York.

Lippmann, R. P. (1987). An introduction to computing with neural nets. *IEEE Transactions on Acoustics, Speech and Signal Processing*, 32:4–22.

McClelland, J. L., and Rumelhart, D. E. (1986). *Parallel Distributed Processing Models, Explorations in Microstructure of Cognitron*, Vol. II. MIT Press, Cambridge, MA.

Minsky, M., and Papert, S. (1969). *Perceptron: An Introduction to Computational Geometry*. MIT Press, Cambridge, MA.

Oja, E. (1989). Neural networks, principal components and subspaces. *International Journal of Neural Systems* 1:61–68.

Pao, Y. H. (1989). *Adaptive Pattern Recognition and Neural Networks*. Addison-Wesley, Reading, MA.

Rosenblatt, F. (1958). The perceptron: a probabilistic model for information storage and organization in the brain. *Psychology Review* 65:386–408.

Rosenblatt, F. (1962). *Principles of Neurodynamics: Perceptron and the Theory of Brain Mechanism*. Spartan Books, Washington, DC.

Rumelhart, D. E., et al. (1986). *Parallel Distributed Processing*, Vol. I. MIT Press, Cambridge, MA.

Tou, J. T., and Gonzalez, R. C. (1974). *Pattern Recognition Principles: Trainable Pattern Classifiers and the Deterministic Approach*. Addison-Wesley, Reading, MA.

Ullman, J. R. (1973). *Pattern Recognition Techniques*. Butterworths, London.

Wasserman, P. D. (1989). *Neural Computing Theory and Practice*. Van Nostrand Reinhold, New York.

6

Unsupervised Classifiers

6.1. INTRODUCTION

In the previous chapter we discussed methods of supervised classification wherein we assumed that training samples are available for training the classifiers. In this chapter we investigate methods of unsupervised classification or learning without a teacher. Unsupervised classification techniques deal with self-learning. Human beings are capable of learning without a teacher.

The problem of unsupervised classification essentially reduces to partitioning the data in the feature space into subgroups or clusters. Many well-known clustering algorithms such as K-means or isodata are available in practice. Clustering techniques essentially try to group data samples in the feature space. Self-organizing neural networks with learning paradigms like competitive learning, adaptive resonance theory (ART), and Kohonen's self-organizing maps are examples of unsupervised learning. Before Hebb's work it was very hard to see how a neural network could learn. Hebb (1949) proposed that a reasonable and biologically plausible change would strengthen connections between elements of the network only when both the presynaptic and post-synaptic units are active simultaneously. The essence of Hebb's idea still persists today in many learning paradigms. Textbooks such as those by Duda and Hart (1973), Tou and Gonzalez (1974), and Hartigan (1975) describe clustering techniques. Textbooks and articles such as those by Rosenblatt (1962), Rumelhart et al. (1986a, b), Lippmann (1987), Grossberg (1988), Kohonen (1988), Pao (1989), Linkser (1988), and Oja (1989) discuss self-organizing neural networks and their implementation. Conventional clustering techniques as well as neural network paradigms used for unsupervised classification are discussed in this chapter.

6.2. CONVENTIONAL CLUSTERING TECHNIQUES

It is a common phenomenon that features belonging to the same class tend to form groups or clusters in the feature space. Let N be the number of samples and characterize each sample by an n-dimensional vector. Each sample is to be placed into one of m classes $(\omega_1, \omega_2, \ldots, \omega_m)$, where m may or may not be known. Let ω_{ki} denote the class to which sample i is assigned. Let a classification Ω be a vector made up of the ω_k and configuration X be a vector made up of x_i; i.e.,

$$\Omega = [\, \omega_{k1} \quad \omega_{k2} \quad \cdots \quad \omega_{kn} \,]^T \tag{6.1}$$

$$X = [\, x_1^T \quad x_2^T \quad \cdots \quad x_n^T \,] \tag{6.2}$$

The clustering criterion J is a function of Ω and X and can be written as

$$J = J(\Omega, X) \tag{6.3}$$

By definition, the best classification satisfies

$$J(\Omega_0, X^*) = \min J(\Omega, X) \quad \text{or} \quad \max J(\Omega, X) \tag{6.4}$$

Many iterative algorithms to obtain the optimum J are available. Neural networks are well suited for optimization problems and can be used for clustering. The most commonly used clustering criterion is the Euclidean distance function. Figure 6.1 shows a two-dimensional feature space with three categories $(\omega_1, \omega_2, \omega_3)$. We may intuitively arrive at the conclusion that an unknown sample x belongs to class ω_i only on the basis that it is "closer" to the patterns of ith class. We may use different measures for "closeness." After a measure of the pattern similarity has been adapted, we need to specify a

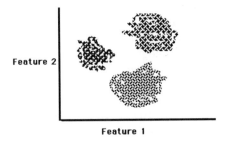

Feature 2

Feature 1

Figure 6.1. *Clusters in feature space.*

procedure for partitioning the input data set into cluster domains. A few similarity measures that are used in clustering follow:

1. Minkowsky metric:

$$d(\boldsymbol{x}_i, \boldsymbol{x}_j) = \left[\sum_{k=1}^{n} (x_{ik} - x_{jk})^{1/2} \right]^2 \tag{6.5}$$

where n is the number of features.

2. Quadratic metric:

$$d(\boldsymbol{x}_i, \boldsymbol{x}_j) = (\boldsymbol{x}_i - \boldsymbol{x}_j)^T \boldsymbol{W}(\boldsymbol{x}_i - \boldsymbol{x}_j) \tag{6.6}$$

where $\boldsymbol{W}$ is an $n \times n$ positive definite matrix.

3. Normalized correlation:

$$d(\boldsymbol{x}_i, \boldsymbol{x}_j) = \left(\boldsymbol{x}_i^T \boldsymbol{x}_j \right) / \left[\left(\boldsymbol{x}_i^T \boldsymbol{x}_i \right) \left(\boldsymbol{x}_j^T \boldsymbol{x}_j \right) \right]^{1/2} \tag{6.7}$$

4. Mahalonbic metric:

$$d(\boldsymbol{x}_i, \boldsymbol{x}_j) = (\boldsymbol{x}_i - \boldsymbol{x}_j)^T \boldsymbol{D}^{-1}(\boldsymbol{x}_i - \boldsymbol{x}_j) \tag{6.8}$$

where $\boldsymbol{D}$ denotes a within-group covariance matrix.

5. Hamming distance: The Hamming distance for two binary vectors $\boldsymbol{x}_i$ and $\boldsymbol{x}_j$ is defined as

$$d(\boldsymbol{x}_i, \boldsymbol{x}_j) = N - \sum_{k=1}^{N} x_{ik} x_{jk} \tag{6.9}$$

where N denotes the number of features in the features vector, and x_{ik} and x_{jk} denote elements of vectors $\boldsymbol{x}_i$ and $\boldsymbol{x}_j$, respectively.

Commonly used clustering algorithms include the K-means, isodata, split and merge techniques, and optimization techniques (Duda and Hart, 1973; Tou and Gonzalez, 1974; Ball and Hall, 1976). In the K-means clustering algorithm the sum of the square distances from all the points in the cluster domain to the cluster center is used as the criterion for grouping the input data samples. The algorithm can be described in the following four steps:

Step 1: Choose K initial cluster centers $\boldsymbol{m}_1(1), \boldsymbol{m}_2(1), \ldots, \boldsymbol{m}_K(1)$.

Step 2: Assign an unknown sample $\boldsymbol{x}$ to class ω_j if

$$\|\boldsymbol{m}_j(k) - \boldsymbol{x}\| < \|\boldsymbol{m}_i(k) - \boldsymbol{x}\| \tag{6.10}$$

for $i = 1, 2, \ldots, K, i \neq j$.

Step 3: Compute new cluster centers

$$m_j(k + 1) = \frac{1}{n} \sum_{x \in \omega_j} x$$

where n is the number of samples in cluster j.

Step 4: If $m_j(k + 1) = m_j(k)$ for $j = 1, 2, \ldots, K$, the algorithm has converged; otherwise go to Step 2.

The behavior of the K-means algorithm is influenced by the number of clusters specified, the choice of the initial cluster centers, and the order in which samples are taken. Although no general proof of convergence exists for this algorithm, it can be expected to yield acceptable results when clusters are far from each other in the feature space (Tou and Gonzalez, 1974).

The clustering problem can be also considered as an optimization problem. Let x_i for $i = 1, 2, \ldots, N$ be input data samples, and $\omega_1, \omega_2, \ldots, \omega_K$ be K categories to which the samples are to be assigned. We may choose any suitable similarity measure as the criterion for clustering. In clustering the N samples are assigned to K categories using some similarity function. The similarity criterion ought to describe the quality of grouping in the sense that the mutual distances between x_i belonging to the same ω_i are as small as possible while the distances between ω_i are large. The function describing the grouping may contain terms such as sums of some powers of the distances. Determination of centers of ω_i is a global optimization problem wherein a set of simultaneous algebraic equations describing the optimality criterion can be solved by direct or iterative methods (Kohonen, 1988).

Kulkarni and Chandrasekhar (1984) have suggested an algorithm for clustering using the sequential simplex optimization technique. They have assumed samples in the feature space to be random variables with a multidimensional normal distribution. To start with, the number of clusters, the mean and variance of each cluster, and the number of data points in each cluster are assumed to be known. With these assumptions histograms with respect to each feature are estimated. The estimated histograms are compared with the actual histograms obtained from the input data samples. The error between the actual histograms and the estimated histograms is used as the optimization criterion. Kulkarni and Chandrasekhar (1984) have used the sequential simplex optimization technique for finding the minimum of the error function. The cluster centers, their mean and variances, and the number of samples in each cluster are adjusted so as to optimize the error function. As an illustration, they considered the problem of multispectral data analysis. Each pixel in the multispectral image is represented by a vector. The obtained clusters are shown in Figure 6.2.

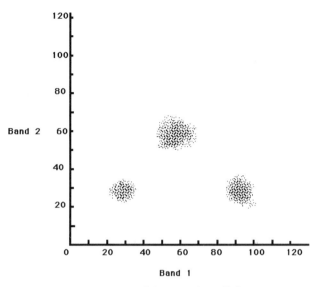

Figure 6.2. *Multispectral data in the 2-D feature space.*

Splitting and merging clustering methods are related to optimization methods. In a splitting method, initially all samples are assumed to belong to a single cluster. The initial cluster is then partitioned into two clusters whereby the interclass distance is maximized. The samples are then reassigned to different clusters. The process is continued to generate more clusters. The method directly produces a binary tree structure. A stopping rule (if the interclass distance falls below a certain threshold) may be applied to prevent further division. In merging methods, one starts with a single element as a cluster. In each successive stage k most similar clusters are merged. Similar to the splitting methods, the interclass distance can be used as the criterion for merging clusters. Several variations of these splitting and merging techniques are used in practice.

6.3. SELF-ORGANIZING NETWORKS

Self-organizing networks adjust themselves with new input patterns. Rumelhart et al. (1986a, b) have classified learning paradigms for neural networks into four classes: autoassociator, pattern associator, classification, and regularity detection. The autoassociator deals with storing a set of patterns in the system and retrieving any pattern from the set with a stimulus pattern. Here, during the storing process, the response and stimulus patterns are identical. While any pattern is being retrieved, the corresponding stimulus pattern may be noisy or incomplete.

The pattern associator is similar to the autoassociator. However, in the pattern associator a set of pairs of stimulus and response patterns are stored.

Here, the stimulus and response patterns are not identical. In the classification paradigm the goal is to classify the stimulus vector into a fixed set of categories.

The classification paradigm is essentially a supervised learning wherein training data need to be provided. In the regularity detector the network is presented with stimulus patterns, and it is supposed to discover statistically salient features of the input population or detect the similarity in the input patterns. Here, the number of categories in which input patterns are to be grouped may not be known. Regularity detector paradigms are similar to a clustering technique. Self-organizing networks with learning paradigms, including the competitive learning, adaptive resonance theory, and Kohonen's self-organizing maps, are well suited for unsupervised classification.

Kohonen (1982, 1988) suggested that one of the important learning mechanisms in the human brain is placement of neurons in an orderly manner. Orderly placement usually does not mean moving units to new places. The units may even be structurally identical; the specialized role is determined by their internal parameters, which are made to change in certain processes. Although much of the low-level organization is genetically predetermined, it is likely that some organization at higher levels is created during learning by algorithms that promote self-organization. Kohonen's learning algorithm creates a feature map by adjusting weights from common input nodes to output nodes in a two-layer network, as shown in Figure 6.3. The Kohonen network provides advantages over classical pattern recognition techniques because it utilizes the parallel architecture of a neural network and provides a graphic organization of pattern relationship. The first layer of the network is the input layer. The second layer is the competitive layer, and it organizes as a two-dimensional grid. The two layers are fully connected. Input vectors are presented sequentially to layer L_1. In Kohonen learning each unit computes the dot product of its weight vector with the input vector. The unit with the largest dot product is declared the

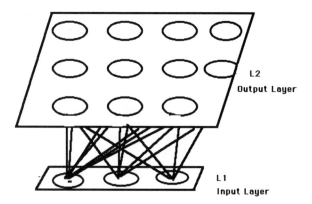

Figure 6.3. *A two-layer network (Kohonen learning).*

winner. The winner unit and its neighbor are the only units permitted to learn. Learning in the Kohonen network is described below.

Let $x = (x_1, x_2, \ldots, x_n)^T$ represent the input vector. Let W represent the weight matrix for the weights between layers L_1 and L_2. Element w_{ij} of matrix W represents the connection strength for the connection between unit j of L_1 and unit i of layer L_2. The first step in Kohonen learning is to compute matching values for each unit in layer L_2. The matching value for unit i is given by

$$v_i = \sum_j (w_{ij} - x_j)^2 \tag{6.11}$$

which is essentially the distance between the vectors w_i and x. Here, the unit with the lowest matching value wins the competition.

The next step is to update the weights. In this algorithm the weights corresponding to the winner unit and its neighboring units are updated. The change in weight w_{ij} is given by

$$\Delta w_{ij} = \alpha(x_j - w_{ij}) \tag{6.12}$$

if unit i is in the neighborhood of the winner unit; otherwise Δw_{ij} is zero. In Eq. 6.12, α represents a learning rate. The weights are updated as

$$w_{ij}(k + 1) = w_{ij}(k) + \Delta w_{ij} \tag{6.13}$$

where k indicates the number of input samples. The weights are updated with each input sample. A neighborhood of any shape can be chosen. Rectangular and hexagonal neighborhoods are commonly used. The neighborhood size for a given network decreases in size with time, as shown in Figure 6.4. The width of the neighborhood decreases over the number of iterations. The initial value of d

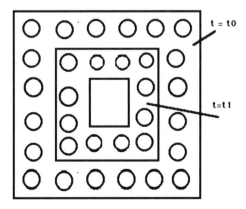

Figure 6.4. *Neighborhood regions (Kohonen learning).*

may be chosen as d_0. Typical values for d_0 may be chosen as a half or a third of the width of the competitive layer of processing units. The value of d is then made to decrease as

$$d = d_0(1 - t/T) \tag{6.14}$$

where t is the current iteration and T is the total number of iterations to be done. Kohonen's network gradually organizes. Kohonen's maps are obtained by plotting weight values. The initial weight values are shown in Figure 6.5a, and points corresponding to the adjacent units are connected. The cluster of points in the center of the graph depicts the randomized initial weight values. Subsequent feature maps are shown in Figures 6.5b through 6.5f. This algorithm performs well in noisy environments because for a given configuration the number of classes is fixed, weights adapt slowly, and adaptation stops after training.

Another important learning paradigm in self-organizing networks is competitive learning. Models with competitive learning have been developed by Malsburg (1973) and Rumelhart and Zipser (1985). There are many ways to implement competitive learning (Desieno, 1988). One of the simplest is the competitive learning scheme described by Rumelhart and Zipser (1985). Here,

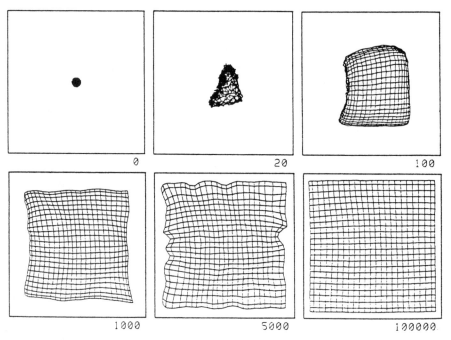

Figure 6.5. *Kohonen's feature maps. (From Kohonen, 1988, with permission. © 1988 Springer-Verlag.)*

each unit in the hidden and output layers receives the input from all the units in the preceding layer. Within the layer units are broken down into a set of inhibitory clusters. The units within clusters compete with one another to respond to the pattern appearing at the input layer. The more strongly any particular unit responds to incoming stimulus, the more it inhibits other units within the cluster.

The unit learns by shifting a fraction of its weight from its inactive lines to active lines. The functioning of a two-layer network with competitive learning can be described. A simple two-layer feed-forward network is shown in Figure 6.6. Layer L_1 is the input layer; it is made up of processing units that receive input patterns. The second layer is a competitive layer, which classifies the input pattern. The two layers are fully interconnected. Each interconnection has an associated weight. The weights between the two layers are represented by elements of matrix $\boldsymbol{W}$. The element w_{ij} represents the connection strength for the connection between unit i of Layer L_2 and unit j of layer L_1. The weights are normalized; i.e.,

$$\sum_{j=1}^{n_1} w_{ij} = 1 \qquad (6.15)$$

where n_1 represents the number of units in layer L_1. The weights are initialized to small random values.

In this algorithm processing takes place in two steps: first the weighted sum for each unit in layer L_2 is calculated, and then the winner is decided. The

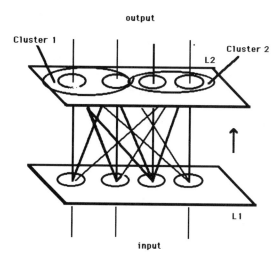

Figure 6.6. *Two-layer feed-forward network (competitive learning).*

weighted sum for unit i in layer L_2 is given by

$$net_i = \sum_{j=1}^{n_1} w_{ij} x_j \tag{6.16}$$

In Eq. 6.16, x_j represents the output of unit j in L_1. The weighted sum for all units in layer L_2 is calculated. The unit with the highest weighted sum is declared the winner, and this unit is then given a new activation value, 1.0, and all other units are given the activation value of 0.0. The weights are updated with each iteration according to the rule:

$$\Delta w_{ij} = \alpha(x_j/m - w_{ij}) \tag{6.17}$$

where α is a learning rate parameter ($0 \leq \alpha \leq 1$), m represents the number of units in layer L_1 that have activation levels of 1.0, and x_j represents the output of unit j in layer L_1. Typical values of α are 0.01–0.3.

With the above method it can be seen that weights connected to the winner unit are updated. The weights that correspond to active lines ($x_j = 1$) are increased, and the weights corresponding to the inactive lines ($x_j = 0$) are decreased. Thus, the network learns by shifting a fraction of its weights from inactive lines to active lines. The adjustment in Eq. 6.17 causes the weighted sum for the input pattern to be slightly higher if the same input pattern is presented again immediately.

In the above algorithm we assumed the input vector $\boldsymbol{x}$ to be binary. However, this restriction can be relaxed, and the algorithm can be generalized to a continuous-valued input vector. Networks with competitive learning can be used as unsupervised classifiers. Kulkarni et al. (1991) have analyzed satellite data using the ANN model with the competitive learning algorithm. The data were obtained using the thematic mapper (TM) sensor. The TM obtains data in seven spectral bands. The TM data for the scene (#y018116055) of January 1983 was analyzed using the competitive learning algorithm. The input layer in the ANN model for the competitive learning algorithm contained seven units that correspond to seven spectral bands. The output layer contained four units. The classified output is shown in Figure 6.7. In this example the input image pixels were grouped into two clusters because feature vectors representing different categories were very close in the feature space.

The main disadvantage of a competitive learning algorithm is that the network's adaptability enables prior learning to be washed away by recent learnings in response to the wide variety of patterns. To overcome this drawback more complex algorithms have been developed; these include the adaptive resonance theory (ART) (Carpenter and Grossberg, 1987a, b; Grossberg 1972,

Figure 6.7. *Classified output (competitive learning).*

1987, 1988), neocognitron models (Fukushima, 1988), and modified competitive learning (Kulkarni and Whitson, 1990).

Carpenter and Grossberg (1987a, b, 1988a, b) have represented a human cognition theory in terms of a neural network model based on the adaptive resonance theory (ART). The ART is divided into two paradigms, ART_1 and ART_2. ART_1 is designed to accept only binary input vectors, whereas ART_2 can classify both binary and continuous input patterns. The ART architecture is complex, and it is impossible to describe details of their research here in a few pages. In this section we present an overview of the ART. ART models have also been reviewed by Lippmann (1987), Wasserman (1989), and Toborg and Hwang (1989). The ART learning algorithm is essentially an unsupervised learning algorithm.

The network implements a clustering algorithm that is very similar to the sequential leader-clustering algorithm described by Hartigan (1975). The algorithm selects the first input as the exemplar for the first cluster. The next input is compared with the first cluster exemplar. If the normalized Euclidean distance is less than the threshold, the exemplar is clustered with the previous exemplar. If the normalized Euclidean distance between the two exemplars is greater than the threshold value, a new category is created, and the exemplar is assigned to the new cluster. The process is repeated for all succeeding inputs. The number of clusters thus grows with the number of input exemplars, and the number of clusters depends on both threshold and distance matrix used.

The core structure of the ART model is shown in Figure 6.8. The ART network consists of two layers, the comparison and recognition layers; $Gain_1$, $Gain_2$, and *Reset* provide control functions needed for training and classification. The comparison layer receives the binary input vector $\boldsymbol{x}$. The recognition layer compares and classifies the input vector. Each neuron in the recognition layer has an associated weight vector $\boldsymbol{b}_j$. Only the neuron with a weight vector best matching the input vector "fires"; all other neurons in the layer are inhibited. Neurons in the recognition layer are interconnected by a lateral inhibition network. The learning algorithm for the ART net can be described in the steps shown below (Lippmann, 1987):

Step 1: Before starting the net all weight vectors $\boldsymbol{b}j$ and $\boldsymbol{t}j$ and the vigilance parameter ρ must be initialized as

$$t_{ij}(0) = 1 \tag{6.18}$$

$$b_{ij}(0) = 1/(N + 1) \tag{6.19}$$

for $0 \le i \le N - 1$ and $0 \le j \le M - 1$; set $0 \le \rho \le 0$. In Eq. 6.19, $b_{ij}(t)$ is the bottom-up and $t_{ij}(t)$ is the top-down connection weight between input node i

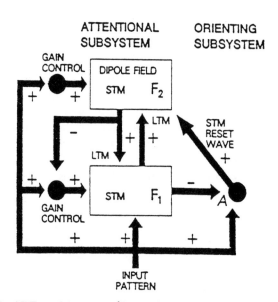

Figure 6.8. *ART architecture. (From Carpenter and Grossberg, 1988b, with permission.)*

and output node j at time t. The fraction ρ is the vigilance threshold and indicates how close an input must be to a stored exemplar to match.

Step 2: Apply new input.

Step 3: Compute output, which is given by

$$\mu_j = \sum_{i=1}^{N-1} b_{ij}(t) x_i \tag{6.20}$$

for $0 \le j \le M - 1$. In Eq. 6.20, μ_j is the output of output node j and x_i is the element i of the input vector.

Step 4: Select the best-matching exemplar

$$\mu_j^* = \max_j \{ \mu_j \} \tag{6.21}$$

This is performed using extensive lateral inhibition.

Step 5: Vigilance test.

$$\|x\| = \sum_{i=0}^{N-1} x_i \tag{6.22}$$

$$\|Tx\| = \sum_{i=0}^{N-1} t_{ij} x_i \tag{6.23}$$

If $\|Tx\|/\|x\| \ge \rho$, then go to step 6; otherwise go to step 7.

Step 6: Disable the best-matching exemplar. The output of the best-matching node selected in step 4 is temporarily set to zero and no longer takes part in maximization of step 4. Then go to step 3.

Step 7: Adopt the best-matching exemplar.

$$t_{ij}(t + 1) = t_{ij}^*(t) x_i$$

$$b_{ij}^*(t + 1) = t_{ij}(t) x_j / (0.5 + \sum_{i=0}^{N-1} t_{ij}^*(t) x_i \tag{6.24}$$

Step 8: Repeat by going to step 2.

Carpenter and Grossberg (1988a), as an illustration, considered 50 analog input patterns, as shown in Figure 6.9. The patterns were categorized using the

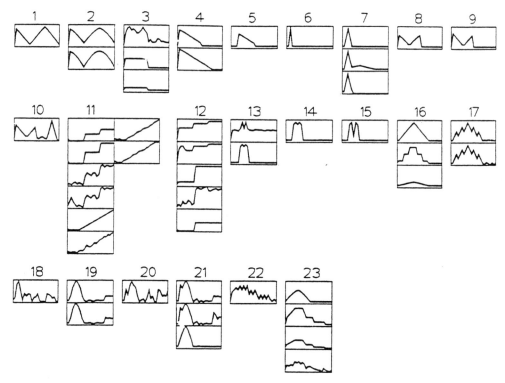

Figure 6.9. Analog input patterns. *(From Carpenter and Grossberg, 1988b, with permission.)*

ART2 architecture, which grouped them into 23 categories. They have also shown that by changing the vigilance factor, fine or coarse grouping can be achieved. Similar analog input patterns are often found in many recognition problems. The ART architecture is very useful in these types of tasks.

Kulkarni and Whitson (1990) have suggested a modified competitive learning algorithm that is essentially similar to competitive learning. The main disadvantage of the competitive learning algorithm is that the network forgets previous learning with new input patterns. The modified competitive learning algorithm overcomes this drawback. The basic idea here is that there are two types of weights: long-term weights (LTWs) and short-term weights (STWs) are used. With each new input pattern only STWs are updated. The LTWs are updated periodically. In this algorithm each unit in the hidden layer is associated with a few auxiliary units. Units with LTWs are called principal units. The auxiliary units are connected through STWs to units in the preceding layer. The weights are normalized. With each input pattern the winner unit is first determined, and the STWs of one of the auxiliary units associated with the winner unit are modified. The LTWs store nontemporary learning and are updated periodically using corresponding STWs. Since with each new input pattern only STWs that correspond to the winner unit are updated, spurious input patterns do not damage LTW values. Thus, stray input patterns do not wash away the prior learning. At the same time, the change in STWs provides the network with plasticity. The LTWs are updated only after STWs of all the auxiliary units associated with any principal unit have been updated.

An ANN model with the modified competitive learning algorithm is shown in Figure 6.10 (Kulkarni and Whitson, 1990). The model consists of four layers. Layer L_1 is an input layer. Layer L_2 is a feature vector layer. Layers L_3 and L_4 represent the recognition and fine recognition layers, respectively. The connections between layers L_1 and L_2 are shown in Figure 6.11. The algorithm is described in the steps shown below. Consider the two layers: the feature layer and recognition layer. Let the strengths associated with LTWs be represented by the elements of the matrix $WLTW(i, j)$, where the subscript j specifies the unit j in the feature layer and the subscript i specifies the unit i in the recognition layer. Let $WSTW(i, j, k)$ represent the short-term weights, where subscripts i and j are the same as in $WLTW(i, j)$. The subscript k specifies the auxiliary unit k associated with the principal unit i. The learning algorithm is described in the following steps:

Step 1: Initialize the weights with random values as

$$\sum_j WLTW(i, j) = 1 \qquad \text{for all } i \qquad\qquad (6.25)$$

$$\sum_j WSTW(i, j, k) = 1 \qquad \text{for all } i \text{ and } k \qquad\qquad (6.26)$$

Step 2: Obtain the output of Oi for units in the recognition layer.

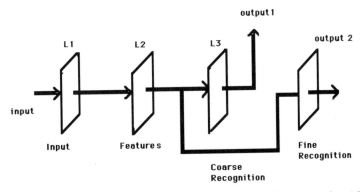

Figure 6.10. *ANN model with modified competitive learning algorithm.*

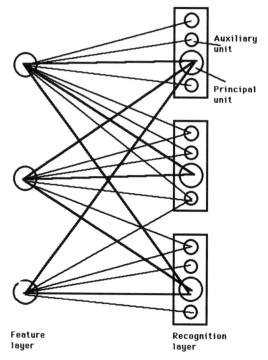

Figure 6.11. *Two-layer network with LTWs and STWs.*

Step 3: The change in $WSTW(i, j, k)$ is given by

$$\Delta WSTW(i, j, k) = 0 \qquad \text{if unit } i \text{ loses}$$

$$= c \cdot g/n - gWSTW(i, j, k) \qquad (6.27)$$

where $c = 1$ if the input line is active, otherwise $c = 0$, and g is the learning factor.

Step 4: Repeat step 1 and step 2 with each input pattern until all the STWs of all auxiliary units associated with any principal unit are updated. The change in $WLTW(i, j)$ is given as

$$\Delta WLTW(i, j) = \beta \left\{ (1/n) \sum_k [WSTW(i, j, k) - WLTW(i, j)] \right\} \qquad (6.28)$$

where β is a constant and n is the number of auxiliary units associated with a principal unit.

Step 5: In step 4 the WLTWs are conditionally updated. The condition for a split is given as

$$WLTW(i, j) - WSTW(i, j, k) > C_1 \qquad \text{for all } k \qquad (6.29)$$

If the condition in Eq. 6.29 is true, the split is said to occur, and the new set of LTWs is generated. If there is no split the LTWs are updated using Eq. 6.28.

Step 6: After each update of LTWs, check for a merge. The condition for a merge is given by

$$WLTW(i,j) - WLTW(l,j) \leq C_2 \qquad \text{for } i \neq 1 \qquad (6.30)$$

If the condition in Eq. 6.30 is true, then merge the two LTWs.

Step 7: Repeat steps 2 through 6 for each new input pattern.

It can be seen from the above steps that the constant C_1 is the threshold for a split, and the constant C_2 is the threshold for a merge. These constants determine the performance of the network. The criteria for determining these constants are discussed by Kulkarni and Whitson (1990). The algorithm has been used successfully for multispectral image analysis.

6.4. SUMMARY

Unsupervised classifiers deal with learning without a teacher. Clustering techniques that detect similarity between exemplars are often used for unsupervised classification. Commonly used clustering algorithms such as K-means, clustering with optimization techniques, and split and merge techniques are described. Self-organizing networks with learning algorithms such as competitive learning, Kohonen learning, and ART are also discussed. In a self-organizing network the weights are often initialized using random values as weight strengths. The network selects the first input as the exemplar of the first cluster. Subsequent inputs are compared with the earlier clusters. Any new input, based on some similarity criterion, is assigned to one of the existing clusters, or if there is no match a new cluster is created. With each input pattern weights are updated. Thus, the network learns with experience. Self-organizing networks are used as unsupervised classifiers for recognition of objects in an image.

REFERENCES

Ball, G. H., and Hall, D. J. (1976). ISODATA, an iterative method of multivariate data analysis and pattern classification. *Proceedings of the IEEE International Communications Conference.*

Carpenter, G. A., and Grossberg, S. (1987a). A massively parallel architecture for a self organizing neural pattern recognition machine. *International Journal of Computer Vision, Graphics and Image Processing* 37:54–115.

Carpenter, G. A., and Grossberg, S. (1987b). ART2: Self organization of stable category recognition codes for analog input patterns. *Applied Optics, Special Issue on Neural Networks.* 4919–4930.

Carpenter G. A., and Grossberg, S. (1988a). ART2: Self organization of stable category recognition codes for analog input patterns. *Proceeding of Joint International Conference on Neural Networks, San Diego,* Vol. II, pp. 727–735.

Carpenter, G. A., and Grossberg, S. (1988b). The ART of adaptive pattern recognition by a self organizing neural network. *Computer* March:77–88.

Desieno, D. (1988). Adding a conscience to competitive learning. *Proceeding of Joint International Conference on Neural Networks, San Diego,* Vol. I, pp. 117–124.

Duda, R. O., and Hart, P. E. (1973). *Pattern Classification and Scene Analysis.* John Wiley & Sons, New York.

Fukushima, K. (1988). Neural networks for visual pattern recognition. *Computer* March:65–74.

Grossberg, S. (1972). Neural expectation: Cerebellar and retinal analogs of cells fired by learnable or unlearnable pattern classes. *Kybernetics* 10:49-57.

Grossberg, S. (1987). Competitive learning: From interactive activation to adaptive resonance. *Cognitive Science* 2:23–63.

Grossberg, S. (1988). *Neural Networks and Natural Intelligence.* Bradford Books, MIT Press, Cambridge, MA.

Hartigan, J. A. (1975). *Clustering Algorithms.* John Wiley & Sons, New York.

Hebb, D. O. (1949). *The Organizational Behaviors.* John Wiley & Sons, New York.

Kohonen, T. (1982). Self organizing functions in neural computing. *Applied Optics* 26:4910–4918.

Kohonen, T. (1988). *Self Organization and Associative Memory.* Springer-Verlag, Berlin.

Kulkarni, A. D. (1991). Neural networks for pattern recognition. In: *Progress In Neural Networks,* Vol. I, O. Omidvar (ed), pp. 197–219. Ablex, New York.

Kulkarni, A. D., and Chandrasekhar, S. C. (1984). Clustering of multispectral data using sequential simplex technique. *Proceedings of IEEE Conference, Bombay,* pp. 649–651.

Kulkarni, A. D., and Whitson, G. M. (1990). Self organizing neural networks with a split/merge Algorithm. *Proceedings of 1990 ACM SIGMALL/PC Symposium on Small Systems,* Arlington, VA, pp. 255–261.

Kulkarni, A. D., et al. (1991). Multi-spectral image analysis using artificial neural network system on a Cray X-MP. *Proceedings of Symposium on Applied Computing,* Kansas City, MO, p. 345.

Linkser, R., (1988). Self organization in perceptual network. *Computer* 21:11–22.

Lippmann, R. P. (1987). An introduction to computing with neural nets. *IEEE Transactions on Acoustics, Speech and Signal Processing* 32:4–22.

Malsburg, V. (1973) Self organization orientation sensitive cells in striate cortex. *Kybernetics* 14:85–100.

Oja, E. (1989). Neural networks, principal components and subspaces. *International Journal of Neural Systems* 1:61–68.

Pao, Y.-H. (1989). *Adaptive Pattern Recognition and Neural Networks.* Addison-Wesley, Reading, MA.

Rosenblatt, F. (1962). *Principles of Neurodynamics: Perceptron and the Theory of Brain Mechanism.* Spartan Books, Washington, DC.

Rumelhart, D. E., et al. (1986a). Learning internal representation by error propagation. *Parallel Distributed Processing Models: Explorations in Microstructure of Cognitron,* Vol. II, pp. 318–362. MIT Press, Cambridge, MA.

Rumelhart, D. E., et al. (1986b). *Parallel Distributed Processing*, Vol I. MIT Press, Cambridge, MA.

Rumelhart, D. E., and Zipser, D. (1985). Feature discovery by competitive learning. *Cognitive Science* 9:75–112.

Toborg, S. T., and Hwang, K. (1989). Exploring neural network and optical computing technologies. In: *Parallel Processing for Super Computers and Artificial Intelligence*, Hwang, K., and Degroot, D. (eds.), pp. 609–660. McGraw-Hill, New York.

Tou, J. T., and Gonzalez, R. C. (1974). *Pattern Recognition Principles*. Addison-Wesley, Reading, MA.

Wasserman, P. D. (1989). *Neural Computing Theory and Practice*. Van Nostrand Reinhold, New York.

7

Associative Memories

7.1. INTRODUCTION

Human memories operate in an associative manner, i.e., a portion of a recollection can produce a larger related memory. Associative memories are content-addressable memories. Associative processing is one of the most fundamental brain functions of our memory and thought processes. Because a human memory is characterized by its associative, distributed, and content-addressable structure, each item is represented by a response pattern of a group of neural elements. According to this notion many artificial neural network (ANN) models have been proposed to represent an associative memory. Linear associative memories have been studied extensively by Kohonen (1972, 1988). Nakano (1972) has also suggested a model for an associative memory called an associatron. A model for an associative processor called a human associative processor (HASP) has been proposed by Hirai (1983). Bidirectional associative memories have been studied by Kosko (1987, 1988a, b; Kosko and Guest, 1989).

The basic functions of an associative memory are to store associative pairs through a self-organizing process and to produce an appropriate response pattern on receipt of the associated stimulus input pattern. An associative network is a network that serves to map stimulus vectors $\{x_1, x_2, \ldots, x_n\}$ to response vectors $\{y_1, y_2, \ldots, y_n\}$. In autoassociative networks the response vectors y_i are equal to the stimulus vectors x_i. In heteroassociative networks the response vectors y_i are not equal to the stimulus vectors x_i

Associative memories are often able to produce correct response patterns even though stimulus patterns are distorted or incomplete. This behavior of associative memories allows recognition and detection of objects under geometric distortions, in the presence of noise, or with partial occlusion. Textbooks such as those by Kohonen (1988), Hinton and Anderson (1989), Wasserman (1989), and Hecht-Nielson (1990) deal with associative memories. Associative memories are also used in pattern recognition (Fuchs and Haken, 1988; Telfer and Casasent, 1991).

7.2. BIDIRECTIONAL ASSOCIATIVE MEMORIES

A bidirectional associative memory (BAM) is the minimal two-layer nonlinear feedback network (Figure 7.1) that behaves as a heteroassociative content-addressable memory. Pairs of vectors (x_i, y_i) can be stored in a BAM by summing bipolar correlation matrices. In a $m \times n$ BAM, n neurons in layer L_1 are represented by the bottom-up field $F_x = \{x_1, x_2, \ldots, x_n\}$, and m neurons in layer L_2 by the top-down field $F_y = \{y_1, y_2, \ldots, y_m\}$. In a BAM the two fields are interconnected by a $m \times n$ synoptic weight matrix W. The neuron states in field A and field B are the units of the short-term memory (STM). The connection matrix W is the unit of the long-term memory (LTM). Information passes forward from one layer to another through the connection matrix W. Information passes backward through the matrix transpose W^T, where W^T represents the transpose of W.

Let (x_i, y_i) for $i = 1, 2, \ldots, N$ be the N pairs of patterns to be encoded in a BAM. One way to memorize the association (x_i, y_i) is by forming a correlation

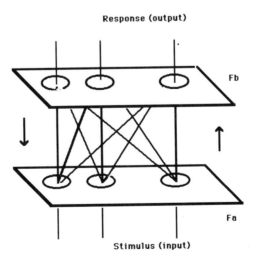

Response (output)

Stimulus (input)

Figure 7.1. *Bidirectional associative memory.*

matrix $y_i x_i^T$. A number of associations can be stored by adding corresponding correlation matrices.

$$W = \sum_{i=1}^{N} y_i x_i^T \tag{7.1}$$

If input pattern vectors $x_1, x_2, \ldots, x_n$ are the orthonormal (i.e., $x_i x_j = 1$ for $i = j$ and 0 otherwise), then the recall is perfect. If the input vectors are not orthonormal, then the output vector may contain crosstalk. In a dual BAM, feedback is achieved with W^T and is given by

$$W^T = \sum_{i=1}^{N} (y_i x_i^T)^T = \sum_{i=1}^{N} x_i y_i^T \tag{7.2}$$

If we assume a nonlinear transfer function for neurons in the BAM, then the recalled output is a nonlinear function of a transformed input vector and is given by

$$y_i = F(W x_i) \tag{7.3}$$

With the feedback, the input vector x_i can be estimated as

$$x_i = F(W y_i) \tag{7.4}$$

The simplest transfer function for a BAM is a step function. The stable reverberation corresponds to a system energy local minimum. When the BAM neurons are activated the network quickly evolves to a stable state of two-pattern reverberation or a nonadaptive resonance. In order to improve recall accuracy, the output vector y_i can be synchronously fed back. The back-and-forth flow of distributed information quickly resonates on a fixed data pair. The sequence can be represented by

$$
\begin{aligned}
x_i(0) &\rightarrow W \rightarrow y_i(0) \\
y_i(0) &\rightarrow W^T \rightarrow x_i(1) \\
x_i(1) &\rightarrow W \rightarrow y_i(1) \\
y_i(1) &\rightarrow W^T \rightarrow x_i(2) \\
&\vdots \\
x_i(i) &\rightarrow W \rightarrow_i (i) \\
y_i(i) &\rightarrow W^T \rightarrow x_i(i+1) \\
x_i(i+1) &\rightarrow W \rightarrow y_i(i+1) \\
&\vdots
\end{aligned}
\tag{7.5}
$$

Linear associative matrices are in general not bidirectionally stable. Kosko (1987) has shown that with a sigmoid transfer function all the matrices are bidirectionally stable. Kosko's stability results are based on the earlier work by Cohen and Grossberg (1983). If the dimensions of the stimulus vector x and the response vector y are n and m, respectively, then an estimate of the BAM storage capacity for reliable recall is given by $p \leq \min(n, m)$, where p represents the number of data pairs to be stored.

Let us consider a simple example of a BAM construction and synchronous operation. Let the number of units in layer L_1 be eight ($n = 8$), the number of units in layer L_2 be five ($m = 5$), and the number of pairs of vectors to be encoded be four ($N = 4$). The stimulus and response vector pairs are given by:

$$x_1^T = (-1 \quad 1 \quad -1 \quad 1 \quad -1 \quad 1 \quad -1 \quad 1)$$

$$x_2^T = (-1 \quad -1 \quad 1 \quad 1 \quad -1 \quad -1 \quad 1 \quad 1)$$

$$x_3^T = (-1 \quad -1 \quad -1 \quad 1 \quad 1 \quad 1 \quad -1 \quad -1)$$

$$x_4^T = (-1 \quad -1 \quad -1 \quad -1 \quad 1 \quad 1 \quad 1 \quad 1)$$

$$y_1^T = (1 \quad 1 \quad -1 \quad 1 \quad 1)$$

$$y_2^T = (-1 \quad 1 \quad 1 \quad 1 \quad -1)$$

$$y_3^T = (-1 \quad -1 \quad 1 \quad -1 \quad -1)$$

$$y_4^T = (-1 \quad 1 \quad -1 \quad 1 \quad -1)$$

The weights between the two layers are given by the correlation matrix W:

$$W = y_1 x_1^T + y_2 x_2^T + y_3 x_3^T + y_4 x_4^T$$

$$= \begin{pmatrix} 2 & 4 & 0 & 0 & -2 & 0 & -2 & 0 \\ -2 & 0 & 0 & 0 & -2 & 0 & 2 & 4 \\ 0 & -2 & 2 & 2 & 0 & -2 & 0 & -2 \\ -2 & 0 & 0 & 0 & -2 & 0 & 2 & 4 \\ 2 & 4 & 0 & 0 & -2 & 0 & -2 & 0 \end{pmatrix} \quad (7.6)$$

The BAM convergence is quick and robust when W is constant. A possible neural network implementation of a BAM is shown in Figure 7.2. Here, the stimulus vector x_i is represented by layer L_1. Layer L_2 represents the response vector y_i. The weights between layers L_1 and L_2 are given by the elements of matrix W. The weights between layers L_2 and L_3 are given by the elements of matrix W^T. The output of layer L_2 is used iteratively as an input to layer L_1.

Output

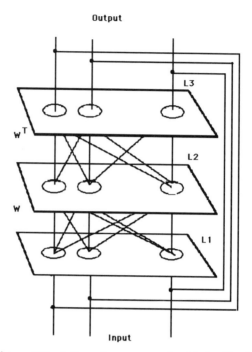

Input

Figure 7.2. *A three-layer network with feedback.*

A software simulation of the network shown in Figure 7.2 has been developed. The network was tested with test images. The results are shown in Figures 7.3 and 7.4. Each image is represented by a matrix of 12×12 pixels. The 12×12 matrices representing binary images were scanned row by row to generate input vectors; each vector thus was of size 144. Layer L_1 representing an input vector contained 144 neurons. Six image patterns that represented the characters **A**, **B**, **C**, **1**, **2**, and **3** were stored in the BAM. In order to generate matrix **W**, six binary orthogonal binary vectors were chosen as output vectors (y_i). Initially, these images were stored by generating appropriate weight matrices. During the recall, noisy and incomplete images were used as the stimulus images. Images of the partial objects shown in Figure 7.3a were used as stimulus images, and the corresponding recalled images are shown in Figure 7.3b. The noisy input images are shown in Figure 7.4a, and the corresponding recalled images are shown in Figure 7.4b. A software simulation of a bidirectional associative memory has also been described by Blum (1990).

In the above examples the weight matrices were initialized to store various stimulus-response patterns. However, human memory is adaptive in nature. The idea behind an adaptive BAM is to let some of the stable STM reverberation slip gradually into the LTM connection matrix **W**. The simplest way to change the weights is to use the Hebian learning rule, i.e.,

$$\Delta w_{ij} = S_e(x_i)S_e(y_j) \tag{7.7}$$

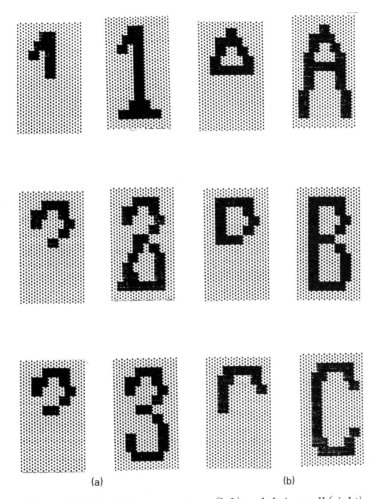

(a)   (b)

Figure 7.3. *Partial image patterns (left) and their recall (right).*

where $-1 \leq S_e(x_i)S_e(y_i) \leq 1$. In Eq. 7.7, S_e represents the neuron output or the neuron state. The signal product is 1 if the signals are both $+1$ or both -1; it is -1 if one signal is $+1$ and the other is -1. Adaptive BAMs have been discussed extensively by Kosko (1988a, b).

7.3. OPTIMAL ASSOCIATIVE MEMORY

A BAM is often characterized by low memory capacity and small basins of attraction for the stored patterns (Schneider and Sigillito, 1991). If we assume units with linear response, then the response $\boldsymbol{y}_i$ for the stimulus $\boldsymbol{x}_i$ is given by

$$\boldsymbol{y}_i = \boldsymbol{W}\boldsymbol{x}_i \qquad (7.8)$$

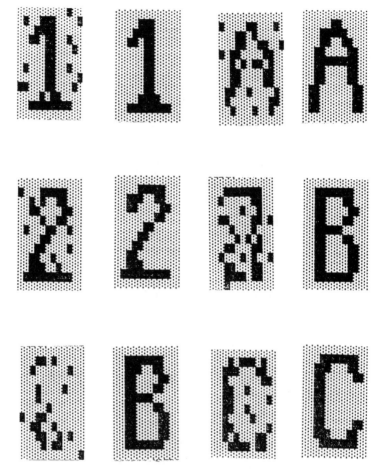

Figure 7.4. *Noisy image patterns (left) and their recall (right).*

The weight matrix W can also be determined by minimizing the mean squared error $\|Wx_i - y_i\|$. Equation 7.8 can be rewritten in a matrix form as

$$Y = WX \qquad (7.9)$$

where columns of matrices X and Y represent the stimulus and response vectors, respectively. Usually, the number of associations, n is less than m, the length of the vector to be associated. If we use the constraint for a unique matrix W that of minimizing $\|Wx_i - y_i\|$, it results in the solution (Kohonen, 1988; Kohonen et al., 1989)

$$W = YX^\dagger \qquad (7.10)$$

where $X^\dagger$ is the Moore-Penrose generalized inverse of X.

It should be noted that the linear mapping is only one representative in an infinite class of mapping functions, some of which are derived from the linear models by adding such nonlinearities as saturation or threshold triggering to signal paths. A recall operation projects an unknown stimulus vector x_i and obtains the associated response vector y_i using Eq. 7.8. The recall can be viewed as the weighted sum of the response vectors. Schneider and Sigillito (1991) made a comparative study of performances of the BAM and OAM. They have shown that the OAM is superior to the BAM in terms of memory capacity and size of radii of attraction. However, the main disadvantages of the OAM is that the connections required for physical implementation of the OAM are twice those of the similar BAM. Schneider and Sigillito (1991) have also suggested an improved bidirectional associative memory (IBAM), which is also a two-layer feed-forward network wherein information flows forward and backward in the same connections. The main difference is in the learning rule. The IBAM is an improved BAM with a bidirectional connection matrix. It uses the learning algorithm for optimizing both the forward and backward flow of the information. Here the weight matrix W is generated such that it minimizes the average mean squared error between the actual output and the desired output and also the mean squared error between the actual stimulus and the input obtained by applying W^T to all output prototype vectors.

7.4. SELECTIVE REFLEX MEMORY

Recently, Loos (1990) has suggested a selective reflex memory (SRM), which is a modified version of a BAM. The main disadvantage of a BAM is early saturation. The ART overcomes early saturation, but at the cost of fault sensitivity of the top layer. The desired characteristics of an ideal associative memory include absence of early saturation, efficient use of the dimension, capacity for local learning, and simple hardware implementation. In an attempt to build such a memory, a selective reflex memory was suggested by Loos (1990). The main idea here is to select back states of the BAM as orthogonal vectors. The SRM consists of two stages: the front end followed by the dominant label selector (DLS) stage (Figure 7.5). The front end is much like a BAM; however, there is no rear thresholding. Because the front end is different from that of the BAM, it is called the bidirectional linear transform (BLT) stage. The BLT connection matrix can be built adaptively by Hebb learning. The DLS itself can be considered an associative memory with N stored states.

Let (x_i, y_i) for $i = 1, 2, \ldots, N$ represent a set of bipolar vectors to be stored in a memory. Here, the input vector x_i is first mapped to vector u_i, which is chosen to be an orthogonal vector such as a row of the Walsh-Hadamard matrix. The connection matrix P that maps x_i to u_i can be obtained from vector pairs (x_i, u_i). Vector u_i is then mapped to the output vector y_i. The connection matrix Q that maps u_i to y_i can be obtained from vector pairs (u_i, y_i). Loos (1990) has shown that the SRM performs perfect associative recall for any one

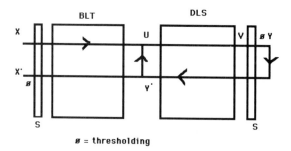

Figure 7.5. *Selective reflex memory. (From Loos, 1990, with permission.*
© *1990 IEEE.)*

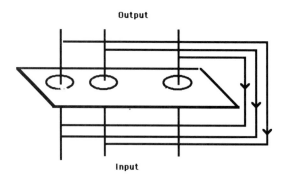

Figure 7.6. *Hopfield network.*

of the N stored bipolar vectors. There are no spurious stable states, and the memory can be loaded up fully to the dimension N.

7.5. HOPFIELD NETWORK AS AN AUTOASSOCIATIVE MEMORY

A Hopfield network has a single layer of processing units as shown in Figure 7.6. The input vector is a binary vector. At any given time the state of the network is represented by a state vector such that $v = (v_1, v_2\ v_3, \ldots, v_n)^T$. The units in the Hopfield network are fully connected. Here, output of each unit is fed into inputs of other units in the same layer. The interconnection topology makes the network recursive. Each interconnection has an associated weight. Let t_{ij} denote a connection from unit i to unit j. In the Hopfield network the weight matrix is symmetrical; i.e., $t_{ij} = t_{ji}$. Hopfield (1982, 1984) has shown that a network with a symmetrical connection matrix and with zero diagonal elements and asynchronous update will always converge. Convergence is necessary for it to be possible to perform useful computational tasks such as optimization and associative recall. Many networks with unequal weights, $t_{ij} \neq t_{ji}$, also converge successfully. The basic procedure to update a binary Hopfield network is as follows.

Each unit calculates the weighted sum that is given by

$$net_j = \sum_{\substack{i=1 \\ i \neq j}}^{n} v_i t_{ji} \qquad (7.11)$$

If net_j is less than zero, the output of unit j is set to zero; otherwise the output of unit j is set to 1; i.e.,

$$\text{if } net_j \geq 0, \text{ then } v_j = 1$$

$$\text{if } net_j = 0, \text{ then } v_j = 0 \qquad (7.12)$$

One system of updating process is to update the units in sequence. The update mechanism posed by Hopfield (1982) chooses the unit randomly. Usually many updates must be done to all processing units before the network reaches a stable state. Each state of the Hopfield network has an associated "energy" value, which is defined as:

$$E = -\tfrac{1}{2} \sum_j \sum_{\substack{i \\ i \neq j}} t_{ji} v_j v_i \qquad (7.13)$$

At a stable state the energy function is the minimum. The minimum may be local or global.

One of the applications of the Hopfield network is as an autoassociative processor. A number of binary vectors representing different patterns can be stored in the Hopfield network. Here, in order to store input vectors, the energy equation is used to assign the weight values such that each memory vector corresponds to a stable state or the minimum energy function of the network. During the recall the network is initialized with a partial or noisy input pattern. The updating process moves the state of the network until it reaches the minimum energy function. If the noisy or partial pattern is close enough to the memory pattern, then the network converges to the correct pattern. The correct pattern is then recovered from the partial or noisy input pattern. Hopfield (1984) has shown that the network settles in about 4 cycle times, and if there are N neurons in the network it can remember $0.15 \times N$ stable states before the error in the recall becomes severe.

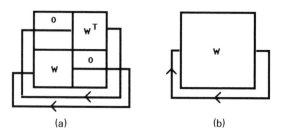

Figure 7.7. *Connection matrices for (a) BAM and (b) Hopfield net.*

A connection matrix between a BAM and Hopfield net is shown in Figure 7.7.

7.6. BIDIRECTIONAL ASSOCIATIVE MEMORIES WITH MULTIPLE INPUT/OUTPUT PATTERNS

A BAM is an associative memory that uses the forward and backward search to recall any associated vector pair $(\boldsymbol{x}_i, \boldsymbol{y}_i)$. Bidirectional memories are often limited to two input/output patterns. Humpert (1990) has generalized BAMs to store several input/output patterns. For the present discussion, we denote a BAM with two input/output patterns as a BAM_2 and a BAM with several input/output patterns as a BAMg (BAM generalized). Some of the possible configurations of a BAMg are shown in Figures 7.8a through 7.8c. Figures 7.8a shows a BAMg with *1* stable states $(A_1, A_2, \ldots, A_1)$. These stable states are reached if the energy function of the system has found a local minimum.

Generalization of the BAM_2 to several vector fields raises questions regarding the updating process. In the BAM_2 all units in a field are asynchronously (or synchronously) updated. The sequence updating weights in a BAMg is not obvious. The generalization of a BAM_2 to several vector fields also raises the question of interconnections. In Figure 7.8a each field is connected to all other fields; another possible alternative could be a tower of fields as shown in Figure 7.8b, and yet another possible alternative for a BAMg with three fields is shown in Figure 7.8c. The BAMg is very useful in image-processing applications, wherein the appearance of two patterns could be needed for a third pattern to be invoked or to store temporal images. A set of related images can be stored a BAMg. During the recall a complete set can be recovered by activating a few member images in the set. Humpert (1990) has generalized a few results of a BAM_2 to a BAMg. However, this research topic is relatively new and has not been fully explored yet.

Kulkarni and Yazadanpanahi (1992) have developed a software simulation of a BAMg. They have considered three sets of test images. The three sets contained images of characters $\{1, 2, 3\}$, $\{A, B, C\}$, and $\{\alpha, \beta, \gamma\}$. Each character was represented by a 12×12 matrix. The three sets were stored in a BAMg with three inputs/outputs. During the retrieval any one image (partial or noisy)

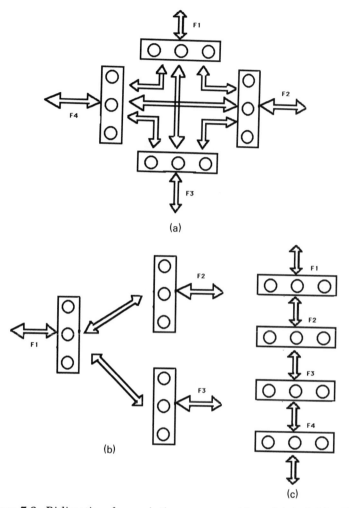

Figure 7.8. *Bidirectional associative memory with multiple fields. Three different schemata are shown.*

from any set was used as the stimulus. The corresponding images from the other set were retrieved. The results are shown in Figures 7.9 and 7.10.

7.7. TEMPORAL ASSOCIATIVE MEMORIES

Temporal associative memories are used in image processing to store a sequence of images acquired at different time instants. Applications of temporal image analysis include remote sensing, and medical image analysis. In remote sensing, temporal images are used for crop yield prediction, observing geological structural changes, etc. In medical image analysis, temporal images are used for applications such as the tumor growth detection. In all these applications we need to store and retrieve sequences of images obtained at different instances of

Figure 7.9. *Partial patterns and their recall (BAM$_g$).*

time. Bidirectional associative memories can be used to store sequences of images. A two-dimensional image can be represented in a vector form by using a scanning or stacking operation. A BAM with two input/output fields can be used as a temporal associative memory (TSM).

Let $\{x_1, x_2, \ldots, x_n\}$ be a sequence of vectors to be stored in the memory. These patterns can be memorized using local contiguities that can be represented by $x_1 \to x_2 \to x_3 \to \cdots x_i \to x_{i+1} \to \cdots$. This local contiguity conjecture can be stored in a connection matrix W of a BAM. A pair of patterns (x_i, x_{i+1}) can be memorized by the correlation matrix $x_{i+1}x_i^T$. For a sequence of n patterns, matrix W is given by

$$W = x_1 x_n^T + \sum_{i=1}^{n-1} x_{i+1}x_i^T \tag{7.14}$$

Kosko (1987) has shown that the memory can store k temporal patterns of length $m_1, m_2, \ldots, m_k$ provided $m_1 + m_2 + \cdots m_k = m \ll n$, where $n \times n$ is the size of the matrix W.

7.8. COUNTERPROPAGATION NETWORKS AS ASSOCIATIVE MEMORY

The counterpropagation network was proposed by Hecht-Nielsen (1987). The network consists of three layers: the input layer, a hidden layer, and the output

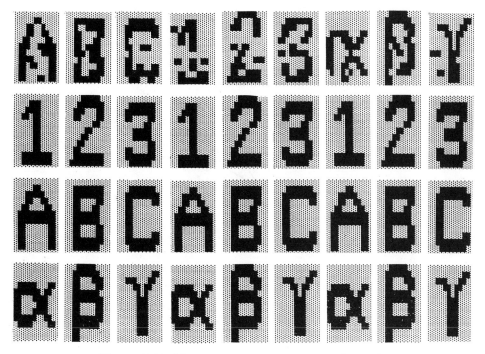

Figure 7.10. *Noisy patterns and their recall* (BAM_g).

layer. The hidden layer is a Kohonen layer with competitive units that do unsupervised learning, and the output layer is a Grossberg layer. The Grossberg layer is trained by a Widrow-Hoff or Grossberg rule. The counterpropagation network can be used as an associative memory to store pairs of vectors $(\boldsymbol{x}_i, \boldsymbol{y}_i)$. Consider the network shown in Figure 7.11. Let $\boldsymbol{x} = (x_1, x_2, x_3, \ldots, x_n)$ be the input vector. The weights between layers L_1 and L_2 are represented by elements of matrix $\boldsymbol{P}$; the weights between layers L_2 and L_3 are represented by elements of matrix $\boldsymbol{Q}$. The element p_{ji} represents the weight from unit i in layer L_1 to unit j in layer L_2. The element q_{kj} presents the weight between unit j in layer L_2 and unit k in layer L_3. The weights vectors $\boldsymbol{p}_j$ are normalized; i.e.,

$$\sum_{i=1}^{n_1} p_{ij} = 1 \tag{7.15}$$

where n_1 represents the number of units in layer L_1. The net input to units in layer L_2 is given by

$$net_j = \sum_{i=1}^{n_1} x_i\, p_{ij} \tag{7.16}$$

The unit with maximum net input wins. After the competition, the hidden layer

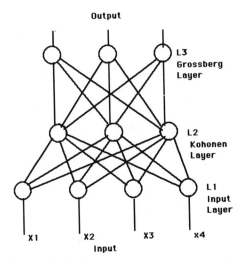

Figure 7.11. *Counterpropagation network.*

activations are

$$z_c = 1.0 \qquad \text{for the winner unit}$$

$$z_c = 0.0 \qquad \text{for other units} \tag{7.17}$$

The output at layer L_3 is given by

$$y_j' = \sum_{i=1}^{n_2} z_i q_{ji} \tag{7.18}$$

where n_2 represents the number of units in the hidden layer. During the training both layers are updated. The incoming weights are updated to the winner unit only. The change in weights is given by:

$$\Delta p_{ji} = \alpha(x_i - p_{ji})$$

$$p_{ji}(k + 1) = p_{ji}(k) + \Delta p_{ji} \tag{7.19}$$

In Eq. 7.17, α is a learning constant $(0 < \alpha \wedge 1.0)$.

The weights between the layers L_2–L_3 are updated as

$$\Delta q_{ji} = \beta z_i(y_j - y_j')$$

$$q_{ji}(k + 1) = q_{ji}(k) + \Delta q_{ji} \tag{7.20}$$

where β is a learning constant, y_j' is the output of unit j in layer L_3, and y_j is the target output or the desired output at unit j. Since $z_i = 1$ only for the winner unit, the outgoing weights are updated from the winner unit only. The counterpropagation network requires that the input vector be normalized; i.e.,

$$\|\boldsymbol{x}\| = \left[\sum_{i=1}^{n_1} x_i^2 \right]^{1/2} = 1 \tag{7.21}$$

It can be seen that with the above learning algorithm the pairs of vectors $(\boldsymbol{x}_i, \boldsymbol{y}_i)$ can be encoded, and the stored pairs can be recalled with noisy or partial input vectors. Thus, the network can function as an associative memory.

7.9. IMAGE-PROCESSING APPLICATIONS

Associative memories are often able to produce correct response patterns even though stimulus patterns are distorted or incomplete. This property of associative memories makes them a valuable tool for many image-processing and pattern recognition applications. Associative memories are used to improve the signal-to-noise (S/N) ratio of an input image. They are used to recognize objects from partial views. If we assume N associations in the memory and each of the stimulus and response vectors have m elements and an additive uncorrelated noise with zero mean and variance $\sigma_i 2$, the response vector is then given by

$$\boldsymbol{y}_k + \boldsymbol{v}_0 = \boldsymbol{W}(\boldsymbol{x}_k + \boldsymbol{v}_i) \tag{7.22}$$

where $\boldsymbol{v}_i$ is the input noise vector and $\boldsymbol{v}_0$ is the output noise vector. The ratio of the average output noise variance to the average input noise variance is (Murakami and Aibara, 1987)

$$\sigma_0^2 / \sigma_i^2 = 1/m \ \mathrm{Tr}[\boldsymbol{W}\boldsymbol{W}^T] \tag{7.23}$$

For an autoassociative memory this simplifies to

$$\sigma_0^2 / \sigma_i^2 = N/m \tag{7.24}$$

This means that when a noisy version of a memorized input vector is applied to the memory, the recall is improved by the ratio of the number of memorized vectors to the number of elements in the vector. For heteroassociative memories a similar formula holds as long as N is less than m.

$$\sigma_0 2 / \sigma_i^2 = 1/m \ \mathrm{Tr}[\boldsymbol{Y}\boldsymbol{Y}^T] \mathrm{Tr}\left[(\boldsymbol{X}^T\boldsymbol{X})^{-1}\right] \tag{7.25}$$

Examples of autoassociative memory image recollection are shown in Figures 7.12, through 7.14 (Casasent, 1989). Figure 7.12 shows images of Phantom

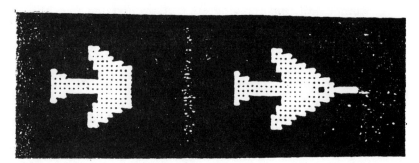

Figure 7.12. *Partial aircraft image and its recall. (From Casasent, 1989, with permission.)*

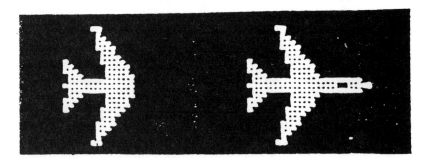

Figure 7.13. *Partial aircraft image and its recall. (From Casasent, 1989, with permission.)*

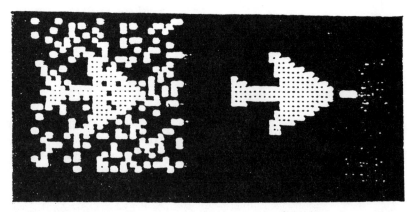

Figure 7.14. *Noisy aircraft image and its recall. (From Casasent, 1989, with permission.)*

aircraft with 15% of the aircraft missing and the corresponding recalled image. Figure 7.13 shows a DC-10 aircraft image (with 17% missing) and the corresponding recalled image. Figure 7.14 shows an image with noise and the corresponding recalled image.

Fault tolerance is a byproduct of the distributed nature and error-correcting capabilities of distributed associative memories. Wechsler and Zimmerman (1988, 1989) have used these properties of an associative memory in their object recognition system. They used the distributed associative memory (DAM) as the recognition component and a complex log-invariant image representation, which, along with the DAM yields a system able to recognize memorized objects regardless of their scale and orientation. The system is fault tolerant and allows noise and overlap. They have tested the system with images of objects: keys, leaves, and mechanical parts. The original objects are shown in Figure 7.15, a recall in the presence of noise is shown in Figure 7.16, and recall with a rotation is shown in Figure 7.17.

Figure 7.15. *Original images. (From Wechsler and Zimmerman, 1989, with permission. © 1989 IEEE.)*

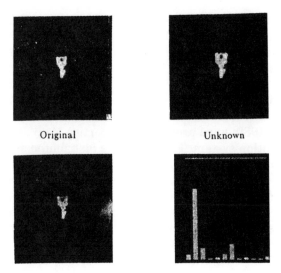

Figure 7.16. *Noisy images and their recall. (From Wechsler and Zimmerman, 1989, with permission. © 1989 IEEE.)*

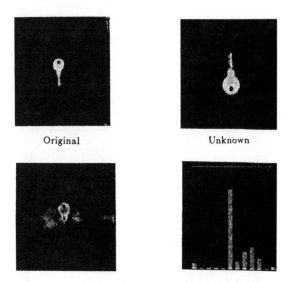

Figure 7.17. *Images with rotation and their recall. (From Wechsler and Zimmerman, 1989, with permission. © 1989 IEEE.)*

7.10. SUMMARY

Associative memories are used to store pairs of stimulus and response vectors. A response vector can be invoked by the corresponding stimulus or the key vector. In this chapter we introduced the basic ideas behind bidirectional associative memories (BAMs), optimal associative memories (OAMs), improved associative memories (IBAMs), temporal BAMs, and generalized BAMs. We also demonstrated use of these memories with the help of examples. Since the associative memories are able to retrieve the stored patterns from noisy or partial input patterns, these memories are extremely useful in image storage and retrieval applications

REFERENCES

Blum, A. (1990). Bidirectional associative memory systems in C++. *Dr. Doob's Journal* April:16–20.

Cohen, M., and Grossberg, S. (1983). Absolute stability of global pattern formation and parallel memory storage by competitive neural networks. *IEEE Transactions on Systems, Man and Cybernetics* 13:815–926.

Casasent, D. (1989). Pattern recognition: Review. Tutorial notes. In *International Joint Conference on Neural Networks*, Washington, DC.

Fuchs, A., and Haken, H. (1988). Pattern recognition and associative memory as dynamic processes in nonlinear system. *Proceedings of Joint International Conference on Neural Networks, Washington, DC*, Vol. I, pp. 217–224.

Hecht-Nielsen, R. (1987). Counterpropagation networks. *Proceedings of the First International Joint Conference on Neural Networks, San Diego*, Vol. II, pp. 19–32.

Hecht-Nielsen, R. (1990). *Neurocomputing*. Addison-Wesley, Reading, MA.

Hinton, G., and Anderson, J. (1989). *Parallel Models of Associative Memory*. Lawrence Erlbaum Associates, Hillsdale, NJ.

Hirai, Y. (1983). A model of human associative processor (HASP). *IEEE Transactions on Systems, Man and Cybernetics* 13:851–857.

Hopfield, J. J. (1982). Neural networks and physical systems with emergent collective computational abilities. *Proceedings of the National Academy of Sciences* 79:2554–2558.

Hopfield, J. J. (1984). Neurons with graded response have collective computational properties like those of two-state neurons. *Proceedings of the National Academy of Sciences* 81:3088–3092.

Humpert, B. (1990). Bidirectional associative memory with several patterns. *Proceedings of International Joint Conference on Neural Networks, San Diego*, Vol. I, pp. 741–750.

Kohonen, T. (1972). Correlation matrix memories. *IEEE Transactions on Computers* 21:353–359.

Kohonen, T. (1988). *Self Organization and Associative Memory*. Springer-Verlag, Berlin.

Kohonen, T., et al. (1989). Storage and processing of information in distributed associative memory systems. In: *Parallel Models of Associative Memory*, Hinton, G., and Anderson, J. (eds.), Lawrence Erlbaum Associates, Hillsdale, NJ.

Kosko, B. (1987). Adaptive bidirectional associative memories. *Applied Optics* 26:4947–4959.

Kosko, B. (1988a). Competitive adaptive bidirectional associative memories. *Proceedings of International Join Conference on Neural Networks, San Diego*, Vol. II, pp. 759–766.

Kosko, B. (1988b). Bidirectional associative memories. *IEEE Transactions on Systems, Man and Cybernetics* 18 49–60.

Kosko, B., and Guest, C. (1989). Optical bidirectional associative memories. *Proceedings of Society for Photo-optical and Instrumentation Engineers: Image Understanding* 758:11–18.

Kulkarni, A. D., and Yazdanpanahi, I. (1992). Generalized bidirectional associative memories for image processing. *Proceedings of Society for Photo-optical and Instrumentation Engineers: Intelligent Robot and Computer Vision 1826:152–159.*

Loos, H. G. (1990). Quadratic Hadamard memories. *Proceedings of International Joint Conference on Neural Networks, San Diego*, Vol. I, pp. 735–740.

Murakami, K., and Aibara, T. (1987). An improvement on the Moore-Penrose generalized inverse associative memory. *IEEE Transactions on Systems, Man and Cybernetics* 17:699–707.

Nakano, K. (1972). Associatron—a model of associative memory. *IEEE Transactions on Systems, Man, and Cybernetics* 2:380–388.

Schneider, A., and Sigillito, V. G. (1991). Two-layer binary associative memories. In: *Progress in Neural Networks*, Vol. I, pp. 87–104, Omidvar, O. M. (ed.), Ablex, Norwood, NJ.

Telfer, B., and Casasent, D. (1991). Neural closure associative processor. *Neural Networks* 4:589–598.

Wasserman, P. D. (1989). *Neural Computing Theory and Practice*. Van Nostrand Reinhold, New York.

Wechsler, H., and Zimmerman, G. (1988). 2-D invariant object recognition using distributed associative memory. *IEEE Transactions on Pattern Analysis and Machine Intelligence* 10:811–821.

Wechsler, H., and Zimmerman, G. (1989). Distributed associative memory (DAM) for bin picking. *IEEE Transactions on Pattern Analysis and Machine Intelligence* 11:814–822.

8

Three-Dimensional Structures and Motion

8.1. INTRODUCTION

Temporal analysis deals with a sequence of images or with images of the same object obtained at different times. The problem of temporal pattern recognition has been studied via both pattern recognition methods and neural network approaches. A substantial amount of work has been devoted to the methods of estimating object motion parameters from a short sequence of images. The problem of temporal analysis occurs in a wide variety of situations such as estimating the rigid-body object structure and motion, navigation, and tracking 3-D motion parameters of a point object. If we consider an image sequence of a moving rigid body from a single camera, we can use various image space data to compute motion parameters. For small interframe object image displacements optical flow or point shifts are used. Many computer-based approaches for estimating 3-D structures and motion parameters have been suggested in practice (Limb and Murphy, 1975; Tsai and Huang, 1981, 1984; Horn and Schunck, 1982; Tsai et al., 1982; Nagel, 1983, Horn, 1986; Broida and Chellappa, 1991; Penna and Wu, 1991).

Optical flow can be used for segmenting an image into regions and estimating the object motion in a given scene. Human beings are sensitive to optical flow, which is defined as the distribution of apparent velocities of motion of brightness patterns in the image. Generally optical flow corresponds to a motion field. Two kinds of techniques are used for motion analysis: the domain-independent and domain-dependent. Domain-independent motion-processing techniques extract information from time-varying images using the weakest possible assumptions about the world, whereas domain-dependent understanding methods make use of models or stronger assumptions about the world. By modeling the imaging system we establish the relationship, in the form of equations, between the coordinates of a point in a 3-D space and its coordinates in the image plane. These equations along with corresponding matching points in various images in the sequence can be used to estimate motion parameters. A few neural network models have been suggested for motion parameter estimation and 3-D surface construction. Conventional methods as well as neural network models used in the 3-D surface construction and motion parameter estimation are discussed in this chapter.

8.2. OPTICAL FLOW

The optical flow or instantaneous velocity field assigns to every point on the visual field a two-dimensional retinal velocity at which it is moving across the visual field. One important feature of the optical flow is that is can be calculated simply using local information. Existing approaches for computation of the optical flow, according to the nature of the primitives used, can be divided into two types: the intensity based and token based. The intensity-based approach basically relies on the assumption that the changes in intensity are strictly a result of the motion of the object and uses intensity values and their spatial and temporal derivatives to compute the optical flow. The token-based approaches consider motion of tokens such as edges, corners, and linear features in the image. Token-based approaches are less sensitive to some of the difficulties associated with variations of image intensities. The main disadvantage of token-based approaches is that they yield information about the object motion and shape only at edges, corners, and linear features. An interpolation procedure has to be included when estimates at dense data are required.

Let image $f(x, y)$ at time t be represented as a function of three variables, $f(x, y, t)$. Using the Taylor series expansion, we get

$$f(x + \Delta x, y + \Delta y, t + \Delta t) = f(x, y, t) + (\partial f/\partial x) \Delta x$$

$$+ (\partial f/\partial y) \Delta y + (\partial f/\partial t) \Delta t + \cdots \quad (8.1)$$

The crucial observation to be exploited is the following: if the image at some time $t + \Delta t$ is the result of the original image at time t being moved by Δx and Δy, we get

$$f(x + \Delta x, y + \Delta y, t + \Delta t) = f(x, y, t) \quad (8.2)$$

$$- (\partial f/\partial t) = (\partial f/\partial x)u + (\partial f/\partial y)v \quad (8.3)$$

where $u = \Delta x/\Delta t$ and $v = \Delta y/\Delta t$. Equation 8.3 implies that the time rate of change in intensity of a point in the image is explained as the spatial rate of change in the intensity of a scene multiplied by the velocity at which points of the scene move past the camera. Standard square error techniques are used to minimize the flow error. An algorithm for computation of optical flow follows:

Step 1: Initialize k, $u(k)$, and $v(k)$ to zero.

Step 2: Find $u(k)$ and $v(k)$ as

$$u(k) = u_{\text{av}(k-1)} - f_x(P/D)$$

$$v(k) = v_{\text{av}(k-1)} - f_y(P/D) \tag{8.4}$$

where $f_x = \partial f/\partial x$, $f_y = \partial f/\partial y$, and $f_t = \partial f/\partial t$.

$$P = f_x u_{\text{av}} + f_y v_{\text{av}} + f_t$$

$$D = \lambda^2 + f_x^2 + f_y^2 \tag{8.5}$$

where λ is a constant and u_{av} and v_{av} represent the spatial averages.

Step 3: Until some error measure is satisfied, iterate step 2.

Horn and Schunck (1981) have demonstrated that the above algorithm derives the optical flow using two time frames; however, the algorithm can be improved to use several time frames, as shown below.

$$t = 0$$

Initialize $u(x, y, 0)$, $v(x, y, 0)$.

For $t = 1$ to maxframes do

$$u(x, y, t) = u_{\text{av}}(x, y, t - 1) - f_x P/D$$

$$v(x, y, t) = v_{\text{av}}(x, y, t - 1) - f_y P/D \tag{8.6}$$

For more detailed discussion of these methods the reader is referred to the papers by Horn (1986), Horn and Schunck (1981), and a textbook by Ballard and Brown (1982).

8.3. COMPUTATION OF OPTICAL FLOW USING NEURAL NETWORKS

Zhou and Chellappa (1988a) have used a Hopfield network for computing the optical flow. Usually the measurement primitives used for computing optical flow from successive images are the image intensity values, their spatial and temporal derivatives, and tokens such as edges, corners, and linear features. Conventional methods based on such primitives suffer from edge sparsity, noise distortion, and sensitivity to rotation. Zhou and Chellappa (1988a), in their approach, have used intensity values and principal curvatures, which are rotation invariant. Hence, the method can detect both rotating and translating objects in the scene. They have used a discrete neural network containing binary neurons representing the disparity values between the two images.

The model consists of $N_r \times N_c \times (2D_i + 1) \times (2D_j + 1)$ mutually interconnected neurons, where N_r and N_c are the image row and column sizes, respectively. $D_i W$ and $D_j W$ represent the maximum velocities in the i and j directions, where W is the width of a subpixel. $V = (v_{i,j,k,l}, 1 \le i \le N_r, 1 \le j \le N_c, -D_i \le k \le D_i, -D_j \le 1 \le D_j)$ denotes a binary state set of the neural network, with $v_{i,j,k,l}$ (1 for firing and 0 for resting) representing the state of the (i, j, k, l)th neuron. When neuron $v_{i,j,k,l}$ is 1, this means that the velocities in i and j directions are kW and lW at point (i, j), respectively. Every point is represented by $(2D_i + 1) \times (2D_j + 1)$ mutually exclusive neurons; i.e., only one neuron is firing and others are resting. This reflects the uniqueness constraint. Let $T_{i,j,k,l;m,n,p,q}$ denote the strength of the interconnection between neurons (i, j, k, l) and (m, n, p, q). With the assumption of symmetry, we get:

$$T_{i,j,k,l;m,n,p,q} = T_{m,n,p,q;i,j,k,l} \tag{8.7}$$

for $1 \le i, \ m \le N_r, \ 1 \le j, \ n \le N_c, \ -D_i \le k, \ p \le D_i, \ -D_j \le l \le D_j$. Zhou and Chellappa (1988a) have assumed the neurons have self-feedback; i.e., $T_{i,j,k,l;i,j,k,l} \ne 0$. In this model, each neuron (i, j, k, l) synchronously receives inputs from all neurons and has a bias input

$$u_{i,j,k,l} = \sum_{m=1}^{N_r} \sum_{n=1}^{N_c} \sum_{p=-D_i}^{D_i} \sum_{q=-D_j}^{D_j} [T_{i,j,k,l;m,n,p,q} v_{m,n,p,q}] + I_{i,j,k,l} \tag{8.8}$$

In order to use the Hopfield network for the optical flow problem, they reformulated the problem of optical flow under the local rigidity assumption as one of minimizing a constrained error function given by Eq. 8.9

$$E = \sum_{i=1}^{N_r} \sum_{j=1}^{N_c} \sum_{k=-D_i}^{D_i} \sum_{l=-D_j}^{D_i} \left(A\{[k_{11}(i,j) - k_{12}(i\Theta k, j\Theta l)]^2 \right.$$

$$\left. + [k_{12}(i,j) - k_{22}(i\Theta k, j\Theta l)]^2\} + [g_1(i,j) - g_2(i\Theta k, j\Theta l)]^2 \right) v_{i,j,k,l}$$

$$+ B/2 \sum_{i=1}^{N_r} \sum_{j=1}^{N_c} \sum_{k=-D_i}^{D_i} \sum_{l=-D_i}^{D_i} \sum_{s \in S} [v_{i,j,k,l} - v_{(i,j)\Theta s,k,l}]^2 \tag{8.9}$$

where $k_{11}(i, j)$ and $k_{12}(i \Theta k, j \Theta l)$ are the principal curvatures of the first image, $k_{12}(i, j)$ and $k_{22}(i \Theta k, k \Theta l)$ are the principal curvatures of the second image, $g_1(i, j)$ and $g_2(i \Theta k, j \Theta l)$ are the intensity values of the first and second images, respectively, and A and B are constants. S is an index set excluding $(0, 0)$ for all neighbors in the window centered at (i, j), and Θ denotes:

$$f_{a \Theta b} = \begin{cases} f_{a+b} & \text{if } 0 \le a + b \le N_c, N_r \\ 0 & \text{otherwise} \end{cases}$$

The first term in the energy function is to seek velocity values such that all points of two images are matched as closely as possible in a least-squares sense. The second term is the smoothness constraint on the solution. The constant B determines the relative importance of the two terms, and the constant A in the first term determines the relative importance of the intensity values and their principal curvatures to achieve the best results. Zhou and Chellappa have mapped the error function to the energy function of the Hopfield network. As an illustration, the algorithm was tested on globally nonrigid disk images of the size 128×128. By setting $A = 5$, $B = 30$, $D_i = D_j = 30$, and $W = 0.1$, a dense optical flow was obtained after 14 synchronous iterations. Figures 8.1a and 8.1b show the first and the second intensity images of a nonrigid disk; Figure 8.1c shows the estimated optical flow.

Recently, Zhou and Chellappa (1990) have also developed an ANN model for motion perception based on physiological and anatomic findings in the visual system. The network is discrete, parallel, deterministic, and locally connected. A set of velocity-selective binary neurons is used for each point in the image. Motion perception is carried out by neuron evaluation using a parallel updating scheme. The network has two important features. It can accurately locate motion discontinuities, and it can use multiple image frames. Zhou and Chellappa (1990) have developed two algorithms: a batch algorithm and a recursive algorithm. The batch algorithm integrates information from all images simulta-

Figure 8.1. *Two time frames and the corresponding optical flow. (From Zhou and Chellappa, 1988a, with permission. © 1988 IEEE.)*

neously, embedding them into the bias inputs of the network, whereas the recursive algorithm uses a recursive least-squares method to update the bias inputs in the network. For detailed discussion of these algorithms, the reader may refer to the paper by Zhou and Chellappa (1990). The results of their experiments are shown in Figures 8.2 and 8.3. They used two frames of a pick-up truck scene (Figure 8.2). The optical flow computed from the frames is shown in Figure 8.3.

8.4. ESTIMATION OF 3-D MOTION PARAMETERS

A human visual system is predisposed to interpret two-dimensional projections of moving 3-D rigid objects. One related area of work is the reconstruction of a three-dimensional structure when the corresponding points in two dimensions are known. Estimation of various 3-D motion parameters is used in applications such as target tracking and obtaining structures from 2-D views. It is possible to estimate three-dimensional motion parameters of a rigid body from time-sequential perspective views. Tsai and Huang (1981, 1984) have considered two frames at time t_1 and t_2. To estimate the motion parameters they used the imaging system model as shown in Figure 8.4.

Let (x, y, z) = object space coordinates at time t_1, (x', y', z') = object space coordinates at time t_2, (x_p, y_p) = image plane coordinates at time t_1, (x'_p, y'_p),

Figure 8.2. *A sequence of the pickup truck scene. (From Zhou and Chellappa, 1990, with permission. © 1990 IEEE.)*

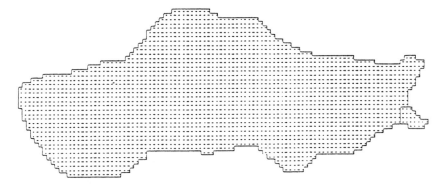

Figure 8.3. *Flow field computed from two frames. (From Zhou and Chellappa, 1990, with permission. © 1990 IEEE.)*

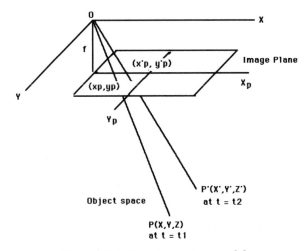

Figure 8.4. *Imaging system model.*

and = image plane coordinates at time t_2. From Figure 8.4 we have

$$x_p = f(x/z)$$

$$x'_p = f(x'/z')$$

$$Y_p = f(y/z)$$

$$Y'_p = f(y'/z') \tag{8.10}$$

They assumed that from time t_1 to time t_2 the three-dimensional object underwent translation, rotation, and linear deformation; then the coordinates

(x, y, z) and (x', y', z') are related by

$$\begin{pmatrix} x' \\ y' \\ z' \end{pmatrix} S \begin{pmatrix} x \\ y \\ z \end{pmatrix} + R \begin{pmatrix} x \\ y \\ z \end{pmatrix} + \begin{pmatrix} \Delta x \\ \Delta y \\ \Delta z \end{pmatrix} \tag{8.11}$$

where

$$S = \begin{pmatrix} s_{11} & s_{12} & s_{13} \\ s_{21} & s_{22} & s_{23} \\ s_{31} & s_{32} & s_{33} \end{pmatrix}$$

$$R = \begin{pmatrix} 0 & -\Psi_3 & \Psi_2 \\ \Psi & 0 & -\Psi_1 \\ -\Psi_2 & \Psi_1 & 0 \end{pmatrix}$$

where $\Psi_1 = n_1 \phi_1$, $\Psi_2 = n_2 \phi_2$, $\Psi_3 = n_3 \phi_3$, $(\Delta x, \Delta y, \Delta z)$ represents the amount of translation, S is the linear deformation matrix, and R is the rotation matrix; the rotations are given by (ϕ_1, ϕ_2, ϕ_3), and the corresponding directional cosines are given by (n_1, n_2, n_3).

Equation 8.11 represents an affine transformation

$$\begin{pmatrix} x' \\ y' \\ x' \end{pmatrix} = \begin{pmatrix} b_{11} & b_{12} & b_{13} \\ b_{21} & b_{22} & b_{23} \\ b_{31} & b_{32} & b_{33} \end{pmatrix} \begin{pmatrix} x \\ y \\ z \end{pmatrix} + \begin{pmatrix} \Delta x \\ \Delta y \\ \Delta z \end{pmatrix} \tag{8.12}$$

Conversely, the affine transformation in Eq. 8.12 can be decomposed into the S and R matrices. Tsai and Huang (1981) have used these mapping equations to estimate the three-dimensional motion parameters of a rigid planar patch from two sequential perspective views. They have defined eight pure parameters, $a_1, a_2, \ldots, a_8$, that are unique for the given mapping from the (x_p, y_p) space onto the (x'_p, y'_p) space

$$x'_p = (a_1 x_p + a_2 y_p + a_3)/(a_7 x_p + a_8 y_p + 1)$$

$$y'_p = (a_4 x_p + a_5 y_p + a_6)/(a_7 x_p + a_8 y_p + 1) \tag{8.13}$$

To evaluate the eight pure parameters we need the coordinates of at least eight matching points in the two images. The eight pure parameters can be obtained by using a least-squares solution method. Tsai and Huang (1981) have shown that the solution is unique and have given a method to evaluate these pure parameters. The motion parameters then are obtained by solving a sixth-degree polynomial relationship.

Broida and Chellappa (1991) have also considered the problem of estimating the kinematics and structure of a rigid object from a sequence of monocular images and developed a model-based approach. They assumed the object to be rigid and the motion to be smooth. Their approach provides a great deal of flexibility by allowing the use of arbitrarily many image frames and feature points. In their experiment they used real images of moving objects in the 3-D space. They estimated 28 unknown translational and rotational motion and structural parameters using 12 images and seven feature points. In their experiment they used the frames of the Bottle images. The Bottle image frames and the corresponding trajectories are shown in Figures 8.5 and 8.6, respectively. They have compared the actual and estimated parameters. The experimental and analytical results presented by them demonstrate the feasibility of the model-based approach.

8.5. NEURAL NETWORKS FOR MOTION ESTIMATION

In order to estimate motion parameters from a sequence of images it is necessary to locate matching points in various frames, but finding the exact location of a match point in various frames is often difficult. Many strategies for locating matching points are described in literature. They include relaxation methods, graph methods, neural network algorithms (Renada and Rosenfeld, 1980; Yen and Huang, 1983; Baird, 1985; Wong, 1986; Shimohara et al., 1990; Sung and Priebe, 1990). In general, three-dimensional motion parameters are uniquely determined by range data for three pairs of asymmetric matched feature points on the object. When data contain noise, more than three pairs of matching points are needed to find motion parameters.

Figure 8.5. *Frames of the bottle image. (From Broida and Chellappa, 1990, with permission. © 1991 IEEE.)*

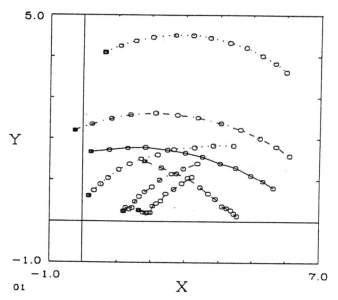

Figure 8.6. *Observed trajectories of feature points in image plane. (From Broida and Chellappa, 1991, with permission. © 1991 IEEE.)*

Zhu et al. (1990) used a Hopfield network to find the best correspondence between three-dimensional point sets. They constructed the energy function of a Hopfield network, the local minima of which correspond to the best matching points. They assumed that the three-dimensional coordinates of a set of feature points on the object at two instances are known and are denoted by $A = \{a_1, a_2, \ldots, a_N\}$, $B = \{b_1, b_2, \ldots, b_M\}$. Let $D_A = \{d(x, i)\}$ and $D_B = \{d(y, j)\}$ be distance matrices of the size $M \times M$ and $N \times N$, respectively. For rigid motion, the distance $D_A(x, i)$ will match the distance $D_B(y, j)$ if the two points match. The correspondence can be found under this constraint. For each point in set A, there are M possible points in set B, but no point in one set is allowed to correspond to more than one point in the other set. Therefore, there are $(M + 1)!/(M - N + 1)!$ possible correspondence relations. Among $(M + 1)!/(M - N + 1)!$ possible matrices, we want to find the one matrix that represents the best match. They have constructed an $M \times N$ permutation matrix V whose rows refer to point set B and columns refer to point set A, such that

$$v_{xi} = \begin{cases} 1 & \text{if point } x \text{ in set } B \text{ matches point } i \text{ in set } A \\ 0 & \text{otherwise} \end{cases}$$

From the above discussion we know that there is no more than one element whose value equals 1 for each row and column for this matrix. Among $(M + 1)!/(M - N + 1)!$ possible matrices, we want to find the matrix that represents the best match. The energy function can be constructed as follows:

$$E = A/2 \sum_{x=1}^{M} \sum_{\substack{i=1 \\ i \neq j}}^{N} \sum_{j=1}^{N} v_{xi} v_{xj}$$

$$+ B/2 \sum_{i=1}^{N} \sum_{x=1, y \neq x}^{M} \sum_{y=1}^{M} v_{xi} v_{yi}$$

$$+ C/2 \sum_{x=1}^{M} \sum_{i=1}^{N} (v_{xi} - N_1)^2$$

$$+ D/2 \sum_{\substack{x=1 \\ y \neq x}}^{M} \sum_{y=1}^{M} \sum_{\substack{i=1 \\ j \neq i}}^{N} \sum_{j=1}^{N} v_{xi} v_{yj} |D_A(x, y) - D_B(i, j)| \qquad (8.14)$$

In Eq. 8.14, the first term equals zero if and only if there is no more than one 1 in each row of V; the second term equals zero if and only if there is no more than one 1 at each column of V; the third terms equals zero if and only if there are N_1 1s in the matrix V and the fourth term refers to the rigidity constraint. Obviously, V represents the best match when E reaches the minimum. The energy function for a Hopfield network is given by (Hopfield and Tank, 1985)

$$E = -\frac{1}{2} \sum_{x=1}^{N} \sum_{i=1}^{N} \sum_{y=1}^{N} \sum_{j=1}^{N} T_{xi, yj} v_{xi} v_{yj} - \sum_{x=1}^{N} \sum_{i=1}^{N} v_{xi} I_{xi} \qquad (8.15)$$

Let v_{ij} be the output of the neuron (i, j); comparing Eq. 8.14 and 8.15, we get

$$T_{xi, yj} = -A\delta_{xy}(1 - \delta_{ij}) - B\delta_{ij}(1 - \delta_{xy})$$

$$- C - D(1 - \delta_{xy})(1 - \delta_{ij})|D_A(x, y) - D_B(i, j)|$$

$$I_{xi} = CN_1 \qquad (8.16)$$

In Eq. 8.16 the first term $T_{xi, yi}$ refers to inhibitory connections within each row, the second term refers to inhibitory connections within each column, the third refers to global inhibition, and the fourth is a data term. Stable state solutions of the network give the best match. Zhu et al. (1990) have developed a simulation of the system and have used it to match N points in one set to another set.

8.6. STEREO VISION

Perception of depth is a central problem in machine vision. Human visual systems perceive three-dimensional spatial relationships effortlessly. One of the methods of depth perception is binocular stereopsis in which two images recorded from different perspectives are used. The stereo vision system allows us to recover information about three-dimensional coordinates of objects. Computational solution for stereo vision involves image acquisition, camera modeling, feature detection, image matching, depth determination, and interpolation (Barnard and Fishcer, 1982).

Stereoscopic images may be recorded from viewing locations and directions that are slightly different or that are radically different. The most important factor affecting image acquisition is the specific application for which stereo computations are intended. Applications of stereo computation involve interpretation of aerial photographs for automated cartography, guidance, and obstacle avoidance for automatic vehicle control. Different applications involve different kinds of scenes. Many computer-based approaches for stereoscopic vision have been developed in practice (Marr and Poggio, 1976; Grimson and Marr, 1979; Barnard and Thompson, 1980; Baker and Binford, 1981; Barnard and Fischler, 1982; Ballard and Brown, 1982; Mohan and Nevatia, 1989).

The key problem in stereo computation is to find corresponding points in stereo images. Corresponding points are the projections of a single point in a three-dimensional space. The difference in positions of two corresponding points in their respective positions is called the disparity and is a function of both the position of the point in space and the position, orientation, and physical characteristics of the stereo cameras. When these camera parameters are known, depth information can be extracted with the help of the camera model, which is a representation of the important geometrical and physical attributes of the stereo camera. A typical camera configuration used in aerial photography is shown in Figure 8.7 (Rao, et al., 1981). Here, O represents the origin of the world coordinate system. O_1 and O_2 represent the perspective viewpoints or camera locations. For stereo images both cameras are located at the same height; however, they are separated in the x direction. IP_1 and IP_2 represent the image planes. The coordinates of point P in the world coordinate system are given by (X, Y, Z). (x_1, y_1) and (x_2, y_2) represent the coordinates of projections of the point P in the planes IP_1 and IP_2, respectively. Figure 8.7 can be simplified to Figure 8.8, from which we get

$$x_1/f = X/(h - Z) \tag{8.17}$$

$$x_2/f = (B - X)/(h - Z) \tag{8.18}$$

where h represents the height of the projection centers from the ground, B represents the separation of the projection centers in the x direction, and f represents the focal length. By subtracting Eq. 8.17 from Eq. 8.18, we get

$$(x_2 - x_1)/f = B/(h - Z)$$

or

$$Z = h - Bf/(x_2 - x_1) \tag{8.19}$$

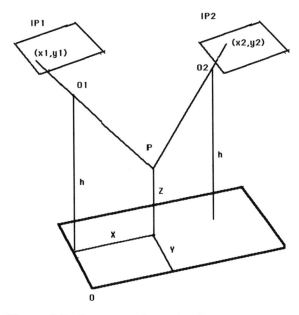

Figure 8.7. *Camera configuration for stereo images.*

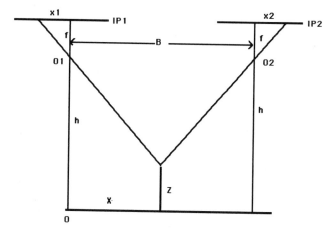

Figure 8.8. *Simplified camera configuration diagram.*

Eq. 8.19 indicates that if the difference between the corresponding image coordinates x_2 and x_1 can be determined, and the baseline (B) and focal length (f) are known, Z can be calculated. The most difficult task in using Eq. 8.19 is to find two corresponding points in the different images of the same scene.

In order to extract three-dimensional information, we need to locate corresponding matching points in the two images. Areas with nearly homogeneous

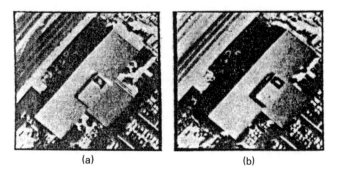

(a)   (b)

Figure 8.9. Stereo pair images. *(From Mohan and Nevatia, 1989, with permission. © 1989 IEEE.)*

brightness cannot be matched with confidence. One needs to use some form of selective feature detection before matching. One way to do this is to select areas that have high image intensity variance. Criteria such as the gray value difference or autocorrelation function have been used for matching. Features used for matching may vary in their size and orientation, and include points, lines, and polygons. One advantage of point-like features is that they can be matched without concern for perspective directions. In area matching, regular-sized neighborhoods of pixels are the basic units that are matched. In feature matching, features such as edges, vertices of linear structures, corners of peaks of buildings, or road surfaces are often used.

Mohan and Nevatia (1989) have suggested perceptual grouping for detecting and describing 3-D objects in complex images. They have considered the problem of matching of structures in aerial images, and proposed collated features as a representation computed by the perceptual organization applied to primitive image elements. The objects are described in terms of component shapes. They have assumed that the individual shape components are well formed and are composed of simpler individual descriptions. The collated features form small local structure descriptions that can then give global object descriptions. As an illustration they have considered aerial images of buildings wherein roof shapes are decomposed into rectangles. The images they considered are shown in Figure 8.9a and 8.9b. Features selected and the 3-D model are shown in Figures 8.10 and 8.11, respectively.

8.7. STEREOPSIS WITH NEURAL NETWORKS

In a human vision system depth perception is achieved by stereoscopic images. Many neural networks architectures have been suggested in practice (Marr and Poggio, 1976; Stewart and Dyer, 1988; Sun et al., 1988; Zhou and Chellappa, 1990). Marr and Poggio (1976) have considered the task of stereopsis from

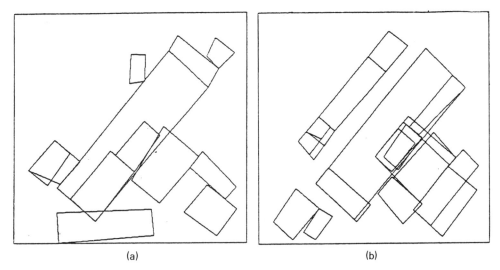

(a)   (b)

Figure 8.10. *Selected features. (From Mohan and Nevatia, 1989, with permission. © 1989 IEEE.)*

Figure 8.11. *Estimated 3-D view. (From Mohan and Nevatia, 1989, with permission. © 1989 IEEE.)*

random dot stereograms and used the uniqueness and continuity constraints for matching. Recently Sun et al. (1988) constructed a high-order recursive network for stereopsis vision from random dot stereograms; in their algorithm the connection weights of the network are learned through the Hebbian rule. Their results confirm the uniqueness and continuity constraints that Marr and Poggio (1976) first postulated to be the working principle of the stereopsis network. Figures 8.12a and 8.12b show two random dot images of left and right edges

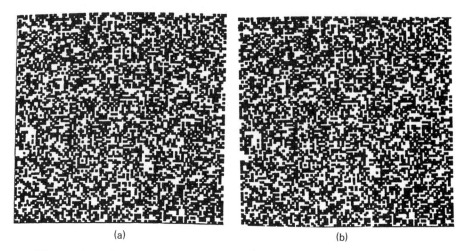

(a)   (b)

Figure 8.12. *Random dot stereograms. (From Mohan and Nevatia, 1988, with permission. © 1988 IEEE.)*

(Julesz, 1971; Sun et al., 1988). Each has 100×100 pixels with an equal probability ($p = 0.5$) to be white and black. The actual 3-D image is shown in Figure 8.13. The uniqueness constraint says that in any given direction we see only one image surface, and the continuity constraint says that the surface is usually continuous. They have shown that these principles can be used to update connection weights in a learning process. The convergence of the network is guaranteed.

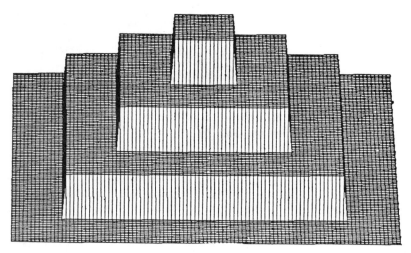

Figure 8.13. *Perspective view for the stereogram. (From Sun et al., 1988, with permission. © 1988 IEEE.)*

Many algorithms for matching have been proposed, each of which uses constraints to help select valid matches. Each of the constraints fails in some circumstances. To address this problem, Stewart and Dyer (1988) have suggested a connectionist model for stereo vision using the general support algorithm, which considers edges in the images and makes use of multiple constraints. The iterations of the network allow the constraints to interact cooperatively to select the most valid match. They considered the uniqueness, intensity, and orientation similarity of edges, multiresolution edges, figure continuity, disparity gradient, and Gaussian support constraints.

8.8. SUMMARY

Human vision systems are sensitive to moving objects. Estimating motion parameters involves analyzing sequences of images. The distribution of apparent velocities of motion of brightness patterns is called the optical flow. Conventional approaches for estimating the optical flow are either intensity based or token based. The basic idea in estimating the optical flow is that the time rate of change of intensity can be expressed as a function of the spatial rate of change of intensity and spatial velocities. The problem of calculating the optical flow can be formulated as an optimization problem. Conventional as well as neural network methods of calculating the optical flow are described in this chapter. A sequence of images can also be used to determine 3-D structures. It is often possible to model the imaging system that related 3-D coordinates in the object space to 2-D coordinates in the image space. A camera model along with the sequence of images can be used to estimate 3-D structures and motion parameters. A camera model is also used to estimate depth information from stereo images. Conventional methods as well as ANN models for stereo image analysis with illustrative examples are also discussed in the chapter.

REFERENCES

Baird, H. S. (1985). *Model-Based Image Matching Using Location.* The MIT Press, Cambridge, MA.

Baker, H. H., and Binford, T. O. (1981). Depth from edge- and intensity-based stereo. *Proceedings of the Seventh International Joint Conference on Artificial Intelligence*, pp. 631–636.

Ballard, D. H., and Brown, C. M. (1982). *Computer Vision.* Prentice Hall, Engelwood Cliffs, NJ.

Barnard, S. T., and Thompson, W. B. (1980). Disparity analysis of images. *IEEE Transactions on Pattern Analysis and Machine Intelligence* 2:330–340.

Barnard, S. T., and Fischler, M. A. (1982). Computation stereo. *Computing Surveys* 14:553–572.

Broida, T. J., and Chellappa, R. (1991). Estimating the kinematics and structure of a rigid object from a sequence of monocular images. *IEEE Transactions on Pattern Analysis and Machine Intelligence* 13:497–512.

Grimson, W. E. L., and Marr, D. (1979). A computer implementation of a theory of human stereo vision. *Proceedings of Image Understanding Workshop, Palo Alto*, pp. 41–47. April Science Application, Arlington, VA.

Hopfield, J. J., and Tank, J. J. (1985). Neural computation of decision in optimization problem. Biological Cybernetics 52:141–152.

Horn, B. K. P. (1986). *Robot Vision*. The MIT Press, Cambridge, MA.

Horn, B. K. P., and Schunck, B. G. (1981). Determining optical flow. *Artificial Intelligence* 17:185–203.

Julesz, B. (1971). *Foundations of Cyclopean Perception*. University of Chicago Press, Chicago.

Limb, J. O., and Murphy, J. A. (1975). Estimating the velocity of moving objects from television signals. *Computer Graphics and Image Processing* 4:311–329.

Marr, D., and Poggio, T. (1976). Cooperative computation of stereo disparity. *Science* 194:283–287.

Mohan, R., and Nevatia, R. (1989). Using perceptual organization to extract 3D structures. *IEEE Transactions on Pattern Analysis and Machine Intelligence* 11:1121–1139.

Nagel, H. H. (1983). Displacement vectors derived from second order intensity variations in image sequence. *Computer Graphics and Image Processing* 21:85–117.

Penna, M. A., and Wu, J. (1991). Recovery of shape and motion parameters for polyhedron like objects. *Proceedings of Symposium on Applied Computing, Kansas City*, pp. 448–456.

Rao, K. R., Kulkarni, A. D., and Chennaiah, G. C. (1981). On stereo pair decomposition of Landsat imagery. *Journal of Photo Interpretation and Remote Sensing* 9:45–48.

Renada, S., and Rosenfeld, A. (1980). Pattern matching by relaxation. *Pattern Recognition* 12:269–275.

Shimohara, K., et al. (1990). Back-propagation networks for event-driven temporal sequence processing. *Proceedings of International Joint Conference on Neural Networks*, Vol. I, pp. 665–672.

Stewart, C. V., and Dyer, C. R. (1988). A connectionist model for stereo vision. *Proceedings of International Joint Conference on Neural Networks, San Diego*, Vol. 4, pp. 215–223.

Sun, G. Z., et al. (1988). Learning stereopsis with neural networks. In: *Proceedings of the International Joint Conference on Neural Networks, San Diego*, Vol. 4, pp. 345–355.

Sung, C. H., and Priebe, C. E. (1990). Temporal pattern recognition. In: *Proceedings of International Joint Conference on Neural Networks, San Diego*, Vol. 1, pp. 689–696.

Tsai, R. Y., and Huang, T. S. (1981). Estimating three-dimensional motion parameters of a rigid planar patch. *IEEE Transactions on Acoustics, Speech, and Signal Processing* 29:1147–1152.

Tsai, R. Y., et al. (1982). Estimating three-dimensional parameters of a rigid planar patch, II: Singular value decomposition. *IEEE Transactions on Acoustics, Speech, and Signal Processing* 30:525–534.

Tsai, R. Y., and Huang, T. S. (1984). Uniqueness destination of three dimensional motion parameters on rigid objects with curved surfaces. *IEEE Transactions on Pattern Analysis and Machine Intelligence* 6:13–37.

Wong, A. K. C. (1986). An algorithm for constellation matching. *Proceedings of the 8th International Conference on Pattern Recognition*, Vol. I, pp. 546–554.

Yen, B. L., and Huang, T. S. (1983). Determining 3-D motion and structure of a rigid body using the spherical projection. *Computer Vision, Graphics, and Image Processing* 21:21–32.

Zhou, Y. T., and Chellappa, R. (1988a). Computation of optical flow using a neural network. *Proceedings of International Joint Conference on Neural Networks, San Diego,* Vol. II, pp. 71–78.

Zhou, Y. T., and Chellappa, R. (1988b). Stereo matching using a neural network. *Proceedings of International Conference on Acoustics, Speech, and Signal Processing,* New York.

Zhou, Y. T., and Chellappa, R. (1990). A network for motion perception. *Proceedings of International Joint Conference on Neural Networks, San Diego,* Vol. II, pp. 875–884.

Zhu, P. Y., et al. (1990). Motion estimation based on point correspondence using a neural network. *Proceedings of International Joint Conference on Neural Networks, San Diego,* Vol. II, pp. 869–874.

9

Neurocomputing

9.1. INTRODUCTION

The new approach for information processing based on the implementation and execution of neural algorithms is called neurocomputing. Neurocomputing is the technological discipline concerned with parallel, distributed, adaptive information-processing systems that develop information-processing capabilities for an information environment (Hecht-Nielsen, 1990). It represents a fundamental shift in computer architecture.

Scientists and engineers have always dreamed of building a machine that mimics the human brain. Conventional computers are based on the Von Neumann approach in which one instruction is executed at a time. The Von Neumann approach has been extended with the introduction of pipelining, array processing, and multiprocessing. In traditional computers, steps involved in the execution of an instruction are fetch, decode, operand fetch, operand decode, and instruction execution.

Parallel processors are still limited in their ability to solve real-time problems in such areas as vision, pattern matching, optimization, speech recognition, and associative storage and retrieval. Neural network researchers are studying the biological properties of the human brain. They are not particularly interested in how the brain works but are interested in designing a new computer that does useful tasks the brain can do by modeling it after the brain itself. Neural network algorithms are basically parallel, distributed in nature. Artificial neural network architectures can take different forms: an electronic, optical, electrooptical, or software simulation. Optical methods for implementation of ANN models have been described (Farhat et al., 1985; Wasserman, 1989). ANN models and algorithms are often implemented and tested on a general-purpose computer. A software simulation of an ANN model on a single processor machine does not exploit the parallel processing capabilities of the neural network model. However, software simulations are useful in developing and testing new algorithms.

Neurocomputing has been in existence a long time. The first successful neurocomputer, the Mark I Perceptron, was built by Rosenblatt in the 1950s (Rosenblatt, 1958); it functioned as a character recognizer. Today a number of neurocomputers are available in practice. Many of them have been configured as coprocessors to standard serial computers. A neurocomputer coprocessor board looks much like any other circuit board, and it is often connected to a host through a shared data bus or standard peripheral interconnection PC bus, Ethernet, or DRV-11. A few neurocomputers, notably those developed at IBM, Texas Instruments, and TRW, can implement several classes of neural networks. Researchers are also trying to develop VLSI chips for neural network implementation.

Both analog and digital implementations are available in practice. Carver Mead (1989) has shown that elementary operations found in the nervous system can be realized in silicon. Analog circuits can perform computations that are difficult and time-consuming when implemented in conventional digital paradigms. Analog implementations include neural network systems from custom analog VLSI "building block" chips developed at California Institute of Technology (Eberhardt et al., 1989), a general-purpose analog neural computer (Mueller et al., 1989), a VLSI image processor using analog programmable synapses and neurons (Lee et al., 1990), and the Lockheed programmable analog neural network processor (Fisher et al., 1990). The main reason to use analog circuits to simulate neural networks is that only a small number of circuit elements are required to simulate a neuron. Although digital circuits require a larger number of circuit elements, it is much easier to implement digital circuits in VLSI. Examples of digital neural network simulators include a digital neurochip (Hirai et al., 1989), a 5-inch wafer-scale neural network LSI developed at Hitachi, Ltd. (Yasunaga et al., 1990), and the X1 architecture by Adaptive Solutions (Hammerstrom, 1990). Some of these neural network processors are described in the following sections.

9.2. DIGITAL NEURAL NETWORK PROCESSORS

Many coprocessors that function as servers for a host computer are available in practice (Hecht-Nielsen, 1988, 1990). Most of these coprocessors have been implemented using commercially available digital signal-processing chips. Examples of these include the Mark III and Mark IV neurocomputers developed at TRW Inc., the Delta floating point processor, the Anza plus, and the X1 architecture. Many researchers have preferred the digital approach for VLSI and wafer-scale integration (WSI) implementation of neural network architectures over the analog approach. Digital neural network implementations are discussed below.

The Mark IV was developed in 1984 with funding from DARPA. The design principles of the Mark IV were similar to that of the Mark III, which consisted of eight 68010-based single-board computers mounted on a broadcast bus back plane. The Mark III functioned as a coprocessor to a Digital Equipments Corporation's (DEC's) micro-VAX as a host. The block diagram of the Mark III is shown in Figure 9.1. The purpose of designing the Mark IV project was to explore a number of ideas for parallel implementation of neural network approaches with an individual processing resource. This neurocomputer was highly pipelined. It had a capacity of 250,000 processing elements and 5,500,000 connections, and a speed of 5 million connections per second (with learning) for any neural network it could implement. The Mark IV was constructed out of signal-processing building blocks (memories, multiplexers, adders, and shifters), TTL logic parts, and memory parts.

Hitachi Ltd. has fabricated a wafer-scale integration (WSI) neural network with 576 neurons interconnected to each other on a 5-inch silicon wafer by using $0.8\text{-}\mu\text{m}$ CMOS (Yasunaga et al., 1990). This WSI neural network can be connected with a host computer and can be used for a wide range of artificial neural network models. Larger ANN models can be realized by simply connecting WSIs. In order to interconnect all of the N neurons in a Hopfield network, $N \times N$ synapses are required. Thus, more than 10,000 synapses are needed in a network for more than 100 neurons. The present hardware does not have sufficient capacity for this large number of synapses. To overcome this difficulty

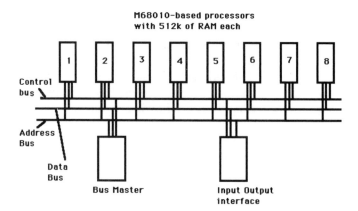

Figure 9.1. *Block diagram of a Mark III neurocomputer.*

Yasunaga et al. (1990) created connections between neurons by time-sharing communication using a digital bus. In this architecture one neuron needs only one synapse. Consequently, only N synapses are needed to interconnect all N neurons, and each neuron has its own address. All neurons are interconnected; therefore, a general-purpose neural network such as a Hopfield net or back-propagation can be developed with the WSI neural network chip. The application software could be developed independently of the WSI hardware. The support software is a set of functions described in the C language and consists of three hierarchical layers. The WSI neural network chip is shown in Figure 9.2.

Adaptive Solutions Inc. has developed a VLSI architecture called the X1 architecture for implementing ANN models (Hammerstrom, 1990). The X1 architecture is one that can be considered a general-purpose "microprocessor" of neurocomputing. The X1 chip consists of a number of simple digital-signal-processor-like processing nodes (PNs) operating in a single-instruction/multiple-data (SIMD) configuration. A broadcast interconnect is used to create inexpensive high-performance communication. The X1 system consists of a linear array of PNs. Each PN is a simple arithmetic processor with its own local memory, and the array is sequenced by a single controller. Each PN executes the same instruction at each clock cycle using single-instruction/multiple-data (SIMD) stream processing.

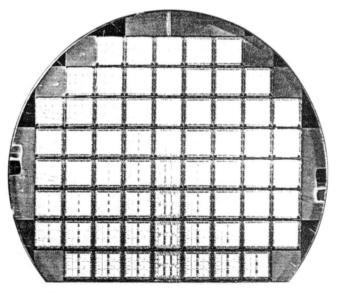

Figure 9.2. *Photograph of the fabricated WSI neural network chip. (From Yasunaga et al., 1990, with permission. © 1990 IEEE.)*

Each PN is connected to three global buses: the input data bus, the command bus, and the output bus. The PN architecture is optimized for traditional neural network applications but is general enough to implement any neural network algorithm and many feature-extraction computations including classical digital signal-processing and pattern recognition techniques. Most neural networks can be created out of one or more basic two-layer systems that perform a matrix vector multiplication to produce an output vector. A layer of connection nodes (CNs) is typically emulated by a layer of PNs. The X1 chip is the first implementation of the X family; it has 64 PNs, and each PN has 4096 bytes of weight storage. Each processor node has internal units connected via control signals and several data buses, as shown in Figure 9.3. The PN consists of an input unit, logic shifter, register file, multiplier, adder, weight memory, and output buffer. This one chip can store 262,144 eight-bit connections. The X1 chip is well suited for use in a variety of research and industrial applications. It represents the first upwardly compatible line of neurocomputer architectures.

Hirai et al. (1989) have fabricated a digital neurochip with the following properties: (1) as with real neurons, inputs and outputs of neurons are represented by impulse densities; (2) each synapse transforms the input impulse density to a density proportional to the synaptic weight, which has 64 levels of modifiable strength; (3) since each neuron operates asynchronously, neural networks of any scale can be developed by simply connecting neurochips, (4) synaptic weights and internal potentials of each neuron can be set and monitored by a control computer; (5) a wide range of neural networks can be

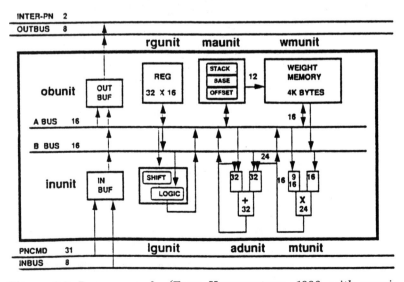

Figure 9.3. *Processor node. (From Hammerstrom, 1990, with permission. © 1990 IEEE.)*

simulated by the neurochips in combination with the computer. A single neuron consists of synaptic circuits, dendrites and cell body circuits. A synaptic circuit transforms the input impulse density to a density proportional to a synaptic weight. A dendrite circuit consists of simple OR gates that spatially sum the impulses from the synaptic circuits connected to the dendrite circuit. The cell body circuit performs the temporal summation. The circuit structure of the digital neurochip is shown in Figure 9.4.

The digital neurochip mounted on a 240-pin grid array is shown in Figure 9.5. There are six neurons in a chip. They are mutually connected by both excitatory

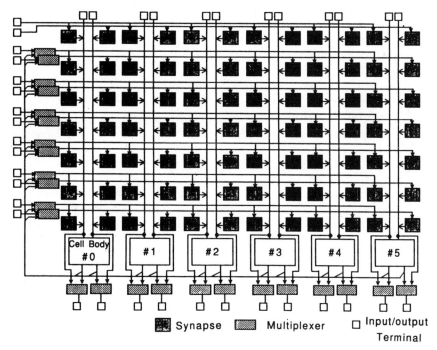

Figure 9.4. *Circuit structure of a digital neurochip. (From Hirai et al., 1989, with permission. © 1989 IEEE.)*

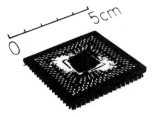

Figure 9.5. *Digital neurochip mounted on a 240-pin grid array. (From Hirai et al., 1989, with permission. © 1989 IEEE.)*

and inhibitory synapses. There are two kinds of outputs from each cell body circuit. One is for standard impulse density and the other is for double density to make the synaptic strength greater than 1. There are six excitatory and six inhibitory synaptic pathways. There are two external input lines. In total there are six neurons with 42 excitatory and 42 inhibitory synapses in a chip. In addition, there is an interface circuit through which the control computer can read and write the up/down counters of six cell body circuits, 84 synaptic weight registers, and control registers. The number of gates required to implement these circuits in a chip is about 18,000. A wide range of neural networks including the back-propagation, Hopfield type, and many others have been simulated using the digital neurochips. With 72 chips, a neural network composed of 54 neurons fully interconnected by 5,832 synapses has been constructed. The processing speed is not affected by the number of chips connected. Hence, the network can be of any scale. A neural network system composed of 72 neurochips is shown in Figure 9.6.

Iwata and Suzumura (1989) have developed an artificial neural network (ANN) accelerator named Neuro-Turbo using a 24-bit digital signal processor (DSP). The Neuro-Turbo is a multiinstruction/multidata (MIMD)-type parallel processor consisting of four DSPs and four dual-port memories (DPM). The

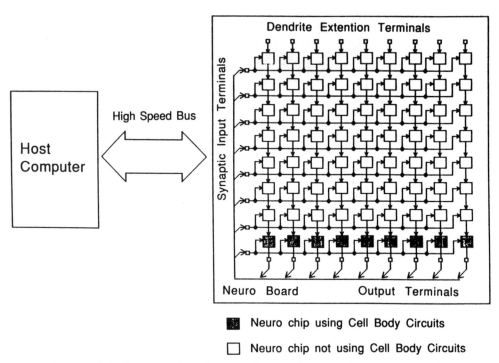

Figure 9.6. *Configuration of a neural network system. (From Hirai et al., 1989, with permission. © 1989 IEEE.)*

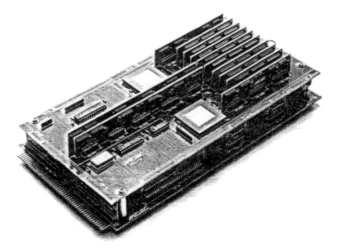

Figure 9.7. *Photograph of a neuroturbo. (From Iwata et al., with permission. © 1989 IEEE.)*

Neuro-Turbo is designed compactly to plug into the extender slots of the NEC personal computer PC98 series (Figure 9.7). Each DSP has its own program memory, working memory, and two dual-port memories. The programs are loaded from the host computer to the program memories. As an illustration, Iwata and Suzumura (1989) implemented the back-propagation learning algorithm on the ring-coupled processors and executed it parallel. A network with 35, 25, and 26 units in the input, hidden, and output units has been implemented. For comparison the same network was simulated on SUN 4/260 workstation. The operation of the Neuro-Turbo was found to be 20 times faster than the simulation on the workstation.

9.3. ANALOG NEUROCOMPUTERS

Human brains derive their efficiency primarily from the analog mode of operation. Analog circuits can perform computations that are difficult or time-consuming when implemented in the conventional digital paradigm. Often simulations of neural networks using digital circuits are slow. Electronic implementations of neural systems based on analog circuits are currently being pursued in a number of laboratories. The basic principles of analog implementations of neural network chips are well described by Mead (1989) in his book *Analog VLSI and Neural Systems*. Mead (1989) has pointed out that a transconductance amplifier computes functions such as *tanh* that are very useful in neural network implementation. He has also shown that we can design networks that can add or subtract currents using Kirchhoff's law, we can multiply two voltage differences using a Gilbert multiplier, and logarithms and exponentials can be computed by the Boltzmann relationship.

One of the common operations a neuron performs is to receive inputs from one or more dendrites and add these inputs to provide a net input. Follower aggregation circuits perform this task (Figure 9.8). The follower implementation of a neural network has great robustness against bad data points. The circuit consists of n follower stages, all driving the single wire labeled V_{out}; V_{out} is the average of the V_i inputs, each input weighted by its transconductance G_i, and is given by

$$V_{out} = \sum_{i=1}^{n} G_i V_i \qquad (9.1)$$

Transconductance amplifiers have a strictly limited current output. This limit is evident in their *tanh* transfer characteristics. The robustness of the collective network is a direct result of this current limitation.

The principles for implementation of a silicon axon are also described in the book. A silicon axon is made up of a number of repeaters connected in cascade. Synapses are central information-processing devices in neural systems. Voltage-dependent conductance devices can be used to develop silicon synapses. Several analog neural network architectures based on these principles are available in practice.

Muller et al. (1989) have suggested an architecture for a general-purpose analog neurocomputer. The machine contains large numbers of neurons, synapses, routing switches, and connection lines. Arrays of these elements are fabricated on a VLSI chip that is mounted on a planar chip. A synapse test chip is shown in Figure 9.9. The machine runs entirely in analog mode. Each neuron chip contains 16 neurons, an analog multiplexer, and the control logic. Connections, synaptic gains, and time constants are set from the central computer manually, or from libraries containing connection architectures for specific tasks. The primary areas of application of such computers include real-time pattern analysis, and robotics. Inputs for the machine can come from sensory transducer arrays such as the electronic retina (Koch, 1989).

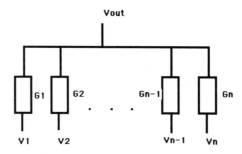

Figure 9.8. Schematic of a follower aggregation circuit.

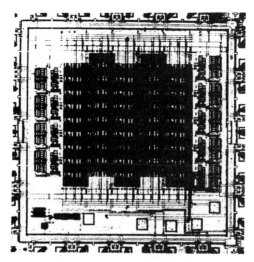

Figure 9.9. *Photograph of a synapse test chip. (From Mueller et al., 1989, with permission. © 1989 IEEE.)*

Lockheed Inc. has developed neural network processors that could be used to study neural network theory and also serve as a massively parallel analog control processor (Fisher et al., 1990). The analog neural network processor consists of 256 operational-amplifier-based neural network circuits with a total of 2048 programmable registers. The registers, which are programmed via an 80286- or 80386-based PC, provide means of training the analog network. The input to the neuron boards can be fed from analog sources or from 12-bit digital sources converted to analog. The heart of the analog network is a digitally programmable register chip. A neuron board is shown in Figure 9.10. A board can be configured to have as few as seven inputs to each of 16 neurons or as many as 128 inputs to a single neuron. The registers (weights) on the board may be reprogrammed at a rate of one per microsecond. The neural network processor has been used to control 69 actuators for a movable mirror.

Several experimental neural network implementations that typically function as direct accelerators for software computations for image-processing applications have been reported. These hardware accelerators consist of main digital processors and associative memories. In most cases, the rich properties of neural networks associated with massively parallel processing using analog neurons and synapses to process digital pictures have not been fully explored yet. To make the neural computing hardware more powerful, the design and implementation of compact and programmable synapses are needed.

Lee et al. (1990) have designed a circuit for a programmable synapse. They used the VLSI neural network circuit for the image restoration problem. The image restoration process essentially finds the improved image x by minimizing

Figure 9.10. *Photograph of a neuron board. (From Fisher et al., 1990, with permission. © 1990 IEEE.)*

the error function ε with respect to the degraded image $\boldsymbol{y}$. The error function is given by

$$\varepsilon = 1/2\|\boldsymbol{y} - \boldsymbol{Hx}\| + \lambda/2\|\boldsymbol{Dx}\| \tag{9.2}$$

where $\|\cdot\|$ is the L_2 norm, $\boldsymbol{H}$ is the blur matrix, λ is a constant, and $\boldsymbol{D}$ is the sharpness matrix. In order to solve the restoration using the Hopfield network, Lee et al. have mapped the error function onto a Hopfield network and minimized the energy function of the network. For VLSI implementation they have partitioned the whole image into subimages of $n \times n$ pixels, and each subimage is processed in a VLSI chip.

9.4. SUMMARY

In this chapter we have discussed neural network implementations. Neural network architectures can take any form: optical, electronic, or electrooptical. In electronic implementation neurocomputers can be designed by analog or digital circuits. Analog implementations are well suited for simulating neurons and synapse circuits and are faster than digital implementations. Digital circuits require a large number of circuit elements. However, digital circuits are easy to design and fabricate. Both approaches have been used in practice to implement ANN models. Examples of both approaches are discussed in the chapter.

REFERENCES

Eberhardt, S., et al. (1989). Design of parallel hardware neural network systems from custom analog VLSI "building blocks" chips. *Proceedings of the International Joint Conference on Neural Networks*, Washington, DC, Vol. 2, pp. 183–190.

Farhat, N. H., et al. (1985). Optical implementation of the Hopfield model. *Applied Optics* 24:1469–1475.

Fisher, W. A., et al. (1990). The Lockheed programmable analog neural network processor. *Proceedings of the International Joint Conference on Neural Networks*, San Diego, Vol. 2, pp. 563–568.

Hammerstrom, D. A. (1990). VLSI architecture for high-performance, low-cost, on-chip learning. *Proceedings of the International Joint Conference on Neural Networks*, San Diego, Vol. II, pp. 537–544.

Hecht-Nielsen, R. (1988). Neurocomputing. *IEEE Spectrum*, March:36–41.

Hecht-Nielsen, R. (1990). *Neurocomputing*. Addison-Wesley, Reading, MA.

Hirai, Y., et al. (1989). A digital neuro-chip with unlimited connectability for large scale neural networks. *Proceedings of the International Joint Conference on Neural Networks, Washington, DC*, Vol. II, pp. 163–169.

Iwata, A., and Suzumura, N. (1989). An artificial neural network accelerator using general purpose 24 bit floating point digital signal processors. *Proceedings of the International Joint Conference on Neural Networks, Washington, DC*, Vol. II, pp. 171–175.

Koch, C. (1989). Seeing chips: Analog-VLSI circuits for computer vision. *Neural Computations* 1:184–200.

Lee, B. W., et al. (1990). VLSI image processors using analog programmable synapses and neurons. *Proceedings of the International Joint Conference on Neural Networks*, San Diego, Vol. II, pp. 575–580.

Mead, C. (1989). *Analog VLSI and Neural Systems*. Addison-Wesley, Reading, MA.

Mueller, P., et al. (1989). A general purpose analog neural computer. *Proceedings of the International Joint Conference on Neural Networks, Washington DC*, Vol. II, pp. 177–182.

Rosenblatt, F. (1958). The perceptron: A probabilistic model for information storage and organization in brain. *Psychology Review* 65:386–408.

Yasunaga, M., et al. (1990). Design fabrication and evaluation of a 5-inch wafer scale neural network LSI composed of 576 digital neurons. *Proceedings of the International Joint Conference on Neural Networks*, San Diego, Vol. II, pp. 527–535.

Wasserman, P. D. (1989). *Neurocomputing: Theory and Practice*. Van Nostrand Reinhold, New York.

10

Applications

10.1. INTRODUCTION

Neural networks represent a powerful and reasonable alternative to traditional approaches for image understanding. Applications of neural networks for image understanding include remote sensing, medical imaging, robot vision, military reconnaissance, cartography, character recognition, fingerprint recognition, and face recognition. Some of these applications are discussed in this chapter.

10.2. REMOTE SENSING

Remote sensing is the science of deriving information about an object from measurements made at a distance from the object. The technique of remote sensing to a great extent relies on the interaction of electromagnetic radiation with matter. Microscopically, the interactions are absorption, reflection, and emission. The remotely measured signal expressed as a function of the wavelength is often referred to as the "spectral signature" of the target object on which the measurements have been made. In principle, spectral signatures are unique; i.e., different objects have different spectral signatures. It would therefore be possible to identify an object from its spectral signature. In brief, this is the principle of multispectral remote sensing, which is a powerful technique for monitoring natural resources and the environment. Remotely sensed spectral measurements can be a source of information for many applications, including agriculture, forestry, mineral resources, hydrology, water resources, geography, cartography, meteorology, and military.

Satellite remote sensing began in earnest with the launching of the first earth resource satellite in 1972 by the National Aeronautics and Space Administration (NASA) of the United States. This was followed by Landsat-2 and Landsat-3 in 1975 and 1978, respectively. Landsat-2 and Landsat-3 carried multispectral scanners (MSS) and return beam vidicon (RBV) sensors. Landsat-4, Landsat-5, and Landsat-6 were launched in 1982, 1983, and 1992, respectively. These satellites, in addition to MSS, have an additional sensor called the thematic mapper (TM). The TM has seven spectral bands of which one is a thermal band. The resolution of the six nonthermal bands is 30 m × 30 m. The spectral bands are shown in Table 10.1.

Multispectral images are often analyzed using conventional statistical techniques. Artificial neural networks (ANNs) represent an alternative to traditional classifiers. Kulkarni and Byars (1991) have used ANN models for multispectral image analysis. They have used the back-propagation (BP) and competitive learning algorithms as supervised and unsupervised classifiers to analyze TM images. A TM scene is usually of the size 5300 scans × 4000 pixels. Conventional methods used for multispectral classification include the maximum-likelihood classifier, minimum-distance classifier, and various clustering techniques.

As an illustration, Kulkarni and Byars (1991) considered a TM scene (#y4018116055, January 1983); the original image for spectral band 5 is shown in Figure 5.7. The scene was analyzed using a three-layer feed-forward network with a BP learning algorithm. The results are shown in Figure 5.8. The same scene was also analyzed using a two-layer feed-forward network with a competitive learning algorithm. In the case of competitive learning, spectral bands 3, 4, 5, and 7 were chosen, as these bands showed the maximum variance and contained the maximum information. The network could recognize only two classes: water and soil. The segmented image with the competitive learning algorithm is shown in Figure 6.7.

Conventional classification techniques are time-consuming because in the conventional classifiers each pixel is tested for all possible classes, and the pixel

TABLE 10.1. *TM SPECTRAL BANDS*

Band Number	Spectral Range (μm)
1	0.45–0.52
2	0.52–0.60
3	0.63–0.69
4	0.76–0.90
5	1.55–1.75
6	10.44–12.56
7	2.08–2.23

is assigned to the class with maximum a posteriori probability. With ANNs once a model is trained the network directly maps the input observation vector to the output category. Thus, for large images ANNs are more suitable than conventional classifiers. Huang and Lippmann (1988) have compared ANN models with conventional classifiers. Eberlein and Yates (1991) have used neural network models for data analysis by a BP learning algorithm in a geological classification system. McClella et al. (1989) have used neural network models with a BP learning algorithm for TM data analysis. Decator (1989) has used ANN models for terrain classification.

A general system for meteorological classification based on a neural network has been developed by the Mitre Bedford Neural Network Research Group of the Mitre Corporation (Smotroff et al., 1990). The system implements a low-level vision system based on a number of biologically plausible theories operating across all input channels. The preprocessing stage is followed by the classification stage. The system generates automated meteorological products in real time. Feature vectors are constructed by appending actual data with derived products. Smotroff et al. (1990) have implemented efficient versions of the boundary counter system (BCS) and the feature counter system (FCS) (Grossberg and Mingolla, 1987) for the purpose of reliably determining coherent regions. The BCS determines boundaries, and FCS constructs regions from them. The regions are used to construct feature vectors for classification. Smotroff et al. (1990) have used 2-D Gabor functions to extract texture features and have employed a BP network as a supervised classifier. Outputs of their sample images from meteorological satellites are shown in Figures 10.1 and 10.2.

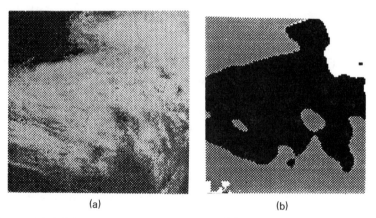

(a)   (b)

Figure 10.1. *Meteorological classification. (a) Raw image. (b) Classified output. (From Smotroff et al., 1990, with permission. © 1990 IEEE.)*

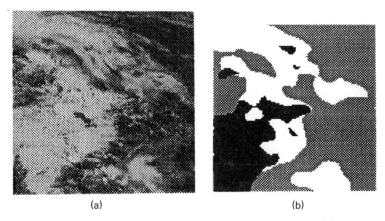

(a)   (b)

Figure 10.2. *Meteorological classification. (a) Raw image. (b) Classified output. (From Smotroff et al., 1990, with permission. © 1990 IEEE.)*

10.3. MEDICAL IMAGE PROCESSING

Conventional statistical techniques have been widely used in practice in the analysis of X-ray, microscopic, and magnetic resonance (MR) images. Neural networks represent a powerful alternative to conventional techniques. Kaufman et al. (1990) have used ANN models for bone fracture healing assessment. Magnetic resonance images have been recently used as a standard diagnostic tool. The accurate and reproducible interpretation of a magnetic resonance image (MRI), as performed by a highly trained physician, remains an extremely time-consuming and costly task. Unlike X-ray images, MRIs permit measurements of three tissue-specific parameters: the spin-spin relaxation tissue (T_2), the spin-lattice relaxation tissue (T_1), and the proton density (PD). Here, each pixel can be represented as a vector in a three-dimensional feature space whose components are the T_1-weighted, T_2-weighted, and weighted PD values. The T_1-weighted, T_2-weighted, and PD images can be treated similarly to spectral band images in a multispectral image analysis. All the classification techniques used in multispectral image analysis can be used for MR images.

Ozkan et al. (1990) have used a three-layer back-propagation network as a supervised classifier to analyze MR images. They used three units in the input layer and four units in the output layer. The three units in the input layer represent the T_1-weighted, T_2-weighted, and PD values for a pixel. The four units in the output layer represent the four tissue types. The segmented images obtained using the neural network classifier and a conventional classifier are shown in Figures 10.3 and 10.4. Neural network models based on boundary counter system (BCS) and feature counter system (FCS) can also be used for medical imaging. Lehar et al. (1990) have used BCS and FCS models for processing MR images. Examples of these are shown in Figure 10.5.

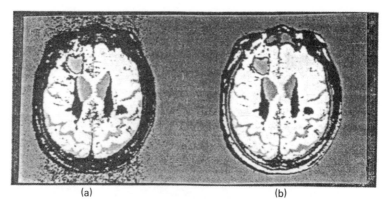

(a)   (b)

Figure 10.3. *Segmented images (pathological case): (a) neural net; (b) maximum likelihood. (From Ozkan et al., 1990, with permission. © 1990 IEEE.)*

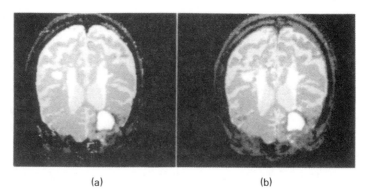

(a)   (b)

Figure 10.4. *Segmented images (normal volunteer): (a) neural net; (b) maximum likelihood. (From Ozkan et al., 1990, with permission. © 1990 IEEE.)*

10.4. FINGERPRINT PROCESSING

It is well known that the human brain outperforms computers when applied to problems such as feature extraction and pattern recognition. One such problem is extraction of minutiae from gray-scale fingerprints. Fingerprints have long been used in identification of individuals because of the well-known fact that each person has a unique fingerprint. The classification is usually performed by noting certain features such as minutiae. Minutiae are places where the fingerprint ridges end or are bifurcated. Conventional approaches for fingerprint analysis include the Fourier transform.

Leung et al. (1990) have developed a system for extraction of minutiae from gray-scale fingerprint images using Gabor filters. A gray-scale image of a typical fingerprint is shown in Figure 10.6, and a small region of a fingerprint with a vertical minutia is shown in Figure 10.7. The Gabor filters are direction sensitive; if one is tuned to edges in the vertical direction, all portions of that figure except the portion immediately surrounding the minutia will closely match the filter and will have equal signal amplitude. A dark spot in the center of a bright surround in these data is therefore a signature of the minutia. The minutia locations are also characterized by regions where there are significant phase

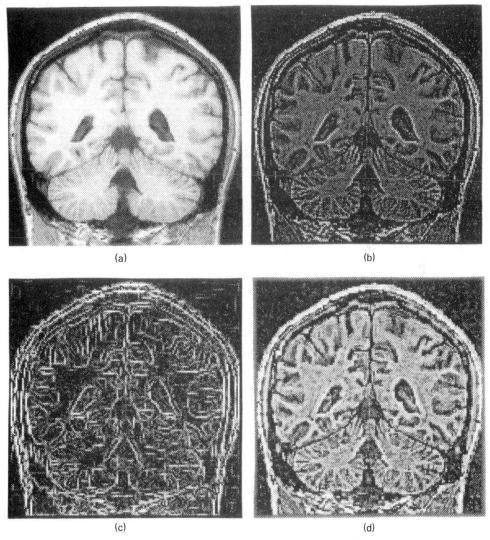

(a)

(b)

(c)

(d)

Figure 10.5. *Application of boundary counter system: (a) original image; (b) direction of counter image; (c) BCS image; (d) FCS image. (From Lehar et al., 1990, with permission. © 1990 IEEE.)*

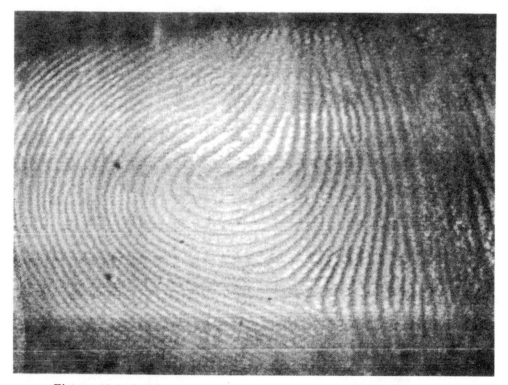

Figure 10.6. *A gray scale image of a typical fingerprint. (From Leung et al., 1990, with permission. © 1990 IEEE.)*

changes. The real output of a zero-degree filter is shown in Figure 10.8. The magnitude and phase of a Gabor-filtered fingerprint image are shown in Figures 10.9 and 10.10, respectively. The final neural network scan of the entire fingerprint is shown in Figure 10.11. The resulting magnitude and phase of filtered images were used successfully to train a BP network to locate and identify minutiae. Leung et al. (1990) could achieve good detection ratios. Their system demonstrated the usefulness of Gabor filters in applications such as fingerprint recognition.

10.5. CHARACTER RECOGNITION

In recent years neural networks have been used for real-time character recognition. Neural networks' parallel algorithms show great promise for providing highly accurate and noise-resistant image recognition applications including character recognition (Omidvar and Wilson, 1991; Jackel et al., 1988). The range of applications for character recognition include postal code reading, automatic data entry, recognition of print and script, automated cartography,

Figure 10.7. *A small region of a fingerprint. (From Leung et al., 1990, with permission. © 1990 IEEE.)*

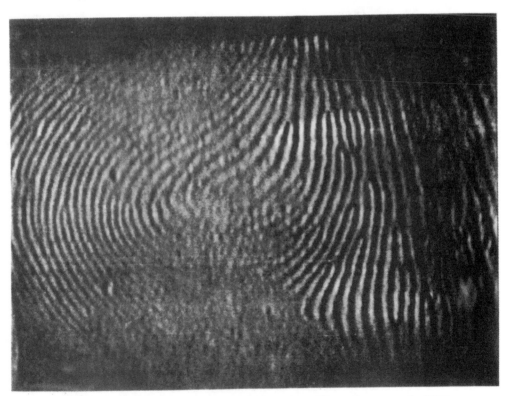

Figure 10.8. *Real output of a 0° Gabor filter. (From Leung et al., 1990, with permission. © 1990 IEEE.)*

banking, and reading services for the blind. Conversion of images of handwritten and machine print characters to computer representation has been studied in detail. Both special purpose hardware and software systems for character recognition have been developed.

Neural networks present an alternative approach for the character recognition problem. One of the critical issues in character recognition is feature selection, as the accuracy of each decision depends on the choice of features. Every character has some features that distinguish it from other characters. Some of the prominent features used for character recognition are loops, holes, strokes, vertical lines, cusps, etc. (Tsuji and Asai, 1984). Most of the existing algorithms involve extensive processing on the image.

The problem of computer recognition of a document is usually broken down into three operations. First, the relevant areas containing the text are located. The global image containing images of one or more characters is broken into images of individual characters. This process is usually referred to as segmentation. These isolated characters form the input for the character recognition system. Rajavelu et al. (1989) have used Walsh functions for extracting features for character recognition. The Walsh functions have been commonly used in signal-processing applications to represent data as a series of orthogonal functions. The number of Walsh functions required to encode image data in an orthogonal series of expansion depends on the accuracy needed for the application. Rajavelu et al. (1989) have used projections in the horizontal and vertical directions and have used the Walsh-Hadamard transform to extract features for character recognition. The feature extraction process resulted in 20 features (expansion coefficients). They then used a three-layer feed-forward network with a BP learning algorithm as a supervised classifier. The BP network had 20 units in the input layer that corresponded to the 20 features extracted in the feature extraction stage. The number of output units in the system represents the number of characters in the standard character set. The system was tested with 20, 30, 40, and 50 units in the hidden layer. The system was used to recognize uppercase alphabets of a Times font. The number of training trials needed for the network to converge was 1215.

Weideman et al. (1989) have also used a BP network for character recognition. They have compared the performance of the BP network with the nearest-neighbor classifier. They used a character set wherein each character is represented by a matrix of the size 32 scans $\times$ 24 pixels. They used features that included the 2-D FT coefficients, geometric moments, and topological features. The topological features included distances from four corners to the first black pixel encountered, the number of loops in the character, the ratio of the energy at the top of the loop to that at the bottom of the loop, the maximum width of the character, etc. They used a three-layer BP network as a classifier. The network contained 100, 90, and 10 units in the input, hidden, and output layers,

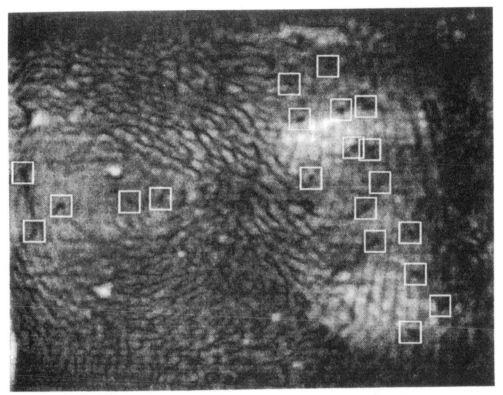

Figure 10.9. *Magnitude of a 0° Gabor filter. (From Leung et al., 1990, with permission. © 1990 IEEE.)*

respectively. They used data from hand-printed numbers generated from 3000 forms from a United States government agency. The character information was digitized and stored in a data base. The data base had approximately 86,000 characters. A training set of 20,000 characters was used to train the network. The characters also were classified by the nearest-neighbor classifier. Weideman et al. (1989) found that the neural network classifier was more efficient than the nearest-neighbor classifier.

Omidvar and Wilson (1991) have suggested a massively parallel implementation of a neural network architecture for character recognition. They used Gabor filters for feature extraction and a BP network as a classifier. They also tried the ART-2 architecture as an unsupervised classifier. Kulkarni and Byars (1991) used the FT domain features with the angular and radial bins for character recognition. As an illustration, they used six types of characters (Figure 10.12). The extracted features were used as an input to a BP network. The network was trained with characters in the first set and was then able to recognize characters in the other sets.

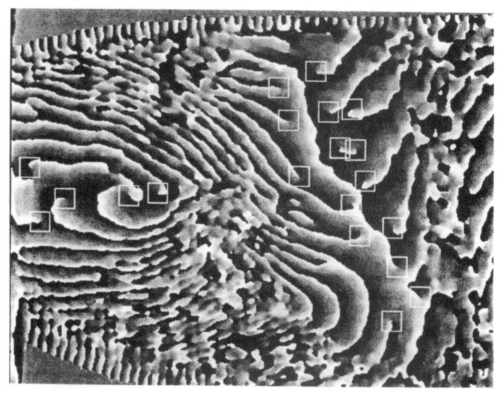

Figure 10.10. *Phase of a 0° Gabor filter. (From Leung et al., 1990, with permission. © 1990 IEEE.)*

10.6. CHARACTERIZATION OF FACES

Recognition of faces is an extremely important skill. The extreme homogeneity of faces, while making it easier to discern them from other objects, greatly complicates the task of recognizing one face as different from another. Conventional methods of face recognition use distances between specific landmarks of the face as features. Fleming and Cottrell (1990) have suggested an approach for face recognition using a neural network. Their model essentially consists of two stages: the feature extraction stage and the recognition stage. They have used a three-layer network with a BP learning algorithm for feature extraction. The network also can be used for image compression (Cottrell and Munro, 1988). The input and output layers in their network are large relative to the hidden layer. This size differential necessitated a more compact representation of the image information at the hidden unit level. By manipulating the ratio of the input/output layer size to the hidden layer size, the necessary data compression is achieved. In the second stage of their recognition system, they used a BP

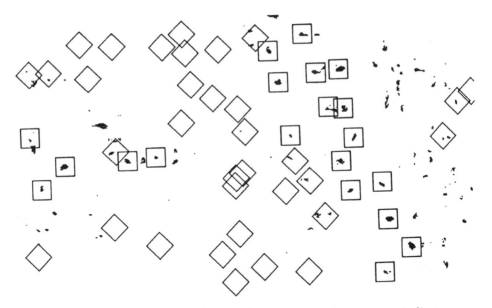

Figure 10.11. *Final neural network output scanning squares indicate minutiae locations. (From Leung et al., 1990, with permission. © 1990 IEEE.)*

network as a supervised classifier. The first stage worked as a large autoassociative network. As an illustration, they used a training set that contained 64 face images. Some of the images are shown in Figure 10.13. The model was found to be highly accurate over a wide variety of stimuli. The classifier output indicated gender, identity, and "faceness" of each input image.

10.7. DATA COMPRESSION

Data compression is basically motivated by reduction of data storage space for storage or transmission. Many conventional methods, including the FFT, DCT, WHT transform, and encoding schemes, are available in practice. Recently neural network algorithms have also been used for data compression (see Figure 10.14). Three-layer feed-forward networks with a BP learning algorithm have been used for data compression. When a three-layer network is adapted for data compression, the number of units in the hidden layer should be smaller than the number of units in the input and output layers. Cottrell and Munro (1988) have shown that a three-layer network in which the input and output layers are large relative to the hidden layer can be used for data compression. Their results demonstrated that by manipulating the ratio of the input/output layer size to the hidden layer size, data compression by a factor of about 8 to 1 can be achieved with little degradation.

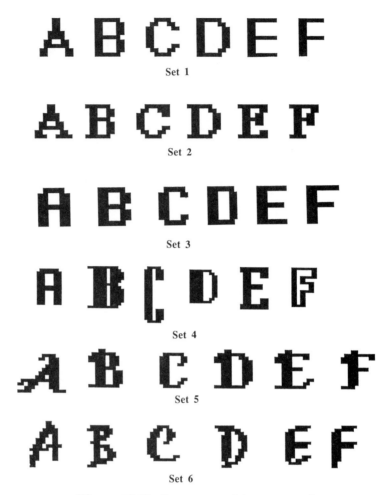

Figure 10.12. *Test patterns (character sets).*

Based on the same principles, Sonehara et al. (1989) have designed a system for data compression using a three-layer network with the BP learning algorithm. The system is divided into two parts: the coder and the decoder. It was simulated on a 512-node processor. The network was trained with a number of training images and was tested with unlearned images. The results are shown in Figures 10.15 and 10.16. Figure 10.15 shows the input and output for learned images, whereas Figure 10.16 shows the input and output for an unlearned image. They have shown that with the increase in the number of hidden-layer units the signal-to-noise ratio (SNR) increases, but the SNR was not as good as those in the conventional schemes. The effects of learning with the DCT coefficients as the initial weights were also investigated and were found to have almost the same SNR characteristics as those obtained by random weights.

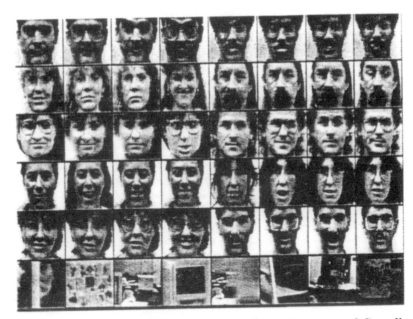

Figure 10.13. *Part of training seg images. (From Fleming and Cottrell, 1990, with permission. © 1990 IEEE.)*

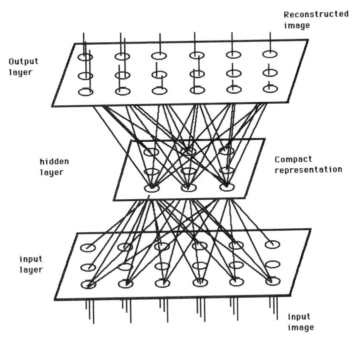

Figure 10.14. *ANN model for data compression.*

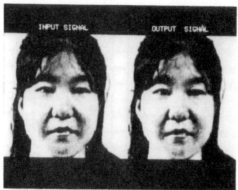

(a) Learned image: SNR =26.98dB,
average SNR =27.12dB

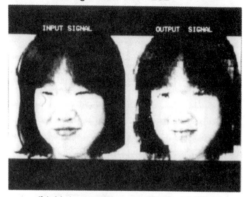

(b) Unlearned image: SNR=14.55dB,
average SNR=14.22dB.

2,000 iterations for each image, 19 learned images,
8-bit quantization, (64,16,64) units.

Figure 10.15. *SNR characteristics of learned images. (From Sonehara et al., 1989, with permission. © 1989 IEEE.)*

10.8. KNOWLEDGE-BASED PATTERN RECOGNITION

Statistical methods of classification as well as neural network models are being successfully used in many pattern recognition applications. However, there are many recognition problems in practice where statistical methods or neural networks with a BP or competitive learning algorithm are inappropriate, and descriptive methods are more suitable. Descriptive methods for classification are based on the rules that map input feature vectors to output categories. These classification rules are often stored in a knowledge base.

The problem of sailing-craft recognition is an example where a descriptive method is more suitable. Images of typical sailing craft are shown in Figure

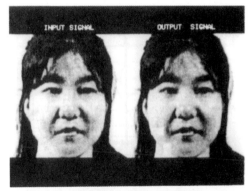

(a) Learned image: SNR=28.69dB,
average SNR=25.93dB for 10 images.

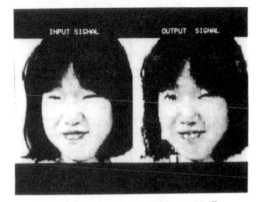

(b) Unlearned image: SNR=14.65dB,
average SNR=14.00dB for 3 images.

400 iterations for each image,
8-bit quantization, (64,16,64) units.

Figure 10.16. *SNR characteristics of unlearned images. (From Sonehara et al., 1989, with permission. © 1989 IEEE.)*

10.17 (George, 1971; Firebaugh, 1988). Sailing craft are often classified by the position of their mast or masts, the height of the mast, and the type of sails (known as the sail plan) they carry. There are two general types of craft: single-masted and double-masted. There are also two general sail plans: the jib-headed and the gaff-headed. A jib-headed rig is one that has a triangular mainsail; the gaff-headed rig is one with a quadrilateral sail. Single-masted sail vessels are called sloops or catters. Two-masted vessels are called yawls, ketches, or schooners. The classification scheme for these sail craft can be represented by the hierarchical tree structure shown in Figure 10.18, which contains categories (entities) and their corresponding features (or attributes). Entities are represented by nodes with incoming arcs, and attributes are represented by nodes with outgoing arcs. The knowledge represented by the tree structure can be encoded in a two-layer network shown in Figure 10.19. The weights connecting

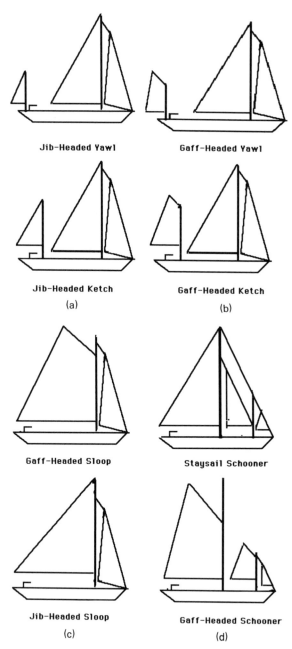

Figure 10.17. *Sailing craft images.*

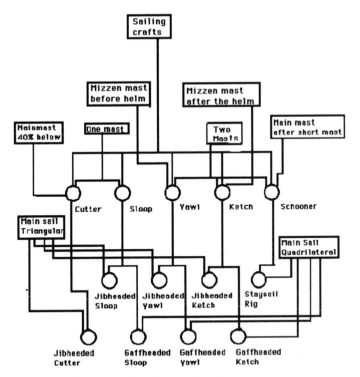

Figure 10.18. *Hierarchical tree structure.*

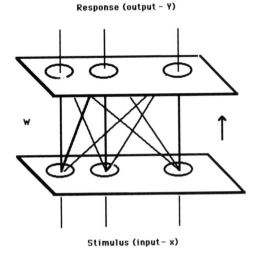

Figure 10.19. *ANN model for autoassociator.*

units in layers L_1 and L_2 are represented by elements of matrix W. Units in layers L_1 and L_2 represent the nodes in the tree (entities and attributes, both). If there is a direct arc between any two nodes, the weight connecting the two units is 1; otherwise it is 0. The matrix W is also referred to as the adjacency matrix (Telfer and Casasent, 1991). The network functions similarly to an associative processor.

A number of operations can be performed with this processor, such as upward closure, downward closure, union, and intersection. These operations can be best explained with the help of an example. If we desire the upward closure of a gaff-headed sloop, we input the vector shown in Table 10.2, column a. We then perform a recall $y = Wx$ and obtain the output as shown in Table 10.2, column b. Here, the matrix W is a binary matrix of the size 22×22. The output vector y is again fed back as input vector x. The process is iterated until the output vector y remains constant. When the number of iterations is equal to the number of levels in the tree minus 1, the processor stops. After this, the output remains the same if the feedback is continued. Column c of Table 10.2 shows the output.

TABLE 10.2. *UPWARD CLOSURE OF GAFFHEADED SLOOP*

	(a)	(b)	(c)
1. sail craft	0	0	1
2. mainmast 40% below	0	0	0
3. one mast	0	0	1
4. two masts	0	0	0
5. mainmast after short mast	0	0	0
6. mizzenmast before helm	0	0	0
7. mizzenmast after helm	0	0	0
8. cutter	0	0	0
9. sloop	0	1	1
10. yawl	0	0	0
11. ketch	0	0	0
12. schooner	0	0	0
13. mainsail triangular	0	0	0
14. mainsail quadrilateral	0	1	1
15. jibheaded cutter	0	0	0
16. jibheaded sloop	0	0	0
17. gaffheaded sloop	1	1	1
18. jibheaded yawl	0	0	0
19. gaffheaded yawl	0	0	0
20. jibheaded ketch	0	0	0
21. gaffheaded ketch	0	0	0
22. staysail rig	0	0	0

Column heads defined in text.

To find the downward closure of the attribute two-masted, the input vector x is applied at L_1 and output $y = W^T x$ is obtained. This output is again fed back as an input to L_1. The process is continued until the output is stabilized (Table 10.3). In order to use the associative processor as a classifier, we need to perform an intersection. A set intersection finds set members common to all of the input sets. The intersection is achieved by performing a downward closure on multiple inputs. The intersection can be performed by downward closure followed by thresholding. The associative processor in this way works as a classifier. In many applications we often want to find a category that possesses the largest number of attributes or that corresponds to the largest number of features. The associative processor is suitable for such applications. Telfer and Casasent (1991) have used the associative processor for an aircraft recognition problem.

A knowledge-based classification approach for multispectral image analysis has been suggested by Carlotto et al. (1984). They used a rule-based expert system for pixel classification starting with a TM scene. The scene is first decomposed into major classes: water, vegetation, and soil-like materials (Fig-

TABLE 10.3. *DOWNWARD CLOSURE FOR TWO MASTS*

	(a)	**(b)**	**(c)**
1. sail craft	0	0	0
2. mainmast 40% below	0	0	0
3. one mast	0	0	0
4. two masts	1	1	0
5. mainmast after mizzenmast	0	0	0
6. mizzenmast before helm	0	0	0
7. mizzenmast after helm	0	0	0
8. cutter	0	0	0
9. sloop	0	0	0
10. yawl	0	1	1
11. ketch	0	1	1
12. schooner	0	1	1
13. mainsail triangular	0	0	0
14. mainsail quadrilateral	0	0	0
15. jibheaded cutter	0	0	0
16. jibheaded sloop	0	0	0
17. gaffheaded sloop	0	0	0
18. jibheaded yawl	0	0	1
19. gaffheaded yawl	0	0	1
20. jibheaded ketch	0	0	1
21. gaffheaded ketch	0	0	1
22. staysail rig	0	0	1

Column heads defined in text.

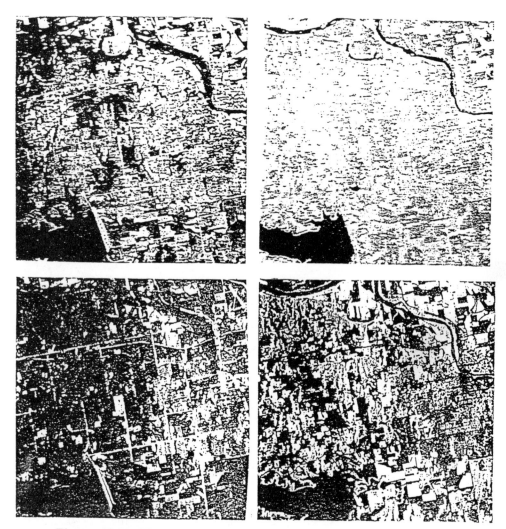

Figure 10.20. *TM data classification using rule-based system. (From Carlotto et al., 1984, with permission from Analytic Science Corporation, Reading, MA.)*

ure 10.20). The rules used to extract three major classes are:

> If (band 4 relative intensities dark),
>   Then (assert water).
> If (band 4 > band 3) AND (band 4 > band 5),
>   Then (assert vegetation).
> If (band 4 < band 5),
>   Then (assert soil-like).

The outputs obtained using these rules are shown in Figures 10.20b through 10.20d. Here, the rules embody knowledge of how a material appears in imagery obtained from a particular sensor. Rules for decomposing a class into subclasses can similarly be obtained and stored in the knowledge base.

10.9. EXTRACTION OF WEAK TARGETS IN A HIGH-CLUTTER ENVIRONMENT

Neural networks have exhibited the capacity for pattern recognition in a very noisy environment. Lippmann (1987) has shown an example of character recognition in a noisy environment with a Hopfield network. The Hopfield net has this capacity for recognition of noisy patterns because the desired patterns represent stable states of a dynamic system. States that are sufficiently similar to the stored patterns are mapped to the stored patterns by repeated iterations of the dynamic system.

Roth (1989) has shown that this capacity for neural networks to extract desired patterns from noisy inputs can be extended to the case of detection of weak targets in high-clutter environments. Here, a feed-forward and graded-response Hopfield network has been implemented as the optimum postdetector receiver. Figure 10.21a shows a simulated target track in a high-clutter field, consisting of 512 × 480 pixels. The target track is a straight line through the center of the field that has a single-cell probability of detection of 10%. The field shown in Figure 10.21a was selected as the initial state of a Hopfield network of 512 × 480 cells. The weight matrix was chosen to be given by a summation of outer products of selected patterns. The selected patterns were all straight line tracks spaced at 10° intervals through the center of the field. Figure 10.21b shows the state of the network after two iterations. After a few more iterations, the clutter is eliminated, and only the straight line corresponding to the weak target tracks is left, as shown in Figure 10.21c.

Figure 10.22a shows a different initial state that corresponds to the presence of two target tracks with a single-cell probability of detection of 10%. Figure

10.22b shows the result after a few iterations. After a few more iterations, as shown in Figure 10.22c, the clutter is completely suppressed, and only the appropriate target tracks remain. The illustration shows that neural networks can implement the optimum postdetection pattern receiver.

10.10. SUMMARY

This chapter describes practical applications of ANN models for image understanding. Remote sensing and medical image processing deal with a multidimensional feature space. ANN models with learning algorithms like BP and competitive learning are used as supervised and unsupervised classifiers for multispectral image analysis. Illustrative examples for satellite images and medical images are provided. Applications such as character recognition, fingerprint processing, data compression, and face recognition, with illustrative examples, are discussed, as are descriptive methods of classification based on the knowledge-based system.

Figure 10.21.

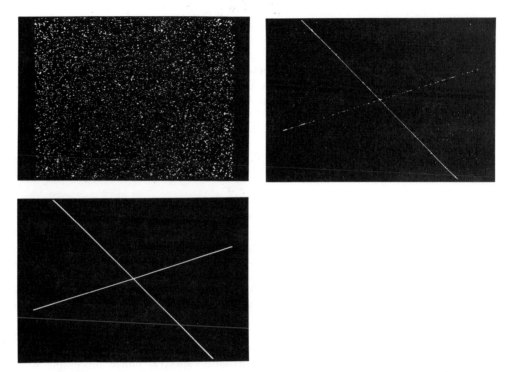

Figure 10.22. *A two-target track simulation. (From Roth, 1989, with permission, © 1989 IEEE.)*

REFERENCES

Carlotto, M. J., et al. (1984). Knowledge based multispectral image classification. *Proceedings of SPIE Conference on Applications of Digital Image Processing*, Vol. 504, pp. 47–53.

Cottrell, G. W., and Munro, P. (1988). Principal component analysis of images via back-propagation. *Proceedings of Society of Photo-Optical Instrumentation Engineering*, Cambridge, MA.

Decator, S. E. (1989). Application of neural networks to terrain classification. *Proceedings of International Joint Conference on Neural Networks, Washington, DC*, Vol. I, pp. 283–288.

Eberlein, S., and Yates, G. (1991). Neural network based system for autonomous data analysis and control. In: *Progress in Neural Networks*, Vol. I, O. Omidvar, (ed.), pp. 25–55. Ablex, New York.

Firebaugh, M. W. (1988). *Artificial Intelligence, a Knowledge Based Approach*. Boyd and Frasier, Boston.

Fleming, M. K., and Cottrell, G. W. (1990). Categorization of faces using unsupervised feature extraction. *Proceedings of International Joint Conference on Neural Networks, San Diego*, Vol. II, pp. 65–70.

George, M. B. (1971). *Basic Sailing*. Motor Boating and Sailing Books, New York.

Grossberg, S., and Mingolla, E. (1987). Neural dynamics of surface perception: Boundary webs, illuminants, and shape from shading. *International Journal of Computer Vision, Graphics, and Image Processing* 37:116–165.

Huang, W. Y., and Lippmann, R. P. (1988). Comparisons between neural net and conventional classifiers. *Proceedings of International Joint Conference on Neural Networks, San Diego*, Vol. 4, pp. 485–493.

Jackel, L. D., et al. (1988). An application of neural net chips: Handwritten digit recognition. *Proceedings of International Joint Conference on Neural Network, San Diego*, Vol. II, pp. 107–115.

Kaufman, J. J., et al. (1990). Bone fracture healing assessment using a neural network. *Proceedings of International Joint Conference on Neural Networks, San Diego*, Vol. II, pp. 53–58.

Kulkarni, A. D., and Byars, P. (1991). Neural network architectures for invariant object recognition systems. *Proceedings of Symposium on Applied Computing, Kansas City*, pp. 336–344.

Lehar, S. M., et al. (1990). Application of the boundary counter/feature counter system to magnetic resonance brain scan imagery. *Proceedings of International Joint Conference on Neural Networks, San Diego*, Vol. I, pp. 435–440.

Leung, M. K., et al. (1990). Fingerprint processing using back-propagation neural networks. *Proceedings of International Joint Conference on Neural Networks, San Diego*, Vol. I, pp. 15–20.

Lippmann, R. P. (1987). An introduction to computing with neural nets. *IEEE Transactions on Acoustic and Signal Processing* 32:4–22.

McClella, G. E., et al. (1989). Multi-spectral image processing with a three layer back-propagation network. *Proceedings of International Joint Conference on Neural Networks, Washington DC*, Vol. I, pp. 151–153.

Omidvar, O. M., and Wilson, C. L. (1991). Massively parallel implementation of neural network architectures. *Proceedings of SPIE Conference on Image Processing Algorithms and Techniques*, Vol. 1452, pp. 532–543.

Ozkan, M., et al. (1990). Multi-spectral magnetic resonance image segmentation using neural networks. *Proceedings of International Joint Conference on Neural Networks, San Diego*, Vol. I, pp. 429–234.

Rajavelu, A., et al. (1989). A neural network approach to character recognition. *Neural Networks* 2:387–393.

Roth, M. W. (1989). Neural networks for extraction of weak targets in high clutter environments. *Proceedings of International Joint Conference on Neural Networks, Washington, DC*, Vol. I, pp. 275–281.

Sonehara, N., et al. (1989). Image data compression using a neural network model. *Proceedings of International Joint Conference on Neural Networks, Washington, DC*, Vol. II, pp. 35–41.

Smotroff, I. G., et al. (1990). Meteorological classification of satellite imagery using neural network data fusion. In: *Proceedings of International Joint Conference on Neural Networks, San Diego*, Vol. II, pp. 23–28.

Telfer, B., and Casasent, D. (1991). Neural closure associative processor. *Neural Networks* 4:589–598.

Tsuji, Y., and Asai, K. (1984). Character image segmentation. *Proceedings of SPIE Conference on Applications of Digital Image Processing*, Vol. 7, pp. 2–9.

Weideman, W. E., et al. (1989). A comparison of a nearest neighbor classifier and a neural network for numeric handprint character recognition. In: *Proceedings of International Joint Conference on Neural Networks, Washington, DC*, Vol. I, pp. 117–120.

INDEX